Contract Terms in International Business

Akhileshwar Pathak

Contract Terms in International Business

Principles and Applications

Springer

Akhileshwar Pathak
Professor of Business Law
Indian Institute of Management Ahmedabad
Ahmedabad, Gujarat, India

ISBN 978-981-96-8145-7 ISBN 978-981-96-8146-4 (eBook)
https://doi.org/10.1007/978-981-96-8146-4

This Springer imprint is published by the registered company Springer Nature Singapore Pte Ltd.
The registered company address is: 152 Beach Road, #21-01/04 Gateway East, Singapore 189721, Singapore

For Ishaan

Preface

Businesses and contracts are synonymous. Businesses happen through contracts. The contract terms make detailed arrangements for the transaction and settle the duties, responsibilities, rights and obligations of the parties on all aspects of the transaction. Understanding the nature and scope of the terms of the contract has been crucial for the business managers, business leaders and the governments to efficiently and successfully formulate, negotiate, manage and perform contracts.

As an academic specialising in law with a business school, Indian Institute of Management Ahmedabad, contracts have demanded attention and engagement. The field has been at the centre of my teaching, research and executive education for over two decades now. A non-law person encounters contract terms as complex, technical and legalistic, almost incomprehensible. But this is only a surface appearance.

The principles of contracts were developed by the common law courts in the prior centuries on the basis of everyday lived experiences of the society, and the prevailing notions of common sense, fairness and justice. The principles got codified as contract law. For this reason, contract law is generalised common sense of the haats and bazars of the prior centuries. Modern businesses are founded on these simple common sense principles. These appear complex and sophisticated because a single transaction may network numerous of these principles together. The complexity dissolves once one goes beneath the surface.

My research and writings over the past two decades have been in doing a narration of the field of contract law in its founding common sense principles. Modern contracts are indeed complex and sophisticated in technology, economy and finance. For the courts and the law, however, a contractual dispute reduces itself to specific contract terms and the common law principles on them. The present book has grown from this engagement with contracts and contract terms for business managers.

From the idea of a book to a published work is a long journey. The journey was made possible with the guidance and coordination of Ms Nupoor Singh of Springer, the Commissioning Editor of the book. I acknowledge and value her help and support. Ms Jayarani Premkumar of Springer very cooperatively and ably coordinated with me towards the production process of the book. I enjoyed writing and I hope it is of use to the readers.

Ahmedabad, India Akhileshwar Pathak

Competing Interests I declare that there is no competing financial and/or non-financial interests in relation to the content of the book.

Contents

About the Author

Akhileshwar Pathak is Professor of Business Law at the Indian Institute of Management Ahmedabad (IIMA). An alumnus of St. Stephen's College and Campus Law Centre, University of Delhi, Professor Pathak did his PhD in law from the University of Edinburgh, UK. He has been researching on contract law and teaching students of management, and training executives for the past 25 years and has authored several books including Contract Law (2011), Law of Sale of Goods (2013), Law Relating to Special Contracts (2013), Law of Sale, Lease and Mortgage (2017) and Business Lawsuits and Disputes (2022). He has authored a textbook Legal Aspects of Business, which is in its eighth edition.

Chapter 1
Introduction

Businesses and contracts are synonymous. Businesses happen through contracts. Contracts can be domestic or international; public or private; consumer or B2B; for sale or service; short term or long term; vertical or horizontal; and online or offline. A company has hundreds of vendors, suppliers and service providers, it contracts with. A business entity contracts with business partners, associates, distributors, franchises and exporters for selling and buying goods and services. The governments do infrastructure development, including highways, power, telecommunications, airports, mines and minerals, and railways through contracts by employing private business entities. The state has been getting into long-term contracts with private businesses through Public–Private Partnerships (PPPs). Immovable properties are leased, mortgaged and sold through contracts. Intellectual property rights, including software and artificial intelligence, are developed, assigned and licenced through contracts.

The contract terms make detailed arrangements for the transactions and settle the rights and obligations of the parties on all aspects of the transactions. Understanding the nature and scope of the terms of the contract has been crucial for the business managers, business leaders and the governments to efficiently and successfully negotiate, manage and performance contracts. The contract terms have got standardised at the global level and are internationally being adapted, revised and adopted. The contract documents setting the terms have come to be called the general conditions of contract (GCC) or standard contract terms.

Contract Terms and Common Law

The contract terms appear complex and legalistic but are based on simple principles. The principles come from the past when trade and commerce was rudimentary. The world has seen trade and commerce for a very long time. As disputes arose in the prior

A. Pathak, *Contract Terms in International Business*,
https://doi.org/10.1007/978-981-96-8146-4_1

centuries, these were taken to the local courts. The courts, on the basis of usage and custom of the community, and the prevailing notions of equity and justice, settled the disputes. As similar cases were decided alike, the reasoning and principles came to be formulated. The courts, thereafter, followed these principles as the law. This court made law came to be called common law. Common law developed everywhere. Due to the British colonial expansion, however, the British took their common law to all the territories they went to, America, Australia, Canada, Africa and Asia, including India. The British common law was used in these territories with some adaptations. Contract law was the most basic and foundational common law. For these reasons, the principles of contracts were generalised common sense prevailing in the 1800s.

The founding principle of contracts is that these are in the domain of individual freedom. Every society has a state, the governing mechanism, which governs through its laws. The state enforces the law with the threat of punishment. The law has to be followed. Beyond the realm of the law, however, individuals are free to do what they like. Contracts fall in this domain of individual freedom. The contract is of the contracting parties and they are free to set the terms of the contract so long as it does not violate the law or encroach in the domain of law.

Contracts are agreements and an agreement is reached between two persons, when there is a meeting of minds. A meeting of minds is secured through a communicative process. One person makes an offer or proposal to the other and if the other were to accept it, the two have become of one mind and an agreement is reached. Agreements for exchanging benefits or imposing obligations on one another came to be contracts. This was to distinguish the transactions of the traders, who travelled great distance for exchanging goods and services, from the mutual help in the realm of social and family. The state and law recognised the contracts and enforced them. If a party failed to do his duty within the contract, the courts awarded damages for the losses suffered to the other party.

Contracts emerged centuries back and were orally made. As the contracts were orally made, the contracting parties could not have spoken out all the details of their transactions. As disputes arose, the courts settled the default principles for the details of the transaction. The courts, thereafter, followed these principles as the law. As a part of this law itself, the courts recognised that contracts were voluntary and the contracting parties were free to replace the default principles formulated by the courts. In several fields, through this process of precedence, a body of principles followed by the judges developed gradually, which came to be called the common law. Contract law was a general law dealing with all business transactions. To systematise the common law, England initiated to codify the principles in the common law countries in the mid-nineteenth century. As it was a shared project, the legislations which emerged in the common law countries were alike. For this reason, Australia, Canada, and most countries of Africa and Asia, including India follow the same contract law. Curiously, while the British enacted laws in the countries they controlled or influenced, for example Indian Contract Act, 1872 in India, they could not enact a codification act in their home country. Till date, contract law in England is based on principles developed by the courts. America developed its own common law, which was very similar to the English common law.

An axis on which we can understand the development of contracts and contract law is the advance of technology for writing and printing. Indeed, the impetus for these advances came from businesses themselves to facilitate contracts and create records of their transactions. As writing and printing became affordable, businesses introduced them in their contracts. A written document brought certainty to what the contract was and bound the parties to it. As written contracts proliferated, the businesses learnt that further certainties could be secured by introducing contract terms than the expenses and the doubts of litigating before the courts. The introduction of a term in a written contract either elaborated the cryptic default principle or ousted it. Every time a court gave a judgment on a default principle, or a contract term, the businesses were quick to introduce a corresponding term, either amplifying the interpretation of the court or ousting it by providing otherwise. Over the decades, the process of introducing contract terms has entirely overrun the contract law and replaced the default common law principles.

The contract terms have become so comprehensive and detailed that these leave no space for the default principles to apply. The digital medium has exponentially accelerated the trajectory as electronic documents can be readily moved and documents generated by copy paste without worrying about the number of pages and the cost of paper and printing. As a result, the contract terms have become free of the national laws and circulate internationally. The terms are picked up, revised, refined and adopted at the global level. The disputes before the courts are no more on the default principles but the meaning and scope of the terms employed in the contract. The only thing which anchors a contract to the law of a country is the contract term specifying the applicable law. The world has come to share the contract terms. The book introduces, explores and details the globally prevalent contract terms.

An international contract is between two parties from different countries. Left to itself, a dispute would arise as to which countries law should apply to the contract. As the contract is of the contracting parties, the contracting parties are free to settle the applicable law. Thus, international contracts always have an applicable law clause settling the law that will govern the contract. The clause is also titled as governing law clause. In addition, contracts have a jurisdiction clause, which settles the court to which a dispute on the contract would be taken to. The jurisdiction of a court can be a different country than the county of applicable law. Thus, if the contract has provided that courts of France have the jurisdiction and the applicable law is English law, the French courts would decide the dispute on the basis of the English law. Further, the contract may provide for arbitration in a particular place. The arbitrators too, say sitting in Singapore, would apply English law to the contract as the applicable law stated in the contract is English law.

English law is most widely chosen applicable law in international contracts. This is even when the contracting parties have no geographical connection with the United Kingdom and the parties are not from the common law countries. There are several reasons for this. The English courts, with the United Kingdom Supreme Court at the apex, are at the forefront in developing the contract law and other foundational aspects of business law. The judgments are valued and cited in the entire common law world and beyond. This is not surprising. The common law countries follow the same legal principles, introduced by England in the prior centuries. As England has maintained its intellectual leadership in the field of common law, the judgments from the English courts are relied on and cited in all the common law countries. As a result, English law provides a high degree of familiarity, certainty and predictability. This makes English law as the market standard for many industries.

The English law recognises the principle of freedom of contract and has no formalities and procedures associated with formation and performance of contracts. This gives flexibility to the parties to structure the transaction and proceed towards its performance. The English courts are continuously and rigorously developing the English law by its application to newer business contexts and circumstances. As a result, the English law becomes most relevant and appropriate. Further, as English remains the default language for international business and commerce, English law gets preferred. The judicial system and the individual judges of the United Kingdom are independent and free from external pressure or influence. This gives confidence in the English law as based on principles, and just and fair. In an international contract, the parties look for neutrality, and English law emerges as a strong contender for the above reasons. Thus, the book will explore contract terms with reference to the English law.

Method of the Book

As the above exploration brings out, while the prevailing contract terms are elaborate, their origin is in simple common sense principles. The book will traverse this journey from simple to the elaborate and contemporary. Each chapter on a contract term will start out by the simple common sense principles and build on it to the current contract term and its application. The chapter will detail out the scope and meaning of the term by exploring latest court judgments on the theme. The reference of the book is to contracts with English law as the applicable law and correspondingly, the court judgments reviewed are from the British courts. We could explore further with the following brief overview of the chapters. We follow this introductory chapter with written contracts and signing clauses.

Chapter 2—Written Contracts and signing clause: The chapter introduces the founding principles of formation of contracts. As contracts are voluntarily made, the contracting parties are free to employ any modality of communication. An oral contract is as binding as a written contract. Businesses for a century have zealously moved to written signed contracts as these bring clarity and certainty. GCCs have a signing clause insisting that there would be a signed contract document confining the parties to its boundaries.

Chapter 3—Entire Agreement Clause: The hope of the businesses that a signed contract would bring certainty and clarity proved illusory. As the contracting parties are free to employ any means of communication, a party not willing to continue with the contract could simply assert the existence of further collateral oral or written agreements. This will rupture the contract. The response to this challenge has been the entire agreement clause. The clause seeks to exclude everything outside the signed contract by insisting that all representations and agreements outside the written signed document are extinguished. This has unfolded to pose a new challenge. Does it mean that all the misrepresentations are also extinguished, vacating the right of a party against misrepresentation?

Chapter 4—No Oral Modification Clause: An entire agreement clause prevents the threat to a signed contract only till the contract is made and not after. A party not keen to continue with a contract can claim that subsequent to the signed contract, the parties had entered into an oral contract modifying the contract or even terminating it. Applying the founding principles of contract, that a contract can be formed by any modality of communication, and a contract is modified by another contract, the claim would be unimpeachable. In response to this, a No Oral Modification (NOM) Clause has been introduced in the GCCs. The clause sets out a formal procedure, invariably insisting on signing, for the parties to be able to modify a contract. As the businesses have come to communicate through electronic means, questions have arisen on the scope of 'signing'.

Chapter 5—Termination of Contract for breach: The common law principle is a party can elect to terminate a contract if the other breaches a core part of the contract or renounces the contract. GCCs have a clause(s) on termination for breach. A party can terminate the contract as provided in the written term. The written term may be at variance with the common law principle. Termination for breach has become an interplay of the general principles and the contract terms. A termination notice must accurately assess the nature of the breaches and clearly state them in the notice. A faulty notice will make the party serving the notice liable for damages for the wrongful termination of the contract.

Chapter 6—Termination of Contract for non-breach: GCCs have clauses giving the right to a party to elect to terminate the contract on the occurrence of an even, without any breach. Examples of these events are, a company appointing an administrator or proceeding to merge or amalgamate. As it is a contractual right, on the occurrence of the stated event, the party can elect to terminate the contract. The contract will come to an end and the parties will get discharged from its further performance. But would the party terminating the contract be able to claim damages for the loss of the contract? He has lost the contract but the other party is not in breach.

Chapter 7—Force Majeure (Impossibility) Clause: No one can do an impossible act or be required to do an impossible act. Recognising this, the courts developed the common law principle that a contract which has become impossible to performance can be terminated on the grounds of frustration by either party. The force majeure clause or the impossibility clause either expands the scope of the impossibility principle or attempts to limit its application by allowing time for the impossibility to subside. Significantly, changes in the market conditions or financial impossibilities cannot be a ground for frustrating the contract.

Chapter 8—General Damages: For every breach of a term of a contract, the other party can claim damages for the losses arising from the breach. The principle for award of damages is rudimentary, dating back to the prior centuries. The principle is to put the parties in a position they would be, by money amount, if the contract had been performed. The damages are only to cover the losses and these cannot be punitive or to profit from. The damages clauses create a mechanics substituting and giving effect to this general overarching principle.

Chapter 9—Liquidated Damages: For claiming damages arising from breach, to bring certainty, the simplest would be to state the amount to be paid in damages for a breach. If this were allowed, the stronger party would stipulate any amount to penalise the other or profit from it. But the general principle is that damages are to cover losses not to penalise the other or to profit from. For this reason, the courts award liquidated damages only if it appears to be a genuine pre-estimate of the losses. The liquidated damages clause finds limited application. Its most common application is for delays in performance of contracts.

Chapter 10—Consequential and Indirect Losses: A breach can have several consequences. The contracting parties would invariably get into a dispute on the extent to which the effect of the breach should be taken. A limitation of liability clause excludes or limits liabilities by employing terms indirect losses, consequential losses and loss of profit. The meaning and scope of these terms have been disputed in the context of the contract.

Chapter 11—Exclusion Clauses: Negligence and Liabilities in torts: The field of tort and negligence is separate from contracts. A person, proximate to another, owes a duty to not cause harm to the person by his action or lack of it. If the person does not take reasonable care and causes harm, the person is negligent and liable to cover the losses. As the contracting parties are proximate, the parties come to owe duties of reasonable care. A party in breach may concurrently be negligent and liable to cover the losses. If the exclusion clause does not specifically exclude liabilities for losses arising from negligence, the party in breach may be liable. Similarly, tort law covers all civil wrong, other than contracts, that cause a person loss or harm. Exclusion clauses should specifically refer to and exclude liabilities from torts and negligence.

Chapter 12—Ownership retention clause: In a sale of goods contract, the seller agrees to transfer the ownership in goods for a price in money. As we live in a material physical world, a sale of goods is an important component of running businesses or business transactions. In a sale of goods contract, the transfer of ownership is a watershed moment. Once the ownership transfers, the buyer can resell or use the goods. If the seller is unpaid, he can only claim the price but not the reverting of the ownership. To protect the seller, the GCCs have an ownership retention clause which insists that the ownership would not transfer to the buyer till the seller is fully paid.

Chapter 13—International Commercial Terms: In a sale of goods contract, the buyer and the seller are mediated by a carrier in the movement of the goods from one to the other. The seller and the buyer have to allocate between them the transportation cost and insurance of the goods in transit. Questions arise as to when the goods are taken to be delivered to the buyer and the risk in the goods passes from the seller to the buyer. The International Chamber of Commerce, a non-governmental world organisation, has developed a menu of terms allocating these factors between the seller and the buyer. The terms are called the international commercial terms (Incoterms). The International Chamber of Commerce publishes the terms every ten years. The prevailing Incoterms are 2020. A sale of goods contract chooses an appropriate incoterm and states it in the contract. The term settles all these varied crucial aspects of the contract.

Chapter 14—Description, Merchantability and Usefulness of Goods: The common law courts developed the principle that in a sale of goods contract, it is implied that the seller will supply goods which are in conformity with the description, of a merchantable quality and useful for the stated person. These came to be termed as implied conditions for whose breach, the buyer could terminate the contract. The implied conditions got codified in the Sale of Goods Act, 1983. The reenactment of the law of sale of goods as the Sale of Goods Act, 1979 has expanded the rights and elaborated them. In a sale of goods contract, the description clause makes express what is implied by law. The clause gets a meaning in the context of the implied conditions.

Chapter 15—Exclusion of Implied Conditions: Sale of Goods: Contracts are voluntarily made and the parties are free to set their own terms. The law of sale of goods vests implied conditions in the buyer but alongside, recognises the right of the contracting parties to oust them by express terms. In a sale of goods contract, where the seller is stronger, the contract excludes the rights of the buyer to terminate the contract on the grounds of the implied conditions of description, merchantability and usefulness. This is done through a warranty clause, where the clause would oust the rights and give limited warranty of repairing the goods for a limited period. Disputes arise whether the warranty clause has clearly ousted the implied conditions or not.

Chapter 16—Reasonable Care and Skill: In a sale of goods contract, the common law principles are developed on the implied conditions, giving protection to the buyer. In other contracts, including service contracts, there was no parallel comprehensive protection for the service receiver. The common law courts developed a basic principle to imply a term in a service contract that the service provider will provide the service with reasonable care and skill. The protection has been codified in the Supply of Goods and Services Act, 1982. Service contracts have warranty clauses stating the deliverables and other parameters specifying the service. The duty of reasonable care and skill can be ousted but only by using clear language. Disputes arise whether the exclusion clause has clearly ousted the implied term.

Chapter 17—Indemnity: The clauses on damages deal only with losses arising from a contractual breach. The parties may suffer all kinds of losses in the course of performance of the contract. These losses are covered by indemnity clauses. The two common indemnity clauses cover losses arising from a party not following the law; and violations in relation to intellectual property rights. In addition, there are indemnity clauses covering specific kinds of losses, if these were to arise. As the indemnity clauses are of a general nature, often, these are subject of interpretation to settle their scope.

Chapter 18—Guarantee: In its classical form, a guarantee is an undertaking to pay a debt on the default of another. Different variations of guarantee have developed, including, see to it guarantee. A guarantee is also misdescribed as an indemnity as it covers losses of another. The financial instruments, indemnity, guarantee and bond form a spectrum but have very different rights and liabilities. GCCs have clauses on these financial instruments.

Chapter 19—Interpretation of Contracts: Three kinds of disputes arise in giving effect to the terms of a contract. One, the meaning of a term of the contract is contested. In this case, the courts put the term in relation to the other terms of the contract and the context of the contract to settle the rival contentions. Thus, rival meanings are resolved by the interplay of text and the context. Two, the contract may be silent, that is, not provided on an aspect. In this case, a term which is so very obvious that it goes without saying or gives the transaction efficacy is implied. Three, a term limiting or excluding the right of a party is interpreted like any other term of the contract. The rider to this is clear and definite words must be used to limit or oust the rights.

Chapter 20—Assignment: A right arising from a contract is like any other right. The person bearing the right in the contract can transfer it to another. Transferring a right is called an assignment. This poses the question whether the transfer is of the future rights or also includes the rights which have already accrued. GCCs have clauses stating that the rights under the contract cannot be assigned without the written permission of the party. For understandable reasons, obligations of a contract cannot be assigned. For transferring both, the rights and obligations of a contract, a novation has to be done. Whether an arrangement is an assignment or novation is not to be determined by labels and descriptions but interpreting the terms of the contract to objectively assess the intention of the parties.

Chapter 21—Non-Disclosure and Restraint of Trade: A non-disclosure agreement (NDA) or a non-disclosure term in a contract protects against an information shared with a contracting party getting disclosed to a third person. The clause is also called a confidentiality agreement or secrecy agreement. A non-disclosure agreement has come to be tied with a restraint of trade agreement. In this agreement, an employee undertakes restraints on his activities after leaving the employment. It also applies to a vendor selling his business and goodwill; and exclusive trade relationships. The common law principle is unless the restraint on trade is reasonable, it is void. The chapter explores the validity and nature and structure of a non-disclosure agreement; and the principles developed by the courts to test the reasonableness of a restraint of trade and to severe void restraints from the others.

Chapter 22—Applicable Law, Jurisdiction and Arbitration: Contracts have a clause stating the law of the country that will govern the contract. This is called the applicable law clause or governing law clause. In addition, the contract will have a jurisdiction clause stating the court of a city or a country that will have the jurisdiction to take up a dispute arising from the contract. The jurisdiction clause may give exclusive jurisdiction to a court or provide for alternate jurisdictions. Where the jurisdiction is not exclusive, disputes arise as to the court which has jurisdiction over a dispute. In addition, the contract may provide for arbitration stating the law that will apply to the arbitration and the seat of arbitration. This could lead to a situation where arbitration is to take place in a country with the substantive law of the contract of another country and the arbitration law of yet another country. This poses challenging and interesting questions on contracts, arbitration and international law.

Chapter 23—Other Contract Terms: The chapter reviews other terms in GCCs including, warranties and representations, order of precedence, good faith and agency. A warranty is a contractual promise, for whose breach, the party can claim damages within the terms of the contract. Representations are statements made towards formation of the contract. The chapter explores the distinct nature of the two. An order of precedence clause lists the order in which the contract documents would be read to resolve conflicts and ambiguities. A contract may have express terms requiring the other to act in good faith. Agency is widely used in contracts. A special aspect of an agency is, even if the contract terms state it to be irrevocable, it can be terminated by the principal. In this case, the principal will need to pay damages to the agent.

The object of the book is to give an engaging accessible conceptual grasp of the meaning, scope and application of the important contract terms. For this reason, for each chapter, only a few contemporary and landmark judgments are taken up and reviewed. Every field of law is vast. Law by its nature and discipline, qualifies a qualified point; makes and exception to an exception; and creates branches to a branch. As a result, a law book is heavily footnoted, with references to numerous court judgments, past and present. The book abstains from this format to avoiding cluttering up the text. The footnotes and references are kept to a minimum. With a conceptual introduction secured, the reader can pursue on one's own through specialised books, blogs and internet sites.

As the book is with reference to the English law, law refers to the English law and common law to the English common law. The apex court of the United Kingdom is the United Kingdom Supreme Court. A reference to the Supreme Court is to this court. The second highest court of the United Kingdom is the Court of Appeal. There is only one Court of Appeal in London. The third layer of the hierarchy of the courts in the United Kingdom comprises High Courts. The High Court system has three divisions and within the divisions, there are several High Courts. The High Courts include Commercial Court which takes up international commercial disputes; and the High Court of Construction and Technology in London. Most cases reviewed have come up from these High Courts. We start our journey of contractual terms with an introduction to written and signed contracts.

Chapter 2
Written and Signed Contracts

All business contracts have now come to be in writing and by signing. There have been two main reasons for this transition to formal written and signed contracts. One, written signed contracts are fully binding on the parties. Two, a written contract creates the space to introduce terms to detail the transaction. Both these aspects bring certainty and efficiency to contracts. For these reasons, businesses have much preferred written signed contracts. As the technologies for writing and reproduction, like printing press, typewriters, photocopiers and computers became affordable, written contracts expanded exponentially in the past century. The digital medium has taken it to an entirely new level. The earlier technologies required the expense of the paper, the digital medium has dispensed with this physicality. Electronic documents can be readily produced, modified and transmitted. The entire commercial, legal and administrative order has now come to be based on the sanctity of the signature. Let us review the court judgments that have secured the sanctity of contracts formed through signing.

L'Estrange V F Graucob, Ltd

L'Estrange was a cafe owner. [L'Estrange v F Graucob, Ltd, (1934) 2 KB 394] The representatives of F Graucob, Ltd, visited her for selling her a vending machine for cigarettes. Following her inclination to buy, the representative entered all the details in a form and gave it to her to sign. A few days later, she received an "order confirmation" from the seller. The seller delivered a machine, but it turned out to be defective. She claimed to return the machine and get her money back. The form she had signed was titled "sale agreement" and contained clauses excluding protection to the buyer against defect in the goods, exempting the seller from liabilities.

The buyer contended that she had not read the form and was not aware of the clause. The court stated the principle that a person signing a contract is bound whether

A. Pathak, *Contract Terms in International Business*,
https://doi.org/10.1007/978-981-96-8146-4_2

they have read or understood the document or not. It is a principle of contracts that a contract formed by a party employing coercion, misrepresentation or undue influence on the other is a voidable contract, giving the right to the innocent party to set the contract aside. In this founding case on the sanctity of signature, the court asserted: [L'Estrange v F Graucob, Ltd, (1934) 2 KB 394: page 394].

> When a document containing contractual terms is signed, then, in the absence of fraud, or … misrepresentation, the party signing it is bound, and it is wholly immaterial whether he has read the document or not.

The court constructed that a party cannot be 'heard to say that she is not bound by the terms of the document because she has not read them' [L'Estrange v F Graucob, Ltd, (1934) 2 KB 394: page 395]. The buyer further claimed that the clause excluding the buyer's rights were in small print. The court recognised that the exclusion clause was 'in regrettably small print' but this was of no consequence as the clause was 'quite legible' [L'Estrange v F Graucob, Ltd, (1934) 2 KB 394: page 395]. A party who has signed a document is fully bound to it so long as it is legible and it was irrelevant that the clause was in small print. The following is the second case on the significance of putting signature on a document.

The Coys of Kensington Case

Coys of Kensington Automobiles Limited (Kensington), a company incorporated in England, conducts auction of classic and vintage cars in different cities in Europe. [Coys of Kensington Automobiles Limited v Tiziana Pugliese, (2011) EWHC 655 (QB). Hereafter Coys of Kensington (2011)] Kensington had a form for an intending bidder to register in an auction. The form gave the option to bid at site or on the telephone. Kensington was conducting an auction in Monaco, a micro-city state in Europe.

Tiziana Pugliese, an Italian national visiting Monaco, downloaded the one-page registration form and completed and signed it opting for telephone bidding for a Bentley car. After the due date of auction, the company sent an auction bill of sale, requiring her to pay the bided price and take delivery of the car. Tiziana refused to proceed and pay. Kensington moved to an English court claiming the price of the car.

Tiziana at first put up that while she registered for the auction, she did not bid for it. But the auction manager, who had conducted the telephone auction, had annotated all the forms with their respective bids. Tiziana's form was annotated with bids and her final bid was the highest. The court concluded that she had bided and the sale was made to her.

In an open auction, the bids are orally made and the auctioneer accepts by striking a hammer. The bids are the offers and the striking of the hammer acceptance, forming a contract by auction. Prior to the auction, the auctioneer and the bidders agree on the terms of the offer. The auctioneer can orally announce these before the auction, display it prominently, circulate it to the bidders or require the bidders to sign on the terms of the auction. Whatever be the modality, the shared terms get incorporated in the offers made by the bidders. In this case, Tiziana had bid orally on the phone and the auctioneer accepted the bid. The parties entered into a contract for the sale of the Bentley car. Tiziana would contest the terms on which this contract was made.

Tiziana claimed before the court that the written signed registration form was not binding, and as a result, the jurisdiction clause which gave the jurisdiction to the English courts alone, did not apply. Within the European Union Directives, the general rule is that a person would be sued at the place where the person is domiciled unless agreed otherwise 'in writing'. Freed from the jurisdiction clause, Kensington would need to pursue the dispute in the Italian courts. In addition to other benefits of the case being pursued in Italy, Tiziana herself was a lawyer!

Tiziana raised several points to claim that the contract was not governed by the signed form. The one-page form stated at the bottom: "All bid shall be treated as offers made within the 'Conditions of business' and 'Important Notice' printed in the catalogue". Kensington had not given a copy of the catalogue to her and she had not seen the catalogue and the terms printed in it. Her first contention was she knew nothing of the catalogue and the conditions of the auction. Thus, the conditions printed in the catalogue were not a part of the contract. The court, thus, dismissed the claim: [Coys of Kensington (2011): para 37].

> The Form on its face referred to the Conditions of Business printed in the catalogue. … such a reference is sufficient for there to be consensus and … there is no need for the actual terms to be in the possession of [Tiziana] and available to her for there to be sufficient consensus.

Thus, if a signed contract has indicated that there are further terms, by annexing it, referring to it or following the common practice of putting a star, followed by 'terms and condition apply', the terms become a part of the document. A signature signifies signature to the entire document, including all the annexures and references in it. It does not matter whether the person has seen or read the documents and the terms or not. A person putting up a document for another to sign is under no duty to make available the further documents referred to in it.

The second contention of Tiziana was, being Italian, she had 'almost no understanding of written or spoken English' [Coys of Kensington (2011): para 36]. As a result, she could not 'read or understand the relevant terms sufficiently' [Coys of Kensington (2011): para 36]. The principle for appraising communications between the parties forming a contract is to see it objectively from the vantage of an ordinary reasonable person and not the subjective intention of the persons making the communication. From a signed document, one understands that the signer is in full concurrence with the content of the document. For this reason, signed documents have become the preferred means for the formation of business contracts. The court noted on the principle: [Coys of Kensington (2011): para 38].

> … as a general principle, a party who completes and signs a document cannot rely on the fact that they have not read the document or have not understood it. Their acts are generally viewed objectively.

The court elaborated on the principle: [Coys of Kensington (2011): para 40].

> Otherwise, to make the question of consensus, in a case based on a document, depend on the intellectual or linguistic capacity of a party would cause great uncertainty which an objective analysis is intended to overcome.

It was evident to the court that she 'understood enough of the Form to complete the boxes including the reference to the lot number and the description of the car' [Coys of Kensington (2011): para 37]. The court was clear that the contention was a weak one and concluded: [Coys of Kensington (2011): para 40].

> I do not consider that there is a strong argument that a person who completes a document such as the Form in such circumstances can avoid its consequences by saying that they did not read it or did not understand it.

In the one-page form Tiziana had signed, the signature was to be put about one quarter from the beginning of the page. But it was the very last line, at the bottom of the page, that had the declaration: 'All bid shall be treated as offers made within the 'Conditions of business' and 'Important Notice' printed in the catalogue'. Tiziana contended that the 'signature was not immediately under or even near the relevant words which were at the bottom of the page' [Coys of Kensington (2011): para 36]. In addition, she contended that the Form did not contain words such as 'I agree to be bound by the terms and conditions' [Coys of Kensington (2011): para 36]. In the absence of this, she contended, her signature cannot be taken to be a concurrence to the terms.

The court, in appraising the contention, emphasised that the principle was 'objective construction' of the meaning and scope of signature. The fact that Tiziana had signed the form was important. The court constructed: [Coys of Kensington (2011): para 44].

> Reading the text of the Form against the background of a person putting a signature on it in the context of wishing to bid in an international car auction, I consider that ... [she] intended the signature to be an acknowledgment of the terms of the Form.

The signature was on the form as a whole. The court was of the view that the 'location of the signature was not near the reference to the conditions of business' was of no consequence [Coys of Kensington (2011): para 45]. Tiziana next contended that the jurisdiction clause, in the catalogue she never saw, was in small print under the heading 'governing law' and not clearly signposted. Thus, she contended that there was no consensus on the jurisdiction clause. The court noted that it was not 'necessary for there to be a specific reference to the jurisdiction clause' or for that matter any clause [Coys of Kensington (2011): para 46].

The entire commercial, legal and administrative system is based on signature being assent to the document. A court, even if it slightly doubted the significance of signature, would prise open and bring the entire system tumbling down. It is no surprise that no court will detract from the significance of the signature. The sanctity of a written document is secured. The founding case, L'Estrange v F Graucob, Ltd [L'Estrange v F Graucob, Ltd, (1934) 2 KB 394.], has been mentioned and relied on in hundreds of cases. In Peekay Intermark Ltd v Australia and New Zealand Banking Group Ltd, the Court of Appeal emphasised the significance of the sanctity of signature to the commercial world: [Peekay Intermark Ltd v Australia and New Zealand Banking Group Ltd, (2006) EWCA Civ 386: page 598].

> [A] person who signs a document knowing that it is intended to have legal effect is generally bound by its terms, whether he has actually read them or not. It is an important principle of English law which underpins the whole of commercial life; any erosion of it would have serious repercussions far beyond the business community.

The Signature Cluse

Both the parties do not have to sign a document to enter into a contract through signing. So long as the offer document is signed and the offer accepted by the other, the parties have entered into a contract through a signed document. The terms in the offer bind both the parties completely. Businesses ensure entering into signed contracts through two means. At times, the parties make it clear to the other that a contract will be made only on both the parties signing a contract document. In this case, till the parties sign, they are only negotiating. There are no rights and obligations for either party till a contract document is signed by both the parties. However, once a contract is signed, they are bonded to the terms of the contract. Other times, a contract may be formed through other modalities, like exchange of letters and emails, quotation, tender or auction. In these cases, the terms shared between the parties have a signing clause. A GCC may have signing clause as follows:

Signing of Contract.

1. The contract will get formed on communication of acceptance by the PURCHASER. Within 15 days of the formation of the contract, the parties will prepare a contract document assimilating all the terms of the contract agreed through the quotation, tender, GCC, SCC and supplementary communications and sign it.
2. The terms in the signed contract document will take precedence over the Seller's bid and all previous correspondence.

The significance of the clause can be illustrated with a tender. A party inviting tender sets the tender document and makes the GCC a part of it. A party submitting a tender becomes the offeror. In a big contract, there could be meetings of the tenders and the party inviting tender. In the light of it, the tender document may have to be supplemented or amended. There may be further clarifications and communications between the potential winner of the tender. Finally, the party inviting the tender would award the contract to a party with a short letter of intent or a purchase order. In this case, the party inviting the tender is the acceptor and the offer is the tender document along will all the supplementary communications that have gone on between the parties.

The contract is a consolidation of all the communications. For this reason, the GCC has a signing clause. It requires the parties to consolidate all the communications in a single document and sign it. In this case, the contract is not made when the parties sign the document. The contract got made when the letter of intent or purchase order was issued. Within this contract, the parties are duty bound to consolidate the contract terms and sign the document. A party refusing to sign would be in breach of its contractual duties. Also, as the signing clause brings out, once the document is signed, it becomes the final terms between the parties. The parties cannot revisit the communications. This would defy the very purpose of the signing clause, which is to bring certainty.

Electronic Contracts

While the electronic medium is new, a contract formed through electronic communication readily falls within the century-old principles of the formation of contracts. Contracts have been formed for long through oral, written and implied communications. The digital medium is merely a means to make oral and written communications. Earlier, people communicated through letters. Nowadays, they communicate through emails, text messages and applications like WhatsApp. Teleconference and applications like Skype and WhatsApp have made face-to-face communication feasible for people while being at a distance. The existing principles have simply to be applied to the new medium.

The digital medium, however, has also brought in entirely new features and ways of contracting. This includes websites, servers, e-stores and digital goods. In these, one person makes an offer and the other accepts it, to form a contract. The United Nations Commission on International Trade Law adopted a UNCITRAL Model Law on Electronic Commerce in 1996. This recognised all electronic records as if these were printed and signed by the person generating the record. Following the wide adoption of the model law in the signatory countries, every electronic data emerging from an electronic gadget, including server, personal computer, laptop, iPad or mobile phone is deemed to be signed. The signature can be a digital signature, email account, pin, password, fingerprints, iris or a scan of a digital signature.

While making a transaction on a webpage, say buying an airline ticket, the customer has to put a tick mark on 'I agree' to the terms of the contract. The terms can be accessed through a hyperlink. The transaction will not proceed unless the customer puts a tick in the box indicating 'I agree'. These are termed as clickwrap terms. Putting a tick mark is equivalent to signature. Most of the court judgments have come from the USA as the technology companies are based there. In Sgouros v. TransUnion Corp. [Sgouros v. TransUnion Corp., 817 F.3d 1029 (7th Cir. 2016)] a state court noted: 'Courts around the [USA] have recognised that this type of electronic "click" can suffice to signify the acceptance of a contract'. In Hines v. Overstock.Com, Inc. [Hines v. Overstock.Com, Inc. 668 F.Supp.2d 362 (2009).], a court noted: [Hines v. Overstock.Com, Inc. 668 F.Supp.2d 362 (2009).]

> It is a basic tenet of contract law that in order to be binding, a contract requires a "meeting of the minds" and "a manifestation of mutual assent." The making of contracts over the internet has not fundamentally changed the principles of contract.

Introducing the distinction between clickwrap and browsewrap, the court noted on browsewrap contracts: [Hines v. Overstock.Com, Inc. 668 F.Supp.2d 362 (2009).]

> [The] "browsewrap" agreements, where website terms and conditions of use are posted on the website typically as a hyperlink at the bottom of the screen. Unlike a clickwrap agreement, a browsewrap agreement does not require the user to manifest assent to the terms and conditions expressly... a party instead gives his assent simply by using the website. In ruling upon the validity of a browsewrap agreement, courts consider primarily "whether a website user has actual or constructive knowledge of a site's terms and conditions prior to using the site."

In Meyer v. Uber Techs., Inc., the Court of Appeal (Second Circuit) recognised: [Meyer v. Uber Techs., Inc., 868 F.3d 66 (2d Cir. 2017)].

> Courts routinely uphold clickwrap agreements for the principal reason that the user has affirmatively assented to the terms of agreement by clicking I agree. Browsewrap agreements, on the other hand, do not require the user to expressly assent. ...Because no affirmative action is required by the website user to agree to the terms of a contract other than his or her use of the website, the determination of the validity of the browsewrap contract depends on whether the user has actual or constructive knowledge of a website's terms and conditions.

Thus, any means by which a person expressly assents to the terms becomes equivalent to signing a document. The terms come to fully apply to the parties whether the person has read the terms or not. However, despite all attempts, the sanctity and certainty of a contract formed by signing is not fully secured. A challenge to it is the claim of collateral oral contracts.

Parole Evidence Rule

The foundational principle of contracts is that these are voluntarily formed. The contracting parties are free to deploy any means of communication. Thus, the contracting parties are free to form a contract which is part written and part oral. The simplest way out then for a party, not willing to perform a written signed contract, is to claim that collateral to the written signed contract, there was an oral agreement too between the parties. The oral agreement supplements and modifies the written document. Should the oral and the written contracts be read together?

The courts reasoned that the very objective of the parties entering into a written contract is to bring certainty, clarity and create a record. The parties would write all that they wanted to be binding. Thus, there is nothing beyond the written terms and only the written contract should be privileged. Thus, the court would not receive oral evidence to qualify a written contract. This came to be called the parol evidence rule. Parol means word of mouth or verbal. The parol evidence rule has been part of 'the common law for over two centuries' [T/A Hamid Properties v Francis Bradshaw

Partnership, [2013] EWCA Civ 470. Hereafter Hamid (2013): Para 46]. It provides that 'where there is a written contract, oral evidence cannot be received to add to, subtract from or vary the written terms' [Hamid (2013): Para 46].

But there was the other side to it. The parties are free to communicate by any means, in writing, orally, impliedly and a combination of these. The parties can create a part oral and part written contract. How would the court know unless it entertains the claim? The courts cannot refuse to explore the claim. This would deny justice to a party. The courts have tried to balance the two sides to the co-existence of a written and oral contract. In Gillespie Bros. & Co. v Cheney, Eggar & Co. [Gillespie Bros. & Co. v Cheney, Eggar & Co., (1986) 2 QB 59. Hereafter Gillespie (1986).], Lord Russell recognised that if there is a written contract, 'presumption is very strong that such contract is intended to contain all the terms of their bargain' [Gillespie (1986): Para 62]. But at the end of it, it is only a presumption. It is 'open to either of the parties to allege' [Gillespie (1986): Para 62] the existence of an oral contract.

As the technology for producing written documents expanded and written documents became omnipresent, the hallow around them too declined. In 2002, the Court of Appeal in Burley v Joseph W Burley Partners Ltd [Burley v Joseph W Burley Partners Ltd (2002) EWCA Civ 1163. Hereafter Burley (2002).] stated that in the modern times 'the mere production of a written agreement, however complete it may look' cannot make evidence of an associated oral agreement inadmissible [Burley (2002): Para 24]. Going further, it emphasised that the court was duty bound to 'look at all the evidence from start to finish in order to see what the bargain was that was struck between the parties' [Burley (2002): Para 24].

Personal computers and laptops have made the production of written records even easier. In 2013, the Court of Appeal in T/A Hamid Properties v Francis Bradshaw Partnership [Hamid (2013)] recognised that the exceptions to the parol evidence rule have increased in recent years. It noted the reason: [Hamid (2013): Para 47].

> This may in part be due to the increasing ease and speed with which documents can be created and dispatched. The temptations of the keyboard, the 'cut and paste' facility and the mouse cannot always be resisted.

To this, we can only add that the judgment too is dated. Documents are now produced on the go on a smartphone with a tap or swipe on the screen. The following is the latest judgment on an oral agreement collateral to a signed written agreement.

Diageo PLC v Vijay Mallya

Vijay Mallya, an Indian businessman, in founding Kingfisher Airlines, diversified from his long-established liquor business [Diageo PLC v Vijay Mallya, (2019) EWHC 2067 (Comm). Hereafter Diageo (2019)]. The airlines failed and to pay the debts for the airlines, Mr Mallya sold a part of his shares in the liquor company he controlled, United Spirits Limited (USL) to the British liquor company, Diageo Plc.

From the purchase and other acquisitions, Diageo came to have a dominant shareholding in USL. The management of the company was with Mr Mallya. Diageo negotiated a deal with Mr Mallya where Mr. Mallya and others will resign from their positions in USL and give the management of the company to Diageo. Diageo in turn will pay him a sum of USD 75,000,000. The contract was termed Deed of Disengagement and finalised in February 2016. It involved several other individuals and group companies.

As a part of the arrangement, an affiliate company of Diageo, Diageo Holdings Netherlands BV (DHN) had stood as a guarantor to Standard Chartered Bank for a loan to Mr. Mallya. Mr. Mallya defaulted and DHN was called upon to pay as a guarantor. Having paid for Mr. Mallya, DHN moved to recover the money from Mr. Mallya. On his failure to pay, DHN moved the UK High Court. Watson Limited was an affiliate of Mr. Mallya. The Deed of Disengagement provided: [Diageo (2019): para 18].

> Watson and Dr Mallya each hereby affirm ... DHN has a valid indemnity claim against each of Watson and Dr Mallya for all and any payments that DHN has made or is required to make in connection with the Third Party Guarantee or otherwise in relation to it.

Before the High Court, Mr. Mallya claimed that alongside the written contract, there were oral contracts between the parties that DHN will not make a claim till certain court proceedings were concluded. The court noted the claim: [Diageo (2019): para 8].

> During discussions on 23 and 24 February 2016 of the terms of the Deed of Disengagement conducted by video conference and by telephone between (amongst others) Mr Menezes and Dr Mallya, Mr Menezes made an oral promise that Diageo and its group companies would take no action to recover from Dr Mallya or his Affiliates as defined in the Deed of Disengagement ... until *"the DRT process moves"*, by which Mr Menezes meant until the attachment of Dr Mallya's shares in the DRT proceedings was released, whereupon Diageo would have further cooperative dialogue with Dr Mallya. ... Diageo's then chairman, Franz Humer confirmed that promise in a subsequent telephone call with Dr Mallya on 24 February 2016.

Diageo had transcripts of the meeting which it submitted to the court. The court appraised the first transcript: [Diageo (2019): para 21].

> The primary transcript, that is the first one that is relied upon, on close review makes clear, in my judgment, that the overall framework identified on both sides was, in summary, that it was acknowledged that it would be difficult to enforce certain obligations in practice. However, no promise about enforcement could be made, not least because of SEC requirements. Therefore, no right to enforce was being released. However, a later conversation would be possible in different future circumstances.

The court appraised the other two transcripts: [Diageo (2019): para 22].

> The subsequent two transcripts convey on both sides an appreciation that there was no promise not to enforce rights. Recognising that that was a situation that he had to live with and was choosing to live with, it is clear that Dr Mallya sought to press the position but it is equally clear that in pressing the position he did not succeed in taking matters further.

The court was of the view the transcripts did not support that there was an oral agreement limiting the rights of DHN. Mr. Mallya claimed that there were further meetings between the parties for which there were no transcripts. His evidence making the claim was recorded by the court as follows: [Diageo (2019): para 25].

> Dr Humer confirmed the promise made by Mr Menezes on 23 and 24 February 2016 in a subsequent telephone call with me on 24 February 2016. This was also confirmed in a conversation which Sunil Mittal, a prominent Indian industrialist who knew both me and Mr Menezes personally, had on my behalf with Mr Menezes. I had told Mr Mittal that Diageo were not acting fairly and properly despite the assurances which Mr Menezes had given me. Mr Mittal spoke to Mr Menezes and informed me that Mr Menezes had told him that Diageo needed to retain the security package in order to obtain a fairness opinion. Mr Mittal also informed me that Mr Menezes had confirmed what Dr Humer and Mr Menezes had told me directly, namely that Diageo had no intention of encashing the securities but could not put it in writing.

The court appraised: 'In my judgment, it does not take matters further than what was in fact the content of the 23 and 24 February exchanges' [Diageo (2019): para 26]. The court concluded that there was no oral agreement made alongside the written agreement limiting the rights of DHN. But what if the parties had agreed? What if indeed Dr Humer had agreed that they would not encash the securities but could not give it in writing? The oral agreement would have been collateral to the written agreement. The two of them put together would have brought out the intention of the parties not to make the demand on Mr Mallya to pay the money. A written signed contract goes only so far. Despite being in writing and signed, it gives limited protection from intrusion by collateral oral agreements.

Businesses sought to have contracts in writing as it served two purposes. It created certainty and clarity. It further created space to add more terms in the contract to detail the transaction and the rights and obligations of the parties. Having secured this, the realisation has come that even this is not full proof. The response to this challenge has been in the insertion of an entire agreement clause or the integration clause. The clause simply states that there is nothing outside the confines of the written contract. We will explore the clause in the next chapter.

References

Burley v Joseph W Burley Partners Ltd (2002) EWCA Civ 1163.
Coys of Kensington Automobiles Limited v Tiziana Pugliese (2011) EWHC 655 (QB).
Diageo PLC v Vijay Mallya (2019) EWHC 2067 (Comm).
Gillespie Bros. & Co. v Cheney, Eggar & Co. (1986) 2 QB 59.
Hines v. Overstock.Com, Inc. 668 F.Supp.2d 362 (2009).
L'Estrange v F Graucob, Ltd (1934) 2 KB 394
Meyer v. Uber Techs., Inc., 868 F.3d 66 (2d Cir. 2017)
Peekay Intermark Ltd v Australia and New Zealand Banking Group Ltd (2006) EWCA Civ 386
Sgouros v. TransUnion Corp., 817 F.3d 1029 (7th Cir. 2016)
T/A Hamid Properties v Francis Bradshaw Partnership (2013) EWCA Civ 470.

Chapter 3
Entire Agreement Clause

Business contracts have come to have a term called the entire agreement clause or the integration clause. The clause attempts to confine the contract to the written signed contract. The clause insists that there is nothing outside the confines of the signed contract. Businesses had hoped that a written signed contract guaranteed certainty and clarity. But the founding principles of contract made this expectation illusory. A contract can be made by any modality of communication. The parties are free to make part written and part oral communications. They can spread their communications in as many segments as they like. The simplest thing for a party then, not willing to get on with the contract, was to say that, alongside the written signed contract, there was a collateral oral agreement or other written agreements. This would reduce the signed document to be only a part of the other communications. The actual contract between the parties would then need to be established before the court. The entire agreement clause prevents this possibility and secures the signed contract. A well-drafted comprehensive exclusion clause can read as follows:

> Entire Agreement: This agreement constitutes the entire agreement between the parties and supersedes and extinguishes all previous discussions, correspondence, negotiations, drafts, agreements, promises, assurances, warranties, representations and understandings between them, whether written or oral, relating to its subject matter.

The clause is of a recent origin. The court has thus explained the reason for its introduction: [The Inntrepreneur Pub Company (GL) v East Crown Limited, High Court of Justice Chancery Division, 2000 WL 1151484. Hereafter Inntrepreneur (2000): Para 7.]

> The purpose of an entire agreement clause is to preclude a party to a written agreement from threshing through the undergrowth and finding in the course of negotiations some (chance) remark or statement (often long forgotten or difficult to recall or explain) on which to found a claim such as the present to the existence of a collateral warranty. The entire agreement clause obviates the occasion for any such search and the peril to the contracting parties posed by the need which may arise in its absence to conduct such a search.

A. Pathak, *Contract Terms in International Business*,
https://doi.org/10.1007/978-981-96-8146-4_3

In the case before the court, the parties had signed a tenancy for 30 years. A term of the contract required the landlord to buy a certain quantity of beer from the tenant for the duration of the tenancy. The landlord claimed that the parties had made an oral collateral agreement that the landlord could free itself from the ties of buying the beer after four years. The court noted that as the parties have signed the contract, the entire agreement clause was fully binding. Following the clause, the 'contractual terms are to be found in the document containing the clause and not elsewhere' [Inntrepreneur (2000): para 7]. The court ruled that even if there was such a collateral agreement, it was of no avail to the landlord as 'the whole purpose of the Entire Agreement Clause that this further exercise should not have to be undertaken' [Inntrepreneur (2000): para 9]. Ignoring any such collateral undertaking, the clauses in the contract would be binding.

The entire agreement clause presents a tricky situation. If all representations, promises and assurances prior to making of the agreement are excluded, it leaves the parties free to liberally and generously misrepresent and mislead as all this too would be excluded! It is a principle of contract law that when a person is induced to get into a contract by a false statement, the person is free to set aside the contract as a voidable contract on the grounds of misrepresentation. While the entire agreement clause helps in securing the contract within the confines of the written signed contract, it seems to take away the remedy against misrepresentation. This is indeed what was claimed in the following case.

AXA Sun Life Services Plc v Campbell Martin Ltd

AXA Sun Life Services plc is an insurance company. [AXA Sun Life Services plc v Campbell Martin Ltd, (2011) EWCA Civ 133. Hereafter AXA (2011).] It sells investment and other insurance products. By separate agreements, it appointed companies as agents to sell its products. The agreements were made on the standard form of the insurance company. AXA terminated the contracts and claimed balance amount from the agents. The agent companies claimed that they were 'induced to enter into the agreement by negligent and fraudulent misrepresentations'. Thus, they would be free to set aside the contract and claim damages for the misrepresentation. Clause 24 of the agreement was an entire agreement clause, which provided:

> This agreement... [constitutes] the entire agreement and understanding between you and us in relation to the subject matter thereof... This agreement shall supersede any prior promises, agreements, representations, undertakings or implications whether made orally or in writing between you and us relating to the subject matter of this agreement...

AXA claimed that even if there was misrepresentation, it was excluded and superseded by the entire agreement clause, making the contract valid and binding on the parties. The Court of Appeal distinguished the realm of representation and agreement from misrepresentation. It noted: [AXA (2011): Para 81].

> The essence of agreement is that it is concerned with matters which the parties have agreed. The essence of misrepresentation, however, is that it is not concerned with what the parties have agreed, but rather with inaccurate statements (innocently, negligently or fraudulently inaccurate statements) which have been made by one party to the other, have been relied on by the representing in entering into their agreement, and which may give the representing rights to rescind that agreement and/or claim tortious or quasi tortious damages by reason of loss arising out of entering into the agreement.

Turning to the entire agreement clause before it, the court noted that the clause was 'concerned with agreements rather than misrepresentations' [AXA (2011): Para 80]. It noted that the clause does use the word 'representations', however, the word is a part of a phrase and 'completely sandwiched between words of contractual import, namely prior 'promises, agreements… Understandings or implications' [AXA (2011): Para 80]. The court concluded that the clause was concerned 'only with matters of agreement, and not with misrepresentation at all [AXA (2011): Para 81]'.

The court explored the meaning and scope of the term 'supersede', and its relationship to 'representations' in the clause. For this, the court referred to the decision in BSyB Ltd v HP Enterprise Services UK Ltd [BSyB Ltd v HP Enterprise Services UK Ltd (2010) EWHC 86 (TCC). Hereafter BSyB (2010).]. In that case, the entire agreement clause provided that the written agreement 'constitute the whole agreement between the parties in relation to its subject matter and supersede any previous discussions, correspondence, representations or agreement' [BSyB (2010): para 359]. The court in the judgment had commented that the clause was concerned with the agreement and it was 'in that context that the Agreement supersedes any previous representations'. The court had explained that 'representations are superseded and do not become terms of the Agreement unless they are included in the Agreement' [BSyB (2010): para 382]. The court thus, read the clause: [BSyB (2010): para 382].

> In this case the statement that the agreement superseded any previous discussions, correspondence, representations or agreement between the parties with respect to the subject matter of the agreement prevented other terms of the agreement or collateral contracts from having contractual effect. It did not supersede those matters so far as there might be any liability for misrepresentation based on them.

The clause does not 'amount to an agreement that representations are withdrawn, overridden or of no legal effect so far as any liability for misrepresentation may be concerned' [BSyB (2010): para 385]. The court further noted that 'while there is reference to representations, there is nothing in the clause that indicates that it is intended to take away a right to rely on misrepresentations'. The following is another case where a claim was made on an entire agreement clause for denying the claims against misrepresentation.

The Nottingham Forest Football Club Case

Nottingham Forest Football Club Limited (the Club) is a professional football team which plays in the English Football League (the "EFL") Championship. [Fawaz Al-Hasawi v Nottingham Forest Football Club Ltd v NF Football Investments Ltd, NFFC Group Holdings Ltd, (2018) EWHC 2884 (Ch). Hereafter Fawaz (2018).] Mr Al-Hasawi, a Kuwaiti businessman, bought the entire share capital of the Club from the shareholders through NFFC Group Holdings Limited (NFF). Since, he invested heavily in the Club, including investment in its training ground, academy and facilities at the ground.

The club bought two players from a leading Greek football club, Olympiacos FC. A dispute arose between the clubs over unpaid transfer fees for the two players. The Geek club was owned by a shipping magnate, Mr Evangelos Marinakis. During discussions between Mr Al-Hasawi and Mr Marinakis on the unpaid fees, Mr Marinakis expressed an interest in buying the Club. The purchase was happening through a company, NF Football Investments Limited (NF). We will call the companies, buyer, seller and the club.

As a part of the exploration, the seller, NFF, created an online data site for the buyer (NF) to see the financial and other details of the club. The data site had a spreadsheet identifying the liabilities of the club. The liabilities stood at £6,566,214. The parties entered into a sale agreement where the buyer bought all the shares in the company for a nominal consideration of £1.

After the sale was performed, the buyer found the debt of the company was far in excess of the amount disclosed in the spreadsheet. The buyer claimed that the seller had misrepresented and must pay in damages the excess amount. The contract had an entire agreement clause which read: [Fawaz (2018): Para 8].

12. Entire Agreement

> This agreement (together with the documents referred to in it) constitutes the entire agreement between the parties and supersedes and extinguishes all previous discussions, correspondence, negotiations, drafts, agreements, promises, assurances, warranties, representations and understandings between them, whether written or oral, relating to its subject matter.

Relying on the clause, the seller asserted that any representation before making of the contract was of no relevance and a claim for misrepresentation could not be made. The clause had used the additional word 'extinguishes' with 'supersedes'. A contention was on the effect of it, if it excluded the effects of misrepresentation. The court disagreeing with the claim, noted: [Fawaz (2018): Para 26].

> In the context of an entire agreement clause, it makes perfect sense to talk about something which might have amounted to a prior agreement being extinguished, just as it could be regarded as superseded by the terms set out in the written agreement. It does not, therefore,

> support any finding that "representations" are "extinguished" in any respect other than that they ceased to have any contractual effect that they might otherwise have borne.

The clause was still about agreements and not misrepresentations. The question then arises is if a clause were appropriately drafted, could it exclude the effects of misrepresentation. The question got answered in the following case.

The Peekay Case

Peekay Intermark Ltd was an investment vehicle for its shareholders. [Peekay Intermark Ltd & Anor v Australia and New Zealand Banking Group Ltd., (2006) EWCA Civ 386. Hereafter Peekay (2006).] The company traded in a variety of investment related products. Mr. Pawani was a director of the company. Investment decisions were taken by Mr Pawani and his fellow directors. The company was a customer of the private banking arm of the ANZ Bank. Mrs Balasubramaniam, an officer of the bank, made representations to Mr Pawani about investing in certain class of bonds issued by the Russian government. Mr Pawani signed up the standard documents of the bank for making investments, including a document containing the detailed terms, titled as final terms and conditions (FTCs). Alongside, he signed a document described as 'Emerging Markets Risk Disclosure Statement'.

The bonds carried a risk and Peekay lost the entire investment. Peekay brought claim against ANZ that there was misrepresentation on the nature of the instrument, following which Peekay got induced to make the investment. Peekay claimed that the contract was voidable and should be set aside. Indeed, the court made a determination.

that Mrs Balasubramaniam had made an innocent misrepresentation. ANZ contended that the Risk Disclosure Statement signed by Mr Pawani excluded the effects of misrepresentation. The Risk Disclosure Statement, which Mr Pawani had signed, had the following: [Peekay (2006): para 55].

> You should also ensure that you fully understand the nature of the transaction and contractual relationship into which you are entering.
>
> The issuer assumes that the customer is aware of the risks and practices described herein, and that prior to each transaction the customer has determined that such transaction is suitable for him.

Referring to the Risk Disclosure Statement which Mr Pawani had signed, the Court noted: [Peekay (2006): para 60].

> The purpose of the Risk Disclosure Statement was both to draw to the attention of the investor the need for caution when investing in emerging markets and to make it clear that ANZ was only willing to enter into a contract with him on the assumption that he had satisfied himself that the transaction was suitable for him.

By signing the statement, Mr Pawani had confirmed as a part of the contract that he was 'aware of the nature of the investment it was seeking to purchase and had satisfied that it was suitable for its needs' [Peekay (2006): para 60]. The statement nullified the effect of the misrepresentation by ANZ. Should a clause like this be valid? The court noted: [Peekay (2006): para 57].

> There is no reason in principle why parties to a contract should not agree that a certain state of affairs should form the basis for the transaction, whether it be the case or not. ... It is common to include in certain kinds of contracts an express acknowledgment by each of the parties that they have not been induced to enter the contract by any representations other than those contained in the contract itself. ... I can see no reason in principle why it should not be possible for parties to an agreement to give up any right to assert that they were induced to enter into it by misrepresentation.

The court was stating the principle that contracts are voluntarily made. It is for the contracting parties to decide the terms of the contract. The right to set aside a contract on the grounds of misrepresentation is also only a civil right. Much the way a contracting party can exchange its rights, say in goods, it can contract out its right to set aside the contract. The court, however, added that provided the intention to waive the right was clear. This was an important point the court was stating. The right to set aside the contract on the grounds of misrepresentation is a right given by law. It is a valuable right. The right should be lost only if stated in clear and uncertain terms. The point was elaborated in a later judgment. Rix in AXA Sun Life Services plc v Campbell Martin Ltd [AXA Sun Life Services plc v Campbell Martin Ltd, (2011) EWCA Civ 133.], emphasised that 'the exclusion of liability for misrepresentation has to be clearly stated' [AXA (2011): para 94]. The judge elaborated the possible ways in which it could be done. He noted: [AXA (2011): para 94].

> ... the exclusion of liability for misrepresentation has to be clearly stated. It can be done by clauses which state the parties' agreement that there have been no representations made; or that there has been no reliance on any representations; or by an express exclusion of liability for misrepresentation. However, save in such contexts, ... talk of the parties' contract superseding such prior agreement will not by itself absolve a party of misrepresentation where its ingredients can be proved.

Thus, the exclusion of liability can be done by three different means. The first is to have a term in the contract that no representation was made. If there is no representation made, the question of there being any misrepresentation does not arise. The second is to state that there was no reliance on any representation. In this case, there may or may not have been a representation but no reliance was made on it. The right of setting aside a contract on the grounds of misrepresentation is available only if it has induced the party to get into the contract. As there is no reliance on the representation, the representation has not induced the person to get into the contract. The third is to state that there will be no liabilities for misrepresentation. In this case, even if there was a misrepresentation and it induced the party to get into the contract, the right to set aside the contract or claim damages is ousted. Whatever the modality followed, it must be stated in clear and definite words.

Implied Terms and Entire Agreement

At times, a contract may have a gap in it and not provide for a situation. The only option may be to set aside the contract on the grounds of uncertainty. The courts in this case imply terms into the contract to make the contract work. The leading judgment on the subject is from the United Kingdom Supreme Court in Marks and Spencer plc v BNP Paribas Services Trust Company (Jersey) Limited. [Marks and Spencer plc v BNP Paribas Services Trust Company (Jersey) Limited (2015) UKSC 72). Hereafter Marks (2015)] In the case, a tenancy clause required the rent to be paid on a quarterly basis while the notice for termination of the tenancy was to be given six months in advance. The tenant gave a notice for termination of the tenancy. The six-month period ended a month short of the quarter. The tenant claimed the rent for the month back. But the contract did not provide for a refund on a pro rata basis. The tenant claimed that a term to this effect should be implied into the contract. The Supreme Court noted A term will only be implied if it satisfies the test of business necessity or it is so obvious that it goes without saying. [Marks (2015): Para 21].

The Supreme Court did not imply a term to refund the rent on a pro rata basis as paying the rent on a quarterly basis did not make the contract unworkable or commercially absurd. The question of implying terms, when the contract has an entire agreement clause came in the following case.

J N Hipwell & Son v Szurek

A lease agreement did not provide in express terms that the landlord would undertake electrical maintenance and keep the property in a state of fitness [J N Hipwell & Son v Szurek (2018) EWCA Civ 674. Hereafter Hipwell (2018)]. Ms. Szurek had rented the premises to run a café for expecting mothers. There was a minor fire in the electric distribution board. The landlord did not satisfactorily attend to it. Following this, the tenant terminated the tenancy. Her claim was while the tenancy did not provide for it, a term should be implied in the contract that the landlord had to take up electrical maintenance and keep the property in a fit condition. The Court of Appeal summarised the principles on implying terms developed by the Supreme Court in the Marks and Spencer Case. The court, thus, summarised the law developed by the Supreme Court: [Hipwell (2018): Para 30].

1. The starting point is to determine whether there is any provision in the agreement in question … which expressly covers the point … it is only after the process of construing the express terms is complete that the issue of an implied term falls to be considered.
2. The court must take into account the possibility that the parties deliberately decided not to include the term sought to be implied: it is tempting but wrong to fashion and interpolate a term simply to reflect the merits of the situation as they appear when the issue arises…

3. The question whether a term is to be implied is to be judged at the date when the contract is made.
4. The test is necessity, not reasonableness; but "absolute necessity" may put the bar too high, and it may be more helpful to ask the question whether without the term the contract would lack commercial or practical coherence.
5. Although the process of construction and the process of implying terms both involve determining the scope and meaning of the contract … the process of implication involves a rather different exercise from that of construction, and calls for strict restraint.

The contract did not in express terms provide that the landlord was to do electrical maintenance of the property. However, there were general clauses on maintenance of the property, casting obligations on the landlord. The landlord was to keep the premises and all the fixtures and fittings in good repair. The landlord was to have the premises fully insured by taking an insurance cover. The tenant had to give access to the property to the landlord and the workmen within 48 h for repair and maintenance. The court recognising the 'plain and obvious gap' on no express provision on electrical maintenance noted: [Hipwell (2018): Para 38].

> In such circumstances I am in no doubt that, to ensure that the Lease does not lack commercial or practical coherence, or, in other words, as a matter of business necessity, the obvious gap should be plugged by implying a covenant on the part of the landlord to the effect that the electrical installation and other service media provided was safely installed and continues to be covered by any requisite certificate.

But the contract had an entire agreement clause. The clause stated that the lease: [Hipwell (2018): Para 3].

> … constitutes the entire agreement and understanding of the parties relating to the transaction contemplated by the grant of this Lease and supersedes any previous agreement between the parties relating to the transaction.

The landlord contended that following the clause, terms could not be implied into the contract. The question before the court was if terms could be implied in a contract which has an entire agreement clause. The Court of Appeal contrasted the different objects and scope of the two. The court noted on implying terms into a contract: [Hipwell (2018): Para 26].

> … it is well established … that a term may be implied where it is necessary to give business efficacy to the contract in question. In such a context, the touchstone is always necessity and not merely reasonableness, and the term is implied as a matter of fact in the particular case, rather than as a matter of law and as a legal incident of contracts of an identified type.

In other words, terms are implied to give meaning to a contract and not bring anything extraneous. The court noted on entire agreement clause: [Hipwell (2018): Para 27].

> In that context … an entire agreement provision does not affect or prevent the implication of a term to be implied on grounds of business efficacy. In my view … a contract lacking business efficacy must, if possible, be supplemented to cure the defect. It cannot be supposed

> that the parties would have intended an entire agreement clause to cause the agreement to fail, and to prevent the court from saving it, if there is an available and appropriate means of doing so consistently with, and indeed to give effect to, what the court finds must have been the true intentions of the parties.

Thus, the object of the two are supporting and supplementary and consistent. Following this, the court implied the term in the contract. Thus, an entire agreement clause does not oust implying of terms in the contract to give business efficacy to the contract.

Undisclosed Principal and Entire Agreement Clause

A person can authorise another to act for him. The one who authorises is the principal and the one authorised is the agent. Thus, a principal-agent relationship is created. The agency relationship is a contract. The agency contract may have authorised the agent to contract with a third party. When the agent contracts with a third party, the contract is of the principal not the agent. The agent only acts for the principal. It is thus said that the agent makes the contract and drops out, creating rights and obligations between the principal and the third party. The principal can sue and be sued by the third party.

The agent, while getting into the contract with the third party, may disclose that he is only an agent for a principal. In this case, the third party knows that the person he is contracting with is only an agent. This contract is with a disclosed principal. The third party may or may not know the identity of the disclosed person. In this case, both the principal and the third party can sue or be sued on the contract. The agent may not disclose to the third party that he is only an agent. This becomes the case of an undisclosed principal. The contract still is of the principal and not the agent, as the agent was only acting for the principal. But should the third party be bonded to a person he was entirely unaware of? The answer to this is yes. The undisclosed principal may declare himself to be the principal and sue and be sued by the third party. The United Kingdom Supreme Court, in Playboy Club London Ltd v Banca Nazionale del Lavoro SpA, noted: [Playboy Club London Ltd v Banca Nazionale del Lavoro SpA, (2018) UKSC 43. Hereafter Playboy (2018): Para 12].

> The rule of English law that an undisclosed principal may declare himself and enter upon a contract is an anomalous legacy of eighteenth and nineteenth century jurisprudence, which survives in the modern law on account of its antiquity rather than its coherence.

Of course, in entering in the contract, the agent must have intended to act for the principal. In the contract that gets formed, the third party can sue the agent and the agent can sue the third party. If it were to emerge that the person was only an agent, the third party 'must irrevocably elect whether to sue the agent or the undisclosed principal' [Playboy (2018): Para 12]. The Supreme Court recognised that the law on undisclosed principal runs counter to the fundamental principles of privity of contract, where only the contracting parties have rights and obligations on one another. The Supreme Court noted: [Playboy (2018): Para 14].

> The whole point about the law relating to undisclosed principals is that a person may be brought into contractual relations with someone with whom he has no factual relationship at all. ...The relationship between A and B's undisclosed principal may not be consensual, but it is at least mutual. The undisclosed principal may not only sue but be sued on the contract. A may elect to sue the agent. If A is sued by the undisclosed principal, he may take any defences which would have been available to him as against B.

The question has emerged whether an entire agreement clause prevents an undisclosed principal emerging and suing on the contract. In Kaefer Aislamientos SA de CV v AMS Drilling Mexico SA de CV, the entire agreement clause provided: [Kaefer Aislamientos SA de CV v AMS Drilling Mexico SA de CV, (2019) EWCA Civ 10. Hereafter Kaefer (2019): Para 11].

1. Agreement: These Terms and Conditions of Business together with this Purchase Order constitute the entire agreement between Atlantic Marine Services BV and its various affiliates and subsidiaries (hereinafter collectively referred to as "the company") and supplier stated in the Purchase Order, (the Seller), for the execution of the work/supply of the goods described in the Purchase Order.

The Court of Appeal noted the principles on undisclosed principal formulated by Lord Denning in Teheran-Europe v Belton: [Teheran-Europe v Belton (1968) 2 QB 545: Page 552].

> It is a well-established rule of English law that an undisclosed principal can sue and be sued upon a contract, even though his name and even his existence is undisclosed, save in those cases when the terms of contract expressly or impliedly confine it to the parties to it.

Thus the undisclosed principal can be ousted from suing only if the contract expressly excludes an undisclosed principal from emerging or the exclusion is implied. The Court of Appeal noted on this aspect: [Kaefer (2019): Para 55].

> ... there is nothing in the contract or surrounding circumstances showing that the agent is the true principal and which excludes the making of a contract with an undisclosed principal. ...For my part I do not think that the entire agreement clause in the terms and conditions necessarily serve to exclude altogether the possibility that there might be undisclosed principals. The language used is not wholly unequivocal and the parties could, had they wished, have expressly stated that the parties thereto were the only parties that could sue and/or be sued. But they did not.

Thus, there being an entire agreement clause in the contract on its own would not oust an undisclosed principal. The entire agreement clause should expressly exclude an undisclosed agent or it should be implied in it.

The question came before the Court of Appeal again in Filatona Trading Limited v Vladimir Anatolevich Chernukhin. [Filatona Trading Limited v Vladimir Anatolevich Chernukhin, (2020) EWCA Civ 109. Hereafter Filatona (2020)]. A shareholder agreement had an entire agreement clause which read: [Filatona (2020): Para 313].

> 14.5 This Agreement together with the preamble, appendices and other documents necessary in accordance with this Agreement is the complete and exhaustive agreement between the Parties in respect of the subject matter thereof, and replaces all previous verbal or written agreements, obligations and arrangements of the Parties in relation to its subject matter that do not comply with the provisions of this Agreement.

The question was whether an undisclosed principal could sue on the contract. The Court of Appeal accepted that the phrase 'the complete and exhaustive agreement' in the indicated that 'the parties intended only to contract with each other' [Filatona (2020): Para 313]. However, to sue and be sued on a contract was a different matter. The court noted: [Filatona (2020): Para 313].

> However, it did not say, as it might that the *only* persons who may sue upon it were the named parties ... and the clause certainly did not unequivocally exclude a disclosed principal from suing on it.

The Court of Appeal stated the principles and measures by which an undisclosed principal could be excluded from suing. It noted: [Filatona (2020): Para 317].

> Whether a contract 'unequivocally and exhaustively' defines the parties or whether the rights of a disclosed and identified principal have been 'clearly excluded by the terms of the contract', may be regarded as two ways of asking the same question; either way there is a heavy burden of persuasion on a party who seeks to argue that a known and identified principal is to be excluded from a contract.

The court did not find that the contract terms had clearly and definite used words to exclude an undisclosed principal from suing.

References

AXA Sun Life Services plc v Campbell Martin Ltd (2011) EWCA Civ 133.
BSyB Ltd v HP Enterprise Services UK Ltd (2010) EWHC 86 (TCC).
Fawaz Al-Hasawi v Nottingham Forest Football Club Ltd v NF Football Investments Ltd, NFFC Group Holdings Ltd (2018) EWHC 2884 (Ch).
Filatona Trading Limited v Vladimir Anatolevich Chernukhin (2020) EWCA Civ 109.
J N Hipwell & Son v Szurek (2018) EWCA Civ 674.
Kaefer Aislamientos SA de CV v AMS Drilling Mexico SA de CV (2019) EWCA Civ 10.
Marks and Spencer plc v BNP Paribas Services Trust Company (Jersey) Limited (2015) UKSC 72.
Peekay Intermark Ltd & Anor v Australia and New Zealand Banking Group Ltd. (2006) EWCA Civ 386.
Playboy Club London Ltd v Banca Nazionale del Lavoro SpA (2018) UKSC 43.
Teheran-Europe v Belton (1968) 2 QB 545.
The Inntrepreneur Pub Company (GL) v East Crown Limited, High Court of Justice Chancery Division, 2000 WL 1151484.

Chapter 4
No Oral Modification Clause

Contracts have a clause classically called, No Oral Modification (NOM) Clause. The clause insists that the contract cannot be modified orally and prescribes a procedure for modifying the contract in writing. Businesses had hoped that a written signed contract guaranteed certainty and clarity. But the principles of formation of contract made this expectation illusory. A contract is modified by another contract, where a party offers modification and the other accepts it. It is a founding principle of contracts that a contract can be formed by any modality of communication including oral communications. Thus, a contract modifying an existing contract can be made orally. As a result, while a contract is written and signed, it can be modified orally. The simplest thing then for a party not willing to get on with a contract is to suggest that the parties have orally modified the contract or even terminated it. The NOM clause prevents this possibility and secures the signed contract.

An entire agreement clause and a no oral modification clause work in conjunction. Both protect the sanctity of the written signed contract. The entire agreement clause deals with the communications between the parties till the contract is made; and the no oral modification clause deals with events after the written contract is signed. However, there is one key difference between the two. The entire agreement clause completely prevents any intrusion into the written contract. A no oral modification clause could not follow the same strategy and state that no modification could ever be made to the contract. Businesses recognise that flexibility is important and the parties may need to modify a contract in the course of its performance. At the same time, a claim of oral modification should not be allowed as this would erode the very sanctity of the written contract. To this end, the clause prohibits oral modification but allows modifications in writing. It may further provide procedures to be followed in a written modification of the contract.

The validity of the NOM Clause, prohibiting oral modifications, however, itself came to be in peril. It is very common for business persons to make face-to-face or telephone conversations to modify a contract, without any reference to the NOM Clause. In fact, they may not even be aware that the contract has an NOM clause.

A. Pathak, *Contract Terms in International Business*,
https://doi.org/10.1007/978-981-96-8146-4_4

They very likely go ahead and follow the modifications. However, in the event a party did not wish to follow the oral modification, would simply claim that the contract could not be modified orally. As contracts are voluntary and the parties are free to set their terms, why should the oral agreement, which is the final wish of the parties, not be binding? In MWB Business Exchange Centres Ltd v Rock Advertising Ltd., (2016) EWCA Civ 553, the Court of Appeal ruled that the oral agreement should be binding. The judgment hereafter is referred as MWB (2016). The effect of this would be that an NOM clause would be of no relevance. The decision came in appeal before the United Kingdom Supreme Court, which addressed this riddle. [MWB Business Exchange Centres Ltd v Rock Advertising Ltd, (2018) UKSC 24. Hereafter MWB (2018).]

The Rock Advertising Case

MWB Business Exchange Centres Ltd (MWB) managed office space in Central London. Rock Advertising Ltd (Rock) was a company which was in the business of providing advertising and marketing services. Rock had rented a premises from MWB for a period of three years. Rock's business did not develop as it had planned and it got into financial difficulties. Rock incurred arrears of the rent and other charges of over £12,000.

Christian Idehen was the sole director of Rock. He proposed to Natasha Evans, the credit controller of MWB, a revised schedule of payments. The proposed arrangement was that for a few months, Rock would pay less than the amount in the lease contract. In the subsequent months, it would pay more and clear the arrears. There was then a discussion between them on the telephone. Idehen reiterated his proposal. Following the phone conversation, Rock paid an instalment in accordance with his proposed revised schedule. Two days later, Evans sent the following email to Idehen: [MWB (2016): para 7].

> Morning Christian, I had a debt review with my finance director last night. … He is not happy to allow you to accumulate any more debt on the account and said [reduced payment] is not acceptable as you are not covering your contractual expectations. Please confirm that you will make payments … as per [the lease terms].

Rock did not pay further to meet the requirements of the lease contract. Following the default, within the terms of the lease contract, MWB terminated the contract and initiated proceedings before Central London County Court claiming the arrears of licence fees, other charges and damages for the losses suffered. Rock disputed the claim and counterclaimed that MWB had wrongfully terminated the contract and that it was MWB which was in breach. Rock claimed that in the telephone conversation on 27 February 2012, Evans had accepted the proposal and an oral agreement was made between the parties to reschedule the payment.

The county judge heard evidence from both the parties. Evans acknowledged the telephone conversation but denied accepting the proposal. The judge concluded that

Evans did accept the proposal and she later realised that she had gone too far and instead treated it merely as a proposal and took it to her superior who rejected it. This led to her email of 29 February 2018 to Idehen. The judge, thus, concluded that an oral agreement to reschedule the payment was made between the parties [MWB (2016): para 8].

MWB next claimed that the oral agreement was not binding as it was opposed to the No Oral Modification clause (NOM Clause) in the contract. Clause 7.6 provided: [MWB (2016): para 13].

> All variations to this licence must be agreed, set out in writing and signed on behalf of both parties before they take effect.

The question before the courts was on the validity of the NOM clause. As the parties are autonomous, they are free to employ any means of communication to express their wish and nothing should come in the way of it. The principle was most eloquently stated more than 100 years back by Cardozo J in the New York Court of Appeals in Alfred C Beatty v Guggenheim Exploration Co: [Alfred C Beatty v Guggenheim Exploration Co (1919) 225 NY 380, pp 387–8.]

> Those who make a contract, may unmake it. The clause which forbids a change, may be changed like any other. The prohibition of oral waiver, may itself be waived … What is excluded by one act, is restored by another. You may put it out by the door, it is back through the window. Whenever two men contract, no limitation self-imposed can destroy their power to contract again.

Indeed, the second highest court, the Court of Appeal, following the principle ruled that an agreement overriding the NOM clause was formed. The effect of it was an NOM clause could not come in the way of the parties forming an oral agreement. The decision was of immense commercial and practical significance. Going with it, a NOM clause would be of no relevance and every contract would be prone to be stalled by a reluctant party on one pretext or the other. The very sanctity of the written contract would collapse. The dispute came before the United Kingdom Supreme Court, which using nuanced arguments, saved the NOM clause.

The UK Supreme Court recognised the dispute to be a riddle and introduced it in these words: [MWB (2018): para 1].

> Modern litigation rarely raises truly fundamental issues in the law of contract. This appeal is exceptional. It raises … whether a contractual term prescribing that an agreement may not be amended save in writing signed on behalf of the parties (commonly called a "No Oral Modification" clause) is legally effective.

The court recognised the party autonomy principle but noted that there were limits to party autonomy: [MWB (2018): para 11].

> Party autonomy operates up to the point when the contract is made, but thereafter only to the extent that the contract allows. Nearly all contracts bind the parties to some course of action, and to that extent restrict their autonomy. The real offence against party autonomy is the suggestion that they cannot bind themselves as to the form of any variation, even if that is what they have agreed.

Thus, the parties are autonomous. However, the very essence of contract is for the parties to bind together and surrender their autonomy for the mutual exchange. The court noted that contracts can be made quickly and informally. However, this flexibility "has been found a mixed blessing by businessmen and is not always welcome" [MWB (2018): para 12]. NOM clauses have been introduced for the very purpose of limiting this flexibility. The court explored the reasons NOM clauses have become common: [MWB (2018): para 12].

> There are at least three reasons for including such clauses. The first is that it prevents attempts to undermine written agreements by informal means, a possibility which is open to abuse, for example in raising defences to summary judgment. Secondly, in circumstances where oral discussions can easily give rise to misunderstandings and crossed purposes, it avoids disputes not just about whether a variation was intended but also about its exact terms. Thirdly, a measure of formality in recording variations makes it easier for corporations to police internal rules restricting the authority to agree them. These are all legitimate commercial reasons…

In this important passage, the court was explaining the reasons for including the clause in contracts. A party to the contract may come along that there was an oral agreement modifying the contract or even terminating it. Other times, in the parties modifying a contract orally, disputes may arise whether the contract was modified and what the modifications to the contract were. Insisting on a written modification brings certainty as to the terms of the modified contract.

A company is a distinct legal person. It is not capable of acting on its own. It acts through the human agency of the directors and its executives. A manager has the authority from the company to perform his function and can readily get a company into an oral agreement. The company, as a policy, may have prohibited this. The manager could have acted being unfamiliar with the policy or deliberately and enthusiastically going beyond to help the company. The formality of admitting only written modifications to a contract helps avoid casual modification of the contract. This makes it easier for the company to 'police internal rules'.

The Supreme Court, in no oral modification clauses, found a parallel in entire agreement clauses. The entire agreement clauses attend to the events till the formation of the written contract and the no oral modification clause, after the formation of the contract. The court noted: [MWB (2018): para 14].

> Such clauses are commonly coupled with No Oral Modification clauses addressing the position after the contract is made. Both are intended to achieve contractual certainty about the terms agreed, in the case of entire agreement clauses by nullifying prior collateral agreements relating to the same subject matter.

The Supreme Court recorded that the no oral modification clause was intended to bring certainty to the terms of the contract. The court found the principles of contract and NOM clause entirely consistent. The judgment reasoned that from an oral agreement, it does not follow that the parties intended to dispense with the clause. Instead, the court noted: [MWB (2018): para 15].

> What the parties to such a clause have agreed is not that oral variations are forbidden, but that they will be invalid. The mere fact of agreeing to an oral variation is not therefore a contravention of the clause. It is simply the situation to which the clause applies.

Thus, the judgment reasoned that the parties are free to make an oral contract modifying the contract. The clause does not say that the parties cannot make an oral agreement and an oral contract in itself is invalid. However, the principal contract refuses to give effect to it as it has a NOM clause. The judge concluded: [MWB (2018): para 17].

> I conclude that the oral variation in the present case was invalid for the … want of the writing and signatures prescribed by clause 7.6 of the licence agreement.

Thus, the court ruled that the no oral modification clause was binding. As the parties had not followed the clause, the contract was not modified. Rock was in breach in not paying the rent according to the schedule in the contract. The judgment of the Supreme Court is truly fundamental. If it were not for the judgment, a NOM clause would be of no value. This would have caused widespread uncertainties in commercial contracts. The Supreme Court has saved the clause. The validity given to the NOM clauses has been deployed in several cases. A review of the cases will bring out the commercial and business context in which, even after a party has orally agreed and morally bound, nevertheless brings the defence of the NOM clause. We would also learn the principles on application of the clause.

Great Dunmow Estates Limited v Crest Nicholson Operations Limited

Great Dunmow Estates Limited (GDEL) owned a plot of land in Essex. It entered into a contract to sell it to Crest Nicholson. [Great Dunmow Estates Limited v Crest Nicholson Operations Limited, (2019) EWCA Civ 1683. Hereafter Great Dunmow (2019)]. The buyer was to develop the property by constructing housing units. The contract set our four conditions to be met for the transfer of land to take place. Three of the conditions were in relation to obtaining the planning permission. These conditions were met. The fourth condition was settlement of the price of the property.

The contract provided a detailed procedure and mechanics as to how the parties will go about settling the price. Clause 6.2 provided for the appointment of a valuer who would value the property based on the Base Revenue Per Square Foot and the Main Infrastructure Costs determined under clause 6.1. As the parties did not agree to a price, within the terms of the contract, a chartered surveyor was appointed to value the property. The two sides had their own valuers. Following the terms of the contract, the Chartered Surveyor, Mr Downham, issued directions to the parties that their valuers should produce a statement of agreed facts in respect of the development site. The valuers were to agree on as many facts as possible. In addition, they were also to set out matters that they had been unable to agree. Further, each party was to present an estimate of the value of the property.

The valuers produced a document entitled "Statement of Agreed Facts". The two valuers produced their respective reports setting out their valuations of the property. The two valuations had a huge difference. The buyer estimated the value of the property to be £29.5 m, and the seller, £43 m. The party whom the report did not suit, under the advice of the lawyers, questioned the very validity of the report. The contract had a modification clause. Clause 30 of the contract read: [Great Dunmow (2019): para 25].

> This Agreement constitutes the entire contract between the Parties and may only be varied or modified in writing by letter or memorandum signed by both the Parties or their solicitors specifically referring to this clause 30 and stating that this Agreement is varied in the manner specified and such variation may be prepared in duplicate or in original and counterpart and reference to such variation shall be endorsed on this Agreement.

The other party insisted that the joint statement of the valuers was not binding as the contract could only be modified by following clause 30, which has not been done. The Court of Appeal referred to the Rock Case [MWB (2018)] and thus summarised it: [Great Dunmow (2019): para 24].

> … the Supreme Court held that there was no reason in principle why the parties to a contract could not bind themselves to a specified method for making any subsequent variation to the contract. The parties are to be taken to have agreed that purported variations which do not comply with the relevant conditions are to be invalid.

The court applied it to clause 30 of the contract in the case before it: [Great Dunmow (2019): para 26].

> … these provisions were not complied with in the present case either in relation to the Statement of Agreed Facts or in relation to any other dealings between the parties that might be relied upon to support the efficacy of what the parties' valuers originally agreed. It is clear therefore that … the effect of the Statement of Agreed Facts … cannot stand and must be set aside.

The parties, through their valuers who were representing them, had communicated and prepared a report in writing. The report, however, did not meet the requirements of clause 30 in two respects, one, it was not signed, and two, it did not refer to being a modification within clause 30. The court concluded that the contract terms were not modified as requirements of clause 30 were not met.

Email and Signed Documents

The NOM clause insists that the modification can only be done by signing in writing. As email and electronic communication have almost entirely replaced paper-based communication, the question has arisen on the nature of email communication and its relationship with the NOM clause. In almost all jurisdictions, on the aegis of a United Nations convention, the law is that any electronic record is deemed as if it is written and signed. The signature can be a digital signature, pin, iris, fingerprint, account password or even an attribution to a person. However, this is only deemed to be for the purposes of general law. The NOM clause is a voluntary contractual requirement set by the parties. The scope of the clause should be given meaning within the text of the contract.

In Golden Ocean Group Ltd v Salgaocar Mining Industries Pvt Ltd [Golden Ocean Group Limited v Salgaocar Mining Industries Pvt Ltd, 2011 WL 197258.] the parties had made email communications and later disputed whether a contract of guarantee was made. The Commercial Court noted that emails forming a contract 'are signed by the electronically printed signature of the persons who sent them' [Golden Ocean Group Limited v Salgaocar Mining Industries Pvt Ltd, 2011 WL 197258: Para 104]. The email which had concluded the contract was sent by Guy Hindley, with he simply ending it with 'Guy'. The Court of Appeal, deciding the dispute noted: [Golden Ocean Group Limited v Salgaocar Mining Industries Pvt Ltd, 2012 WL 608695. Hereafter Golden (2012): para 31.]

> The document which confirms the conclusion of the contract of guarantee is the final e-mail... It contains the name Guy, indicating that it was sent by Mr Hindley.

It was contended that merely writing name at the bottom is 'not a signature at all.' It is 'no more than a salutation'. The Court of Appeal disagreed and concluded: [Golden (2012): para 32].

> ... an electronic signature is sufficient and that a first name, initials, or perhaps a nickname will suffice. In my judgment Mr Hindley put his name, Guy, on the e-mail so as to indicate that it came with his authority and that he took responsibility for the contents. It is an assent to its terms. I have no doubt that that is a sufficient authentication.

Thus, in formation of a contract by an email exchange, merely putting one's name to an email is adequate authentication for it to be a signature. With this, we review the following judgment on the theme of NOM clause and electronic communication. The judgment predates the Rock Advertising Case.

C&S Associates UK Limited v Enterprise Insurance Company Plc

C&S Associates UK Ltd (C&S) was a motor insurance claims handler based in the UK. [C&S Associates UK Limited v Enterprise Insurance Company Plc, (2015) EWHC 3757 (Comm). Hereafter C&S (2015).] Enterprise Insurance Company Plc (Enterprise) was an insurance company incorporated in Gibraltar. Enterprise provided specialist motor insurance for fleet vehicles, taxis and high value or classic cars. The parties entered into a contract titled Claims Management Delegated Authority Agreement. Within the contract, C&S provided claims handling services to Enterprise. The contract provided that it could be terminated by either party by giving a three months' notice.

After working for about a year, C&S sought to increase the fee payable by Enterprise and also introduce a minimum two-year term for the contract. Following various negotiations, Mr Ellis of Enterprise emailed to C&S: [C&S (2015): para 116].

> Hi Mike

> Yes I was in Gibraltar last week and have had the opportunity to discuss fees in detail with Andrew. … I have discussed providing a minimum 2 year agreement, this is something that Andrew would be agreeable to in consideration for a discount on the above fees of say 10%.
>
> I look forward to your comments.
>
> Kind regards
>
> Myles Ellis LLB (Hons), FCILEx.
>
> Head of Claims UK

The arrangement was not acceptable to C&S. It wanted the two-year period for the agreement without any discount in the fee. It emailed this to Enterprise the next day. Mr Ellis responded on 4 October 2013: [C&S (2015): para 117].

> I am pleased to confirm that following further discussion with Keith [Newing, Enterprise's Finance Director] and Andrew [Stone, its Chief Operating Officer] we are happy to agree the fees outlined in my e-mail of the 23rd September with a 2 year agreement to take effect from 1st October 2013 with no discount. …
>
> Kind regards,
>
> Myles Ellis LLB (Hons), FCILex
>
> Head of Claims UK
>
> Enterprise Insurance Company Plc

Mr Smith accepted these terms, as he had said he would, by an email sent on 5 October 2013: [C&S (2015): para 118].

> "Many thanks Myles, much appreciated. Mike"

Later, Enterprise claimed that C&S had committed a repudiatory breach of the contract and terminated the contract. C&S claimed that the terms of the contract were varied by the email exchange and it was not in breach. The court appraised the email communication: [C&S (2015): para 126].

> … it is clear in my judgment that the parties did objectively intend to be bound by their exchange of emails … They used the language of offer and acceptance; there was no expression such as "subject to contract" to negative an intention to be bound; on the contrary Mr Ellis's email used the language of contract confirmation ("We are pleased to confirm"), while Mr Smith's response "Many thanks Myles, much appreciated" suggests strongly that agreement had been concluded.

Thus, the parties had modified the contract by email communication. The contract had the following no oral modification clause: [C&S (2015): para 121].

> *Clause 24.1:* "Any variation of this Agreement shall not be effective unless made in writing and signed by or on behalf of each of the Parties to this Agreement."

The court noted on the clause: [C&S (2015): para 123].

> This introduces a degree of formality into any variation of the contract and ensures that the parties will not be bound by oral agreements or even by informal unsigned written documents. However, it does not go so far as to insist on manuscript signatures, paper documents, or that both parties' signatures must be on the same document.

The court, relying on the Golden Ocean case, [Golden (2012)] observed: [C&S (2015): para 123].

> I see no reason as a matter of construction of clause 24.1 why documents in electronic form, in particular an exchange of emails, signed on behalf of both parties should not satisfy the requirements of the clause.

The court applied the principle to the email communications before it: [C&S (2015): para 124].

> Each of the relevant emails in this case was signed, by Mr Smith on behalf of C&S and by Mr Ellis on behalf of Enterprise.

The court concluded that the email exchanges met the requirements of the modification clause and the parties modified the contract by their email exchanges. We next review the following case on no oral modification from the New York Supreme Court.

Stevens v Publicis S.A.,

Arthur H. Stevens sold his New York-based public relations firm, Lobsenz-Stevens (LS) to Publicis S.A. (Publicis), a French global communications company, and its American subsidiary. [Stevens v Publicis S.A., Judgment, Supreme Court, New York County, 2008 NY Slip Op 02880 [50 AD3d 253]. Hereafter Stevens (2008).] The sale involved two contracts, a stock purchase agreement and an employment agreement. Under the stock purchase agreement, Stevens sold all the shares of LS to Publicis. Under the employment contract, he was to continue as chairman and CEO of the new company, named Publicis-Dialog, Public Relations, New York (PDNY), for three years. In the employment contract, his duties were listed to be the "customary duties of a Chief Executive Officer". Under the employment contract, Stevens was to earn "earn-out" payments of up to $4 million contingent upon PDNY achieving certain levels of earnings.

Within six months of the acquisition, signs of financial problems appeared. Stevens admitted that revenue and profit targets were not met. Stevens was removed as CEO of the business, and was given several options, including leaving the firm, staying and working on new business, and a third option to come up with another alternative. Bob Bloom, former chairman and CEO of Publicis USA, became involved to work out an arrangement. Bloom and Stevens exchanged several emails. Bloom suggested that Stevens spent majority of his time in new business development and that this would be the best opportunity for him to earn his full earn-out. To the email Stevens responded: [Stevens (2008)].

> Bob, to begin with, I want to thank you again for helping me restore the dignity and respect that I'm entitled to as a senior professional. Things were really getting out of hand until you intervened. ... I accept your proposal with total enthusiasm and excitement . . .
>
> I'm psyched again and will do everything in my power to generate business, maintain profits, work well with others and move forward.

Bloom replied the same day: [Stevens (2008)].

> I am thrilled with your decision. You have my personal assurance that all of us will continue to work in the spirit of partnership to achieve our mutual goal and function together as close senior collaborators in a climate of respect and dignity for all.

Publicis later went back on the email exchange and the arrangement. The employment contract had a clause that any modification to the contract be signed by the parties. Publicis claimed that the email exchange did not meet the requirement and the contract was not modified. Noting that the email exchanges bore the typed name of the sender at the foot of the message, the court noted:[Stevens (2008)].

> The e-mails from [Stevens] constitute "signed writings" since [Steven's] name at the end of his e-mail signified his intent to authenticate the contents. Similarly, Bloom's name at the end of his e-mail constituted a "signed writing" and satisfied the requirement of section 13 (d) of the employment agreement that any modification be signed by all parties.

Thus, the court concluded that the email exchanges met the requirement of the modification clause and the contract was modified.

The Estoppel Protection

The protection of the NOM clause can lead to unfair results. To illustrate, a sale of goods contract has a no oral modification clause. Despite this, the parties get on the phone and the buyer requests three more unit of the goods to be delivered. The seller obliges but when the goods reach the buyer, the buyer refuses to accept the goods and claims that, with reference to the NOM clause, the contract is not modified. Undoubtedly, the contract is not modified. But this is unfair on the seller, who on the promise of the buyer has acted on it. In the Rock Case, the Supreme Court noted that 'the safeguard against injustice lies in the various doctrines of estoppel' [(MWB (2018): para 16]. The Court of Appeal explored and stated the principle of estoppel that if a party relies on the promise of the other then: [MWB (2016): para 61].

> … the party who might otherwise have enforced those rights will not be permitted to do so where it would be inequitable having regard to all of the circumstances.

The Supreme Court added that the test for applying the estoppel has to be stringent: [MWB (2018): para 16].

> … the scope of estoppel cannot be so broad as to destroy the whole advantage of certainty for which the parties stipulated when they agreed upon terms including the No Oral Modification clause. At the very least, (i) there would have to be some words or conduct unequivocally representing that the variation was valid notwithstanding its informality; and (ii) something more would be required for this purpose than the informal promise itself.

In the Rock Case, following the oral agreement, Rock had paid the rescheduled rent and MWB had accepted it. Rock contended that as it had acted on the promise of MWB and paid a rescheduled amount, estoppel should apply. The court ruled that there was no inequity in it as Rock was any way bound to pay a larger sum. There was no detriment in paying the sum. The court thus ruled that estoppel did not apply.

Contracts have a modification clause which prohibits oral modification of the contract. Invariable, the clause introduces further procedures and requirements to be followed in being able to modify the contract. This can include the requirement of referring to the modification clause and both the parties signing the modification documents. As the purpose of the clause is to bring certainty, the courts appraise the requirement of the clause technically and stringently.

The wording of the NOM clauses needs updating. The clause comes from the context where the contract documents were written, printed and signed on paper. As all communications have increasingly come to be by the electronic medium, disputes have arisen whether electronic communications modifying a contract meet the formality of the NOM clause. Whatever be the context from which the NOM clause has arisen, natural meaning has to be given to the words employed in a contract document. Undoubtedly, electronic communication, for example, an email, is in writing. The courts have constructed that 'signing' is only an authentication for a person to attribute the text to oneself. Writing one's name at the bottom of the email is attributing it to oneself. Thus, the requirement of writing and signing may be met in using the electronic medium. However, if the clause states that both the parties would sign the amending document, an exchange of emails may not meet this requirement. The NOM clauses need to clearly provide on modification of the contract employing electronic communications.

References

Alfred C Beatty v Guggenheim Exploration Co (1919) 225 NY 380, p 387–8.

C&S Associates UK Limited v Enterprise Insurance Company Plc (2015) EWHC 3757 (Comm).

Golden Ocean Group Limited v Salgaocar Mining Industries Pvt Ltd, 2011 WL 197258.

Great Dunmow Estates Limited v Crest Nicholson Operations Limited, (2019) EWCA Civ 1683.

MWB Business Exchange Centres Ltd v Rock Advertising Ltd, (2018) UKSC 24.

MWB Business Exchange Centres Ltd v Rock Advertising Ltd., (2016) EWCA Civ 553.

Stevens v Publicis S.A., Judgment, Supreme Court, New York County, 2008 NY Slip Op 02880 [50 AD3d 253].

Chapter 5
Termination for Breach

Most contracts get performed and not terminated. Parties come together to get on with the exchange and not get into disputes. Beyond this basic motivation, performance and not termination, is in no small part due to elaborate termination clauses which make the parties diligently and cautiously perform the contract and not risk termination of the contract. Termination of a contract has severe implications for both the parties, particularly the party in breach. For these reasons, a GCC has several elaborate clauses on termination. This includes termination for breach, termination for convenience, termination on the happening on an event and the force majeure (the impossibility) clause. Each of the themes will be developed in the subsequent chapters. Termination is an intricate play of the general law, that is, the common law and the terms stated by the parties in the contract. To recall, the common law is the default principle the courts set over the centuries. We first develop an understanding of the common law principles on termination.

Common Law Principles

Contracts started out centuries back as rudimentary exchanges—to give with one hand and take with another. If a party failed to perform its part, there was nothing left for the other party. The other party got a right to terminate the contract. The party could elect to terminate the contract and communicate it to the party in breach. On the communication of the termination, the contract got terminated and both the parties were discharged from further performance of the contract. The party terminating the contract claimed damages from the party in breach for the loss of the contract.

As the economy developed, contracts came to have multiple duties for the parties. The courts extended the principle by segmenting the duties of the parties in core parts of the contract and subsidiary parts of the contract. If a party breached a core part of the contract, the whole contract was lost. The party suffering the breach could elect

A. Pathak, *Contract Terms in International Business*,
https://doi.org/10.1007/978-981-96-8146-4_5

and communicate termination of the contract for breach to the other party. On the communication of election to terminate, the contract got terminated. Both the parties got discharged from the duties under the contract. Of course, if the suffering party did not make a communication to the other terminating the contract, the contract subsisted. On the other hand, if the breach was of a subsidiary part of the contract, the suffering party did not get a right to terminate the contract. The core part of the contract came to be called condition and the subsidiary part of the contract, warranty. The other names for the core part of the contract were heart of the contract; root of the contract; essence of the contract; or substance of the contract.

Another situation is B, a party to a contract, communicates in advance to the other party C, that he would not perform the contract. In this case, B has not breached the contract as yet. The occasion for breach will arise only when the time to perform comes. B has only renounced the contract in advance. For this reason, a communication renouncing a contract in advance is called anticipatory breach. In this case, C has a choice, he can accept the anticipatory breach or reject it. If C communicates his acceptance of the anticipatory breach, the contract is terminated. Both the parties are discharged from the further performance of the contract. The party suffering the breach will claim damages for the loss of the contract. If C does not accept the anticipatory breach, the contract subsists.

In both, breach of a condition of the contract or anticipatory breach, the suffering party has lost the entire contract or the bargain. In the first case, the core part of the contract is lost and in the other, the contract itself is abandoned. The damages will be for the loss of the entire contract. For this reason, the breach of a condition of a contract or an anticipatory breach is called a repudiatory breach.

In the latest leading case on termination, Newland Shipping and Forwarding Limited v Toba Trading FZC [Newland Shipping and Forwarding Limited v Toba Trading FZC, (2014) EWHC 661 (Comm). Hereafter Toba (2014).] (hereafter the Toba Trading Case), the court stated the principles of common law on termination of contract: [Toba (2014): Para 50].

> Under the general law, a party has the right to terminate a contract if the other party commits a 'repudiatory breach'. I use this term to refer compendiously to the three situations where a party (a) commits a breach which 'goes to the root of the contract' or deprives the other party of substantially the whole benefit of its performance, (b) commits a breach of a term which the parties have agreed will be a 'condition', i.e. a term any breach of which is treated as repudiatory, or (c) renounces the contract by making it clear that it is going to commit a breach of one of these two kinds.

Thus, a party can be in repudiatory breach in any of the three situations. One, the party breaches a term of the contract which is a core part of the contract. Two, the party breaches a term which is not a core part of the contract but the contract provides that it is a core part of the contract. Three, the party in advance announces that it would not perform the contract. In this case, the party has not breached a term but only announced in advance that it would not perform the contract. This is anticipatory breach. A repudiatory breach, that is, any of the three breaches above, does not bring a contract to an end on its own. It gives the right to the suffering party to elect to terminate the contract. The court noted: [Toba (2014): Para 50].

> When a repudiatory breach occurs, the other party has a choice whether to terminate the contract or to affirm it (and thereby lose the right to terminate the contract for the relevant breach). Any communication which clearly conveys an election to terminate (or affirm) the contract will have that effect.

Thus, no formality is needed for communicating the termination of the contract. Any communication, valid within the contract terms, which clearly conveys the election to terminate the contract is adequate. On a valid termination of the contract, 'both parties are released from their primary obligations which are not yet due for performance' [Toba (2014): Para 50]. The primary obligation is substituted by 'a secondary obligation to pay monetary compensation to the other party for the loss sustained by him in consequence of their non-performance in the future' [Photo Production Ltd v Securicor Transport Ltd (1980) AC 827: Page 849]. The imposition of this 'secondary obligation reflects the repudiatory nature of the breach' [Toba (2014): Para 50].

Termination for Convenience

Under the common law principles, a party can get out of a contract only if the other party breaches a core part of the contract. But there would be many occasions where, having got into a contract, a party would like to get out of the contract. Take the case of a contract for supply of cement for three years every month, where the construction contract itself is abandoned. To address this concern, 'termination for convenience' clause got introduced. The clause provides that a party can terminate the contract, when it likes, for its convenience. As the termination for convenience has no reference to breach or is not based on a breach, there is no question of either party paying damages to the other. What about the losses suffered by the other party due to termination of the contract?

The party terminating the contract was not liable as he was not in breach. He was only exercising his right under the contract terms. The clause brought in a risk to a party subject to the clause. The contract could be brought to an end at any point of time by the other for his convenience. To mitigate the harshness of it, a buffer period was introduced. The contract could be terminated only with weeks of advance notice. A termination for convenience clause would read as follows:

> **Termination for Convenience:** The purchaser may, by written notice of thirty days sent to the seller, terminate the contract, in whole or part, at any time for his convenience. The notice of termination shall specify that termination is for the purchaser's convenience, the extent to which performance of work under the contract is terminated and the date upon which such termination becomes effective.

The contracting parties are free to set their own terms. A contract may give the right to terminate the contract for convenience to either the parties or only one of the parties. This will depend on the relative strength of the parties and the party whose GCC is being adopted for the contract.

Termination Clauses

The common law principles developed over the centuries, where contracts were mostly oral. But most business contracts are now in writing and have elaborate clauses. The contract is of the contracting parties and terms of the contract must be given effect to. Thus, the termination clause in a contract should be followed. The court in the Toba Trading Case stated the principle: [Toba (2014): Para 49].

> In principle, a contractual right to cancel or terminate a contract (these terms generally being interchangeable) arises when the contract says it arises. No particular formality is necessary (unless the contract so provides) to exercise the right. Any communication which clearly conveys that the right is being exercised will suffice. ... The general meaning of cancellation or termination of a contract ... is termination of all the primary legal obligations imposed by the contract of which performance is not yet due.

Thus, a contract term, on the happening of an event, may give a right to terminate the contract. The party can exercise the right by making a clear communication to the other of the termination. At this, the contract stands terminated. The parties will be discharged from the performance of further obligations under the contract. At this stage, the clause can be forked into two categories. One, the clause is on breach or has a relationship with breach. Two, the clause is not based on a breach. An example of termination for non-breach is, if a party turns insolvent. In turning insolvent, the party has not breached a term of the contract but the stated event has matured for the other to terminate the contract. In this chapter, we will take up the first one, that is termination clauses which are on a breach or related to a breach.

The consequences of termination 'are again in principle whatever the contract says they are.' [Toba (2014): Para 49] Thus, the party in breach will pay damages as stated in the contract. But here comes the limitations on following the terms of the contract. Contractual damages are only to cover losses suffered by the party due to the breach and not a penalty to be imposed on the other or to profit from it [Ruxley Electronics & Construction Ltd v Forsyth (1995) UKHL 8]. Thus, the damages stated in the contract will not be awarded if these are punitive. To illustrate the point, a contract for fabrication of a machinery provided that the buyer could terminate the contract for any breach by the seller and claim damages for the loss of the entire contract. The seller in breach used ten steel screws than copper-plated screws for the casing of the machine. This was entirely superfluous and made no impact on the performance or the life of the machine. Following the terms, however, justifiably, the buyer terminated the contract. Further, within the terms of the contract, the buyer claimed damages for buying a machine of the same description at a higher price from another seller. The claimed damages, while stated in the contract, are punitive and should not be awarded. The breach by the seller is in use of ten steel screws than copper-plated screws. The loss arising from the breach is the price difference between the two kinds of screws and not of the entire machine.

Interplay of the Principles and Clauses

There are, thus, two sources of termination. The first is the common law principle, that a party can elect to terminate a contract for the breach of a core part of the contract. The second source is a contract term that may provide on breach and termination. As a result, termination for breach has become an interplay of the common law principles and clauses on breach and termination.

Contract are voluntarily formed and the contracting parties are free to set their terms. At the same time, the common law principles are laws established by the courts. The law itself recognises and grants that the contracting parties are free to oust the common law principles or substitute them. As the common law principles are law, however, the courts insists that express and clear language must be used to oust the terms. That is, unless the clause clearly and unambiguously states to oust the common law principles, the principles would not get ousted. The court in the Toba Trading Case stated the principle: [Toba (2014): Para 51].

It is also clear that the inclusion in a contract of an express cancellation clause will not be treated as excluding the right to terminate the contract under the general law upon a repudiatory breach unless the contract clearly says so.

Thus, merely that there is a termination clause in the contract would not oust the common law principles. The clause must clearly oust the common law principle for it to be excluded. This point on ousting of the common law principles is of huge significance. The clause for termination for breach in a GCC where the buyer is the stronger party may read:

> **20.1 Termination for Default:** The seller fails to perform any obligation under the contract. In this case, the purchaser will give a written notice to the seller that he has defaulted. The notice will give the seller 30 days or more to cure the default. The purchaser can terminate the contract if the seller fails to cure the defect within the period given in the notice.

The clause is tilted in favour of the buyer and presumably, the parties have contracted on the GCC set by the buyer. The buyer, who has set the GCC, takes that the seller cannot terminate the contract for any breach by the buyer as the clause provides only for the buyer to terminate the contract. It makes no mention of the seller ever being able to terminate the contract. The understanding of the scope of the clause has been that the seller cannot terminate the contract, no matter what be the breach by the buyer. In the light of the Toba Trading Case, this is an incorrect view. The clause is only silent on the rights of the seller to terminate the contract. But this is not good enough to oust the right of the seller to terminate the contract for a breach of a condition by the buyer. The right of the seller to terminate the contract, if the buyer breaches a condition, remains intact. To secure the intended result, the termination clauses need to be amended with the additions to the effect that the seller cannot terminate the contract for any breach by the buyer, whether the breach is a condition of the contract or a warranty. In the coming decade, a clause to this effect would increasingly get introduced in the termination clauses in the GCC.

We next come to the interplay of the common law principles and the termination clauses related to breach. We would do this, with a review of the Toba Trading Case, which is the latest case consolidating the principles.

The Toba Trading Case: The Contract

Newland Shipping and Forwarding Ltd is a company engaged in trading gasoil and gasoline. In August 2010, the company entered into a contract to sell gasoil and gasoline to Toba Trading FZC. Toba Trading FZC is a company incorporated in the UAE. This company too is engaged in the trading of gasoil and gasoline. We will call the companies Newland and Toba. Following the terms of the contract, Toba made an advance payment of USD 3.2 million but Newland failed to supply the goods. It stated that there were no stocks available at Turkmenbashi Oil Refinery, from where the products were to be sourced. Toba then asked to reimburse the payment that was made but Newland replied that it was experiencing problems to immediately return the money as all their money was 'stuck with different suppliers' [Toba (2014): Para 1].

As a solution, Newland suggested that they enter into new contracts for supplies of gasoil and gasoline where Toba would make a 20% deduction from all invoices. Through this arrangement, the amount already paid by Toba would be partially utilised to fund the new contracts. Toba agreed to the suggestion. The parties entered into a contract on 17 March 2011 for delivery of 5000 MT of gasoil. This contract too ran into problems and got terminated. The contract was subject to English law and jurisdiction of the UK courts. The parties came before the High Court of the UK in dispute.

The contract was for the sale and purchase of 5000 MT $\pm$ 10% of hydro-purified gasoil. Within the contract, the goods were to be sourced from the Turkmenbashi Oil Refinery. The refinery is in the west of Turkmenistan. Turkmenistan borders Afghanistan, Uzbekistan and Tehran. The delivery terms were CPT Serkhetabad Railway Station, Turkmenistan. In a CPT contract, the seller bears the cost of the carriage to the destination. It is the seller's responsibility to arrange carriage to the appointed destination but the risk passes to the buyer when the goods are delivered to the carrier. Thus, it was the seller's responsibility to transport the goods by rail from Turkmenbashi Railway Station to Serkhetabad. Serkhetabad is in the east of Turkmenistan, near the Afghanistan border. The price was fixed according to a formula based on a published Platt's price. Platt provides information on energy sources which is used for assessing and benchmarking price.

Clause 11 of the contract provided that the title to the product was to be 'transferred from seller to buyer after the 100% payment is effected as per seller's instructions'. Thus, the ownership in the goods was to pass only on the seller receiving the full price. Clause 7 of the contract provided on the buyer making the payment. It read: [Toba (2014): Para 11].

Clause 7: Payment.

> Payment for each shipped lot … to be done within 2 (two) banking days after the final price will be known, against the seller's invoice …
>
> In case if buyer fails to pay for cargo in period more than 5 days then the seller has the right to cancel the contract and to sell the cargo to other customers, and buyer will be obliged to compensate to seller all the losses and demurrage connected with such failure.

The Toba Trading Case: Performance of the Contract

Towards performance of the contract, Newland loaded gasoil in railway tankers at Turkmenbashi Railway Station and sent invoice dated 23 March 2011 for payment. Under clause 7 of the Contract payment, the payment was to be made within 2 working days of the raising of the invoices. Newland sent several emails for payment but no payment came from Toba. Toba explained that it was selling the cargo to a party called Mahmood & Jalil Co (M&J) and waiting for them to do the advance payment. On 7 April 2011 Toba informed Newland that it had received the payment from M&J. The email, however, added: [Toba (2014): Para 20].

> … in order for us to be able to effect the payment to your account, we need to have the confirmation from M&J that they have received the cargo, or at least are in total control of the cargo. In that way their account with us will be debited for this cargo, and accordingly we can consider you credible as per our agreements.

Newland replied almost immediately that all these were 'your internal issues with M&J' and reiterated: [Toba (2014): Para 21].

> As per contract, you should pay in 2 banking days after loading from Turkmenbashi. Please arrange payment ASAP. Waiting for your SWIFT confirmation.

Newland reiterated with another mail: [Toba (2014): Para 21].

> Please act accordingly to the signed contract and do not put any additional requirements. Awaiting for the SWIFT confirmation.

No payment was received. The following day, that is, 8 April 2011, Newland sent a notice terminating the contract. Following the termination, Newland claimed damages before the court. Toba already had its money stuck with the seller. It was now completely stranded with the prospect of paying damages for being in breach. Toba claimed that the termination notice issued by Newland was invalid and the termination unlawful. Thus, Toba contended that it was Newland who should pay damages for the unlawful termination of the contract.

The court noted that there are two sources of terminating a contract for breach, the common law principles and the contract terms on breach. The court noted that there will be an interplay between the two: [Toba (2014): Para 52].

> There is therefore generally no inconsistency between exercising a contractual right of cancellation and enforcing its contractual consequences on the one hand and, on the other hand, terminating the contract for a repudiatory breach. It follows that, where both rights are available, a party can generally elect to exercise both rights at the same time.

A contract will get terminated and the parties discharged whether the right is exercised on the grounds of repudiation under the general law or a term on breach in the contract. But it is important to clearly bring out the basis for the termination. The reason for this is, if the termination is done under the terms of the contract, the damages would be awarded as provided in the contract for that breach. On the other hand, if the termination is done for a repudiatory breach, the damages would be awarded under the damages clauses for the loss of the entire contract. The damages under the two rights may be identical. In this case, it would not matter the right under which the termination was done. The damages under the two rights may be different but not inconsistent with each other. In this case again, there would be no difficulty. In other cases, the damages under the two rights may be inconsistent. In this case, conflicts and uncertainties would arise. The party would have to choose between one of the rights and clearly state it while electing to terminate the contract. The court noted on the situations where the two rights led to inconsistencies: [Toba (2014): Para 53].

> There can, however, be cases … where exercising one of these rights is inconsistent with exercising the other because the consequences of their exercise conflict. In such a case a party who has a contractual right to cancel the contract and a right to terminate the contract under the general law cannot exercise both rights and will necessarily have to elect between them. In accordance with general principle, to make a valid election, a party in this position must clearly communicate its choice to exercise one of the rights rather that the other.

With this elaboration of the principles, the court reviewed the termination notice issued by Newland.

The Toba Trading Case: The Termination Notice

Newland had terminated the contract by sending a notice on 8 April 2011. The termination notice by Newland read as follows: [Toba (2014): Para 61].

> Due to the not fulfilment of obligations by your company in terms of payments for cargo loaded as per your instructions …
>
> As per our sale contract: 'in case if buyer fails to pay for cargo in period more than 5 days then the seller has the right to cancel the contract ….
>
> Due to:

(1) Non-payment for the already loaded cargo within aforesaid contractual time period;
(2) Endless additional requirements (which are not mentioned in the contract at all) from your side in order for you to make a payment; we found ourselves in difficult situations….

> In connection with your breach of contract, we recognise it as a repudiatory breach, therefore we consider the contract as null and void.
>
> It discharges our company from further performance of the contract, whilst allowing us to sue for damages for loss of the benefit of the contract, including all losses of future profit.

The court concluded that the notice had based the termination on two grounds, under clause 7 and as a repudiatory breach under the general law.

The Toba Trading Case: Was Toba in Repudiatory Breach?

The question in the case then was, what kind of breaches Toba had made? Clause 7 of the contract gave the right to terminate the contract if Toba did not pay within five days of raising the invoice by Newland. As Toba had not paid in time, Newland certainly had the right to terminate the contract under clause 7. Newland was right in referring to clause 7 for terminating the contract. But it had also stated that Toba was in repudiatory breach as a basis for the termination. Was Toba in a repudiatory breach?

It is a principle of sale of goods that unless 'a different intention appears' from the terms of a contract, a time set for payment is not a condition of the contract. Applying the principle, court noted: [Toba (2014): Para 56].

> There is no reason to infer from the inclusion in the contract of a provision giving a right to cancel if the buyer fails to pay for the goods within a specified period that a failure to pay within that period is to be treated as a repudiatory breach of the contract. Rather, the natural inference is that a contractual right of cancellation is being provided because failure to pay within that period would not (or would not clearly or necessarily) give rise to a right to terminate the contract under the general law.

Thus, the court concluded that Toba was not in a repudiatory breach in its failure to pay within 5 days of the raising of the invoice. But Toba got stuck elsewhere. Toba in its email of 7 April 2011 had declared that it would not make the payment unless and until the sub-buyer M&J obtained the cargo. In other words, Toba declared that it was abandoning its duties under the contract. The court, analysing the email, noted: [Toba (2014): Para 57].

> By that email, Toba made it clear that it would not comply with the contractual payment obligation and was not going to pay for the goods until its buyer received or was in total control of the cargo. There was nothing in the Contract which justified that position. It was an anticipatory breach which was in my view sufficiently substantial to amount to a repudiation and give rise to a right of termination under the general law.

The refusal to pay by Toba, thus, was an anticipatory beach, abandoning and repudiating the entire contract. The court concluded: [Toba (2014): Para 58].

> In these circumstances I consider that, as at 8 April 2011, Newland had a contractual right to terminate the contract under clause 7 and also a right under the general law to terminate the contract on account of Toba's repudiatory breach.

Thus, Toba was in breach of clause 7 and also a repudiatory breach.

The Toba Trading Case: Were the Damages Inconsistent?

The only thing that could now rescue Toba was that the consequences of clause 7 and the repudiatory breach were inconsistent. Clause 7 provided damages for breach of the clause in not paying in time as follows: [Toba (2014): Para 11].

> … to sell the cargo to other customers, and buyer will be obliged to compensate to seller all the losses and demurrage connected with such failure.

This was not inconsistent with the damages clauses for general losses as the clause waived all other damages. It read: [Toba (2014): Para 11].

> Clause 12: limitation of liability
>
> Except as expressly provided for in this contract, neither seller nor buyer shall be liable for any direct or indirect, consequential or special losses, damages or expenses of any kind, directly or indirectly arising out of or in any way connected with the conclusion, performance, failure to perform or the termination of this contract.

Thus, other than the losses and demurrages under clause 7 (except as expressly provided for in this contract), clause 12 waived all other losses and liability. There was no inconsistency between the two rights. Thus, Toba failed to establish that the termination notice was invalid and the termination unlawful.

Newland and Toba seemingly acted as ordinary reasonable business parties. Once Toba's money was stuck, the best it could do was get into new contracts. It did not want more accidents so it was insistent on paying only after getting delivery. But this was a grave folly within the contract terms. We next explore anticipatory breach, where a party to a contract renounces the contract.

Anticipatory Breach: Bunge V Nidera

Bunge SA is a Geneva, Switzerland-based organisation involved in the production and distribution of cereals and grains. [Bunge SA v Nidera BV (2015) UKSC 43. Hereafter Bunge (2015).] It operates as a subsidiary of Bunge Limited. Nidera BV is a Rotterdam, Netherlands-based company, engaged in the distribution of agricultural commodities. It operates as a subsidiary of China National Cereals, Oils and Foodstuffs Corporation (COFCO), one of China's state-owned food processing companies.

The companies entered into a sale contract, through brokers in Milan, for the sale of 25,000 Metric Tonnes of Russian milling wheat. Bunge SA was the seller and Nidera BV, the buyer. The sale was for: '25,000 mt of Russian milling wheat, 2010 crop, f.o.b. Novorossiysk'. The shipment period was from 23 to 30 August 2010. Nidera SA was to arrange for a ship to take the delivery of the goods at the Russian port Novorossiysk from 23 to 30 August 2010. It would notify the seller of the name of the ship and the seller would thus deliver the consignment.

The contract incorporated Grain and Feed Trade Association (GAFTA) form 49. GAFTA is an international trade association that aims to promote international trade in agricultural commodities. It was the duty of the buyer to arrange for a ship to take the delivery at the Russian port. Considering this, the buyer communicated to the seller on 5 August 2010 that a vessel named 'Royal' would take delivery of the goods from the designated port Novorossiysk during August 23 and 30. On the same day, Russia introduced a legislative embargo on exports of wheat from its territory, which was to run from 15 August to 31 December 2010. The seller, understandably, was alarmed at the prospect of the contract failing.

On 9 August 2010, the seller sent an email to the buyer informing them of the export embargo and stating that the contract was, therefore, 'cancelled' under Clause 13 of the contract. On 11 August 2010, the buyer responded with a curious email. The buyer stated that the sellers' email was an anticipatory breach which the buyer accepted. The seller replied on 12 August 2010, expressing puzzlement over the buyer's position. The seller asserted that their earlier email had been sent in accordance with the prohibition clause and that under the embargo, it would not be possible to deliver the goods. The seller declared that they would perform the contract if the ban were lifted or changed. The seller queried whether the buyer truly believed that it was sensible to incur the costs of chartering a vessel and presenting it for loading, knowing well that the goods could not be delivered. Further, the seller formally offered to reinstate the contract on the same terms. The buyer plainly declined the seller's offer.

The buyer proceeded to claim damages for the claimed breach. The first question before the courts was whether the seller had made an anticipatory breach of the contract. Clause 13 of the contract read:

> 13. *Prohibition* —In case of prohibition of export ... restricting export, whether partially or otherwise, any such restriction shall be deemed by both parties to apply to this contract ... to prevent fulfilment ... by shipment ... and to that extent this contract ... shall be cancelled. Sellers shall advise buyers without delay ... to justify the cancellation.

Referring to the clause, the Commercial Court concluded that the seller had made an anticipatory breach by its email communication: [Bunge SA v Nidera BV, (2013) 1 CLC 325: p 333].

> ... it could not be said on 9 August 2010, when sellers purported to declare the contract cancelled, that there was a prohibition restricting such export. ... there was at the time a prohibition which might or might not do so. It depended on whether it was revoked or modified so as to permit some element of performance before the shipment period expired, something which was 'always possible'.

The United Kingdom Supreme Court, before which the dispute came in appeal, The United Kingdom Supreme Court, in Bunge SA v Nidera BV [Bunge SA v Nidera BV, (2015) UKSC 43. Hereafter Bunge (2015)], suggested that anticipatory breach 'probably more accurately' should be referred as "renunciation" [Bunge (2015): Para 12] It saved the waste of economic resources for both the parties from requiring 'the parties to go through the motions of performing a contract which was for practical purposes dead' [Bunge (2015): Para 12]. The court noted on anticipatory breach: [Bunge (2015): Para 12].

> … the effect of the renunciation of a contract in advance of the time agreed for performance was (i) to confer on the injured party an option to accept the renunciation as bringing the contract to an end and to treat himself as discharged from that time onward from further performance; (ii) to enable the injured party to deal with the financial consequences by suing for damages at once, without waiting for the time fixed for performance; and (iii) to bring forward the injured party's duty to mitigate to the time when the renunciation was accepted.

The Supreme Court agreed with the commercial court that the seller 'jumped the gun by their unqualified statement that the contract was cancelled' [Bunge (2015): Para 41].

Termination of a contract is a challenging subject for the contracting parties and needs utmost care, expertise and diligence. The learning from the chapter can be summarised as the following points. One, the existing understanding on a contract term on termination for breach is incorrect and incomplete. Unless the termination clause in clear and express terms oust the rights of termination of a party, the rights do not get vacated. Two, if a party claims breach and terminates a contract, and it turns out that there was no breach, the party terminating the contract would be in wrong. The party would have to pay damages for bringing the contract to an end to the other. Three, if there is only a breach of a term of a contract and this does not constitute a repudiatory breach, a repudiatory breach must not be alleged. This will be a wrongful termination of the contract. Four, if there is a breach of a clause of a contract and also a repudiatory breach, the implications of the two should be thoroughly analysed for drafting the termination notice. A final decision on termination and the drafting of a termination notice is best left to the law specialists. Five, improved means of communication have led to surplus of communications and increased the prospects of a party being in anticipatory beach.

References

Bunge SA v Nidera BV, (2015) UKSC 43.
Newland Shipping and Forwarding Limited v Toba Trading FZC, (2014) EWHC 661 (Comm).
Photo Production Ltd v Securicor Transport Ltd (1980) AC 827.
Ruxley Electronics & Construction Ltd v Forsyth, (1995) UKHL 8

Chapter 6
Termination on Non-breach

It is a common law principle that a party can elect to terminate a contract for a breach of a core part of the contract. The GCCs have clauses on termination for breach by a party. The common law principle and the termination for breach clause have an interplay. GCCs also have express terms on termination for convenience. This gives the right to a party to terminate the contract if the party does not wish to continue with the contract. The key difference between termination for breach and termination for convenience is that for termination for breach, damages can be claimed and for termination for convenience, damages cannot be claimed. In addition, GCCs may provide several other grounds for termination of the contract. It is for the contracting parties to project changes in the context and introduce terms to terminate the contract on the happening of a certain event. A common ground in this category is a party moving towards insolvency. Another ground is a party merging or amalgamating with another company. A simple clause on insolvency may read as follows:

> **Termination for Insolvency:** The purchaser, may at any time, terminate the contract by giving written notice to the seller, without compensation to the seller, if the seller becomes bankrupt or otherwise insolvent or files for insolvency. Further, such termination will not prejudice or affect any right of action or remedy which has accrued or will accrue thereafter to the purchaser.

If the seller becomes insolvent, he is not in a breach of a term of the contract. The clause does not depend on or relate to a breach. It is also distinct from a termination for convenience clause. The convenience clause is available to a party when the party likes. In contrast, the insolvency clause can be invoked only if the stated event, that is, the company turning insolvent, arises. The clause also provides on the consequences of the termination. It states that the purchaser will not be liable to provide any compensation to the seller for the losses suffered from the termination. Further, the termination will not affect any right or remedy of the purchaser.

Exploring the application of the clause, we take the situation where the seller becomes insolvent. The purchaser terminates the contract under the clause. As a result of this, the purchaser loses the bargain or the contract. The purchaser claims

A. Pathak, *Contract Terms in International Business*,
https://doi.org/10.1007/978-981-96-8146-4_6

damages for loss of bargain or loss of the contract. Should the damages be awarded for the loss of the contract? In Phones 4U Ltd (in administration) v EE Ltd, [Phones 4U Ltd (in administration) v EE Ltd, [2018] EWHC 49 (Comm). Hereafter Phones 4U (2019).] the UK High Court explained the basic legal principles of damages for loss of bargain at common law. The judge referred to a repudiatory breach to be a breach of the core part of the contract and renunciation as an anticipatory breach. The court further noted: [Phones 4U (2019): Para 72].

> … it is common to say that in the case of a repudiatory breach or renunciation, the innocent party may "accept the repudiation", or "accept" it "as terminating the contract", and sue for damages for loss of bargain.

The principle is, when a repudiatory breach occurs, the innocent party can elect to terminate the contract or affirm the contract. The judge noted: [Phones 4U (2019): Para 73].

> More precisely: (i) the cause of action is for damages for the repudiatory breach of contract committed by the guilty party or anticipated by its renunciation; (ii) those damages are, or include, damages for the loss of the innocent party's bargain; (iii) such damages are recoverable only if that loss resulted from the breach;

The termination does not happen on its own, the innocent party needs to elect to terminate the contract. While the 'communication requires no particular form, but it must be clear and unequivocal' [Phones 4U (2019): Para 73] The judge stated: [Phones 4U (2019): Para 74].

> It is said that the innocent party has an election, that is to say a free choice, whether to treat itself as discharged from its bargain. … Where the innocent party does have a free choice to treat the bargain as at an end, and so chooses, the law treats the repudiatory breach or renunciation as causing the loss of bargain notwithstanding that freedom of choice. That both reflects and informs the requirements set by the law for there to be a repudiatory breach or renunciation in the first place.

Repudiatory breach and loss of bargain are the two sides of the same coin. The judge stated: [Phones 4U (2019): Para 75].

> … only if an actual breach has deprived the innocent party of substantially the whole of its bargain, or is set to do so, does it seem appropriate in principle to treat the innocent party's decision to walk away as caused by the breach; and then if the decision to walk away is appropriately treated as caused by the breach, damages for that breach should rightly include damages for the loss of the bargain.

Thus, repudiatory breach and loss of bargain go hand in hand. And the reverse, if the termination is not for a repudiatory breach but arises from an express provision in the contract, there cannot be a claim for loss of bargain. In other words, while there will be a termination of the contract, damages will not be payable. We will explore the theme of termination under express provisions with the leading case, Phones 4U Ltd (in administration) v EE Ltd. [Phones 4U (2019)].

The Phones 4U Case: The Trading Agreement and Termination

EE Ltd was a major mobile network operator in the UK. [Phones 4U (2019)] It provided connections under the brand EE, Orange and T-Mobile. EE sold its subscriptions to the customers through intermediaries. Phones 4U (P4U) was a very well-known intermediary for the network operators, including EE. The trading relationship between the parties was governed by a written contract. The contract provided for three different activities, getting new customers on pay monthly plans, managing the plans of the existing customers; and Pay As You Go (PAYG) connections. The contract was dated 8 October 2012. We will call it 'the Trading Agreement'.

From 2012, P4U faced a series of financial difficulties. In 2012, Three, a UK Network operator, ended its trading relationship with P4U. O2, another Network operator, in February 2012, under its contract terms, prohibited P4U from selling new connections. In January 2014, O2 decided not to renew its trading contract with P4U. Vodafone, another operator, issued a termination notice in August 2014, terminating its trading contract with effect from February 2015.

On Friday, 12 September 2014, EE notified P4U that it would not renew or replace the Trading Agreement when it expired on 30 September 2015. The same day in the afternoon, the board of directors of P4U met and resolved to seek the appointment of administrators for the liquidation of the company, as the company had run out of business partners. P4U's retail shops and outlets remained open and traded over the weekend of 13–14 September 2014. On the morning of Monday, 15 September 2014, however, the retail shops and outlets did not open for business and online trading was suspended. Appointment of administrators requires court approval. P4U applied to the court for the appointment of administrators on Monday, September 15 morning and secured it by the afternoon. On Wednesday, 17 September, at 1.02 PM, EE sent the administrators an email indicating that it was terminating the contract. The termination letter was attached with the email. The termination letter stated as follows: [Phones 4U (2019): Para 8].

> We refer to the agreement [the Trading Agreement].
>
> In accordance with clause 14.1.2 of the agreement, we hereby terminate the agreement with immediate effect.
>
> As a result, we hereby terminate with immediate effect your authority to sell and promote all EE products and services contemplated by the agreement …
>
> This notice is governed by English law.

Clause 14.1 of the Trading Agreement gave either party the right at any time to terminate the contract by giving notice in writing. It provided: [Phones 4U (2019): Para 78].

14.1. Either party may at any time by giving notice in writing to the other terminate this Agreement with immediate effect:

14.1.1 if the other party commits a material breach of this Agreement and either such breach is incapable of remedy or, if capable of remedy, has not been remedied to the reasonable satisfaction of the other party within 30 days of a written request from the other party to remedy such breach; or

14.1.2 if the other party is unable to pay its debts … or takes any steps (or any third party takes any steps in respect of the other party) to: initiate a composition, scheme, or other arrangement with any of its creditors (including any voluntary arrangement); resolve or petition to wind up that other party; appoints an administrator, receiver or manager over all or any part of that other party's business undertakings or assets; pass a resolution for that other party's winding up, or has a petition presented to any court for its winding up or for an administration order or if any analogous event occurs in any jurisdiction.

P4U was not prohibited from appointing an administrator. In appointing administrators, it was not in breach of the contract. At the same time, P4U appointing an administrator gave the right to EE to elect to terminate the contract. EE had done this only by its termination letter. It had terminated the contract under clause 14.1.2.

While the contract was terminated immediately, EE would need to pay commissions to P4U till 2021 on the connections P4U had already secured under the trade agreement. P4U estimated the amount to be £120 m. The parties developed a dispute over payment of the amount. EE had a different understanding of its claims. It understood that it would get damages for the loss of the entire remaining period of the contract. Following these, in 2017, P4U filed a claim before the Commercial Court for its commissions and EE responded with a counterclaim for £200 m in damages for loss of bargain.

The court found the counterclaim of EE 'seriously deficient in its analysis' [Phones 4U (2019): Para 20]. EE simply stated that on or about 14, September 2014, the Board of Directors of P4U resolved to cease trading. But EE did not allege it to be a breach of the contract. Nor did it claim that P4U communicated this to it to be able to claim it to be an anticipatory breach. EE claimed, that 'since that time, in breach of the Key Obligation' P4U has not 'undertaken any of the Key Activities' and 'has not procured any new PAYG connections' [Phones 4U (2019): Para 20]. But the contract was terminated on 17 September 2014. A termination discharges both the parties from further performance of the contract. The only days on which there was a breach in P4U not doing its business under the trading agreement was Monday 15 September 2014, Tuesday 16 September 2014 and the morning of Wednesday 17 September 2014. In the light of these serious analytical shortcomings, the court allowed EE to amend its claim and arguments for a counterclaim. The revised claim now stood on the fact that P4U was in breach in not doing the business, which included marketing the products and getting new connections, for two and half days till EE terminated the contract.

The court noted on P4U not doing marketing or promotion of the product in those two and half days: [Phones 4U (2019): Para 38].

> I think it fanciful to suppose that the failure by Phones 4U to engage in any marketing or promotion, for any of the mobile networks, for 2½ days … caused EE any identifiable or quantifiable loss or damage.

On the second aspect of the business, that is, P4U getting new subscriptions, the judge noted: [Phones 4U (2019): Para 39].

> In the context of a Trading Agreement with just over a year to run … in my judgment it is equally fanciful to suppose that this 2½ days of lost connections might be held … to have deprived EE of substantially the whole benefit of the respective contract.

The Phones 4U Case: Repudiatory Breach

Yet another perspective emerged on P4U not doing the business for the two and half days. If there was a 'likelihood of Phones 4U's cessation of trading continuing for substantially the whole of the remaining contract term', the breach for the two and half days indicated the breach for the entire remaining period [Phones 4U (2019): Para 40]. As a result, 'the breach went to the root and justified termination at common law.' [Phones 4U (2019): Para 40] On this point, the judge noted: [Phones 4U (2019): Para 42].

> It seems to me there may be an important issue of principle here … that on the facts as they were at termination the probability was, that is to say it was more probable than not that, breach would continue or be repeated sufficiently to deprive it of substantially the whole benefit of its bargain.

The court recognised that the exercise was a fact-sensitive exercise: [Phones 4U (2019): Para 42].

> … the question whether a breach of contract was or was liable to become sufficiently serious in its consequences as to go to the root of a contract is inherently a fact-sensitive evaluation.

P4U made the following contentions that on the date of termination, that is, 17 September 2014, there was not a strong possibility that the suspension of the business would continue forever.

1. The administrators were just appointed and had emphasised in their public statement that 'the initial focus would be assessing whether the business could be rescued so they could reopen the stores and trade' [Phones 4U (2019): Para 50].
2. The administrators, in their communications with the existing or other possible trading parties, 'showed the administrators to have been pursuing an attempt to rescue the business as a going concern to enable trading to resume and the stores to reopen.' [Phones 4U (2019): Para 50]
3. It was the statutory duty of the administrators 'with continuation of the business as a going concern if possible as a first statutory priority.' This was 'not constrained by any views that may have been expressed by others, including the Board of Directors' [Phones 4U (2019): Para 50].

EE made the following claims as to how it was probable that the breach was a continuing one:

1. P4U in its board meeting on Friday 12 September 2014 stated that it was left with no viable business and resolved to appoint administrators for the company. This was 'an unqualified decision to cease trading indefinitely after the weekend ahead' [Phones 4U (2019): Para 52].
2. In the application to the court on 15 September 2014, for the appointment of administrators, the directors gave evidence that: [Phones 4U (2019): Para 52]

> … without trading contracts with the major mobile networks Phones 4U had no viable business and they did not believe it would be possible to conclude any such trading contracts before the Trading Agreement expired on 30 September 2015, so that they could see no reasonable prospect of avoiding insolvent liquidation.

3. The directors further gave evidence that 'it was too early to say whether any sale of the business as a going concern might be achievable' [Phones 4U (2019): Para 52].
4. It was submitted to the court for the appointment of the administrators by the counsel for the directors: [Phones 4U (2019): Para 52]

> … it was not expected that rescuing Phones 4U as a going concern or achieving a better result for its creditors than winding it up would realistically be achievable, administration rather than liquidation nonetheless being sought on the basis that it would better facilitate the realising of property to make a distribution to secured or preferential creditors.

5. The actions of the administrators in the early days of their appointment indicated that 'the possibility of any substantial resumption of trading was at best a remote one' [Phones 4U (2019): Para 52].

At this stage, we need to note that the judge was doing a summary proceeding. In a summary proceeding, the court has to make a decision whether there is a realistic possibility of a party being able to establish a point to take the case to trial. If there is no realistic possibility, it becomes a waste of time of the court and resources of the other party. The judge noted on the contentions of P4U: [Phones 4U (2019): Para 51].

> Those points seem to me fairly made, so far as they go. However, they do not go so far as to render fanciful the prospect that upon the full investigation of the facts that only a trial can achieve the court may conclude that as matters stood at the time of termination on 17 September 2014 in all probability the cessation of trading by Phones 4U would persist for (at least) all of the remaining period … or the vast majority of the remaining period of the Trading Agreement.

The court noted that even if there was a real possibility of the stores reopening, the initial closure itself could be for a long period: [Phones 4U (2019): Para 53].

> … it is not clear that EE would therefore fail in its claim of repudiatory breach. The question of the probable longevity of the cessation of trading by Phones 4U … is not apt for determination by summary judgment.

The judge was of the view that only after a detailed factual and expert examination the court would be able to make a determination of the question. The court concluded: [Phones 4U (2019): Para 54].

> I am not persuaded that EE does not have a realistic prospect of establishing the existence at the time of its termination letter of repudiatory breach on the part of Phones 4U.

The Phones 4U Case: Anticipatory Breach

Another point the court explored was whether P4U was in anticipatory breach by renouncing the contract. EE contended, in the words of the court: [Phones 4U (2019): Para 55].

> Phones 4U had so conducted itself towards EE and/or communicated with EE as to make it unequivocally to appear that Phones 4U intended no longer to honour its contractual obligations.

The court noted on the contention: [Phones 4U (2019): Para 56].

> … the requirement for a renunciation to be clear, absolute and unequivocal may be very difficult to satisfy by reference to the first couple of days of a large administration in which … the observable conduct of and communication on behalf of Phones 4U might be said to have left distinctly open the possibility of a resumption of trading, perhaps even in the shorter term.

The judge was of the view 'provisionally that the suggestion that Phones 4U had by 1 pm on 17 September 2014 renounced its contractual obligations owed to EE is flimsy' [Phones 4U (2019): Para 56]. But a determination of the question had become irrelevant. The judge had decided on the question of repudiatory breach, which required a trial.

The Phones 4U Case: The Termination Letter

We now move to the significance of the termination letter. The termination letter terminated the contract on the grounds of P4U appointing administrators. It did not refer to any breach or repudiatory breach. Could EE then claim a repudiatory breach and loss of the contract and claim damages?

The appointment of the administrators by P4U gave the right to EE to terminate the contract. There was no breach in P4U appointing administrators. The breach of the business being shut for two and half days happened after the administrators were appointed. The breach did not cause the appointment of the administrators. The features of the case, therefore, were:

1. The contract gave the right to terminate the contract on the happening of an event which was not triggered by a breach.

2. The above right was expressly exercised.
3. At the time of termination, a repudiatory breach and/or anticipatory breach existed but it was not mentioned in the termination notice.

This raised for the judge 'a pure point of principle, whether a claim for loss of bargain is bad in law'. In deciding the question, the judge asked: [Phones 4U (2019): Para 86].

> The key question emerging ... was whether it is necessary, for the common law claim for damages for loss of bargain made ... that EE terminated for breach (actual or anticipatory) by Phones 4U.

The judge answered the question: [Phones 4U (2019): Para 117].

> As a matter of first principle ... I would say that is indeed what EE must show. The loss of bargain damages claim requires EE to show that the termination of the contract, which created the loss of bargain, resulted from the repudiatory breach or renunciation by Phones 4U ...That in turn requires EE to show that the contract was terminated by its exercise of its common law right to terminate for that breach, respectively that renunciation.

The judge recognised that the termination letter terminated the contract siting appointment of administrators and made no mention of any breach: [Phones 4U (2019): Para 117].

> EE's termination letter communicated only a termination under clause 14.1.2 independent of the repudiatory breach or renunciation now alleged, then the contract was not terminated at common law for repudiation. That it could have been so terminated ... cannot be used to re-characterise the facts.

The judge noted that a contract is terminated for what the termination letter states. If a termination letter terminates the contract under a contract term, the party cannot later claim the contract was terminated for breach. The judge stated the principle: [Phones 4U (2019): Para 121].

> To my mind, none of that affects the correctness in principle of the proposition that if a termination letter communicates clearly a decision to terminate only under an express contractual right to terminate that has arisen irrespective of any breach, then it cannot be said that the contract was terminated for breach and so a claim for damages for loss of bargain at common law cannot run.

The court noted on the connection between use of express terms on termination and repudiatory breach. At times, a breach of the contract may have triggered the termination clause in the contract. In this case, the judge recognised: [Phones 4U (2019): Para 76].

> Where the contractual right is triggered by breach, the innocent party can say that by terminating it treated the guilty party's breach as discharging the contract, albeit it expressed itself as relying in that respect on its express contractual right rather than the common law.

In the other cases, however, where the contract term is independent of any breach, the benefit of the loss of bargain cannot be afforded to the party. The judge contrasted: [Phones 4U (2019): Para 76].

> Where however the contractual termination is independent of any breach, the innocent party has not treated the contract as discharged by breach; if treating the contract as discharged by breach is a pre-requisite of the cause of action, the loss of bargain damages claim will fail.

EE could not establish that the notice of termination indicated its intention to accept a repudiatory breach. This in itself was not fatal. EE could still succeed if it could establish that the appointment of administrators was caused by the repudiatory breach. This, however, was not the case. The administrators were appointed first and the repudiatory breach happened later. The issue was only of constructing the notice of termination 'whether by its termination letter EE purported to exercise a common law right to terminate for the repudiatory breach and/or renunciation' [Phones 4U (2019): Para 131].

The termination letter of EE was 'entirely clear' that EE was 'terminating in exercise of, and only of, its right to do so under clause 14.1.2, a right independent of any breach' [Phones 4U (2019): Para 132]. The termination letter did not accuse P4U of any breach. The judge concluded: [Phones 4U (2019): Para 132].

> EE can still sue upon any breach of contract committed by Phones 4U prior to termination. For any such breach, it may pursue all remedies that may be available to it bearing in mind that the contract was terminated under clause 14.1.2 and not for breach. But what EE cannot do is re-characterise the events after the fact and claim that it terminated for breach when that is simply not what it did. Nor can it say that it treated Phones 4U's renunciation (as now alleged) as bringing the contract to an end when that, again, is just not what actually happened.

The Phones 4U judgment is a leading one on the relationship between termination for non-breach and award of damages. A party to a contract can terminate the contract by giving a notice of termination when a stated event matures. This will bring the contract to an end. However, the party cannot claim damages for loss of bargain. Alongside the maturing of the non-breach event, however, if the party has committed a repudiatory breach, the termination letter must state the repudiatory breach to be a basis to claim damages for the loss of bargain. If the termination letter omits it, it cannot subsequently re-characterise the termination to be on the grounds of the breach. A termination happens on the grounds stated in the termination letter. It needs utmost caution and expertise in preparing the termination notice.

Reference

Phones 4U Ltd (in administration) v EE Ltd (2018) EWHC 49 (Comm).

Chapter 7
Force Majeure (Impossibility) Clause

Contracts are voluntarily made. It is for the contracting parties to decide the exchange. Law leaves alone the parties to settle the terms of the contract. From very early on, however, it was clear that no one could do an impossible act, even if the person had contracted to do it. Common law recognised it as the principle that a contract to do an impossible act was void. Void is nothingness, and a void contract is one which never got made or existed. A contract which was fine when it got made but became impossible to perform later, got resolved by an extension of the principle. It was stated that the contract was frustrated on the grounds of impossibility. In other words, the contract on encountering the impossibility became void. Neither party could demand enforcement of the contract, as there was no contract to enforce.

The impossibility manifested in yet another way. A contract is part performed and then, the impossibility arises. It was clear that a party could not do or be made to do, what was impossible to do. For this reason, common law formulated that on an impossibility arising, either party could declare the contract frustrated. Frustration was another name for terminating a contract on the grounds of impossibility. On termination, the parties got discharged from further performance of the contract and neither paid damage as there was no breach. The courts founded the impossibility principle on the basis that it was unjust or unfair to require a party to do an impossible act.

The parties responded by introducing terms on impossibility in the contract. As contracts are voluntary, the principle emerged that if the parties had agreed themselves that a certain event was beyond their control or impossible, even if it was not, the parties could frustrate the contract. The opposite, however, was not true. If a contract required a party to do an act, which had become impossible to perform, either party was allowed to frustrate the contract as it was the just thing to do. The test for determining whether something had become impossible to perform was to compare the situation when the contract was made and the contract came to be performed and ask, if the situation was the similar or totally different. In National Carriers Ltd.

A. Pathak, *Contract Terms in International Business*,
https://doi.org/10.1007/978-981-96-8146-4_7

v. Panalpina (Northern) Ltd, the Court noted: [National Carriers Ltd. v. Panalpina (Northern) Ltd, (1981) A.C. 675: Page 700].

> Frustration of a contract takes place when there supervenes an event (without default of either party and for which the contract makes no sufficient provision) which so significantly changes the nature (not merely the expense or onerousness) of the outstanding contractual rights and/or obligations from what the parties could reasonably have contemplated at the time of its execution that it would be unjust to hold them to the literal sense of its stipulations in the new circumstances; in such case the law declares both parties to be discharged from further performance.

As contracts came to be in writing, the parties started providing on impossibility in the contract to reduce uncertainties. Natural disasters and spread of disease were the common ones. As no one can violate the law, any law prohibiting an act was an impossibility. As impossibilities are fact and contract specific, the impossibility clauses and their scope and application are not standard. The best way to explore the impossibility clauses are by taking up different illustrations and cases.

Airlines carriage contracts have clauses giving the airlines the right to divert, reschedule or cancel a flight for 'circumstances beyond its control' and circumstances beyond its control could be defined to include 'weather, air traffic control, mechanical failure, acts of terrorism, acts of nature, force majeure, strikes, riots, wars, hostilities, disturbances, government regulations, orders, shortage of critical manpower, shortage of parts or material etc.'. A clause of this kind expands the scope of impossibility. It gives the space to claim impossibility to the airline, even if the event is in its control. Of course, the law has stepped in and provided for compensation in the case of delays, rescheduling or cancellation. As law overrides contract clauses, the regulations have to be followed. Thus, in some contracts, the clauses expand the scope of impossibility in favour of a party.

At times, an impossibility clause simply recognises the impossibility principle and elaborates it out in relation to the contract. For example, a GCC developed by Grain and Feed Trade Association (GAFTA), on international export of food grain has the following clause: [Bunge SA v Nidera BV, (2015) UKSC 43. Para 2].

> 13. *Prohibition* —In case of prohibition of export, blockade or hostilities or in case of any executive or legislative act done by or on behalf of the government of the country of origin of the goods, or of the country from which the goods are to be shipped, restricting export, whether partially or otherwise, any such restriction shall be deemed by both parties to apply to this contract and to the extent of such total or partial restriction to prevent fulfilment whether by shipment or by any other means whatsoever and to that extent this contract or any unfulfilled portion thereof shall be cancelled. Sellers shall advise buyers without delay with the reasons therefor and, if required, sellers must produce proof to justify the cancellation.

A clause on impossibility can go with any name. It does not have to use the word impossibility. What matters is the essence or substance of the clause. The above clause recognises three kinds of impossibilities. A blockade is when the passage to a port is blocked for whatever reasons. The second is hostilities. This refers to a war which prohibits the movement of a ship on a route. The third is any law (this includes legislative or executive act), which prohibits exports. If any of the events arises, restricting exports, the contract 'shall be cancelled'. As the export has to happen from the seller's end, the clause requires the seller to advice the buyer and cancel the contract.

Force Majeure: Lebeaupin v Richard Crispin and Company

The impossibility clause is often written as a 'force majeure' clause. The term 'force majeure' does not have a settled meaning, as brought out by Lebeaupin v Richard Crispin and Company, [Lebeaupin v Richard Crispin and Company, (1920) 2K.B. 714. Hereafter Crispin (1920).] is an early case on the clause. Richard Crispin & Co. entered into a contract with M. Lebeaupin to sell 2500 cases of 'British Columbia Fraser river salmon.' [Crispin (1920): Page 717] A clause made the contract 'subject to force majeure.' The seller could not supply as the tins for packing supplied to him by the manufacturer were defective. By the time proper packing material could be secured, the salmon season had got over. The seller disclaimed liability for the breach on the ground the contract was subject to 'force majeure'. The contract had simply stated that the contract was subject to 'force majeure'. The judge explored the meaning of the term 'force majeure': [Crispin (1920): Page 719].

> This phrase "force majeure" has been introduced into many English commercial contracts within recent years. It is employed not only with increasing frequency, but without any attempt to define its meaning or any effort to co-ordinate the phrase to the other provisions of documents. It is a phrase employed in the Code de Commerce of France.

The judge commented on its meaning: [Crispin (1920): Page 719].

> ... the phrase "force majeure" was not interchangeable with "vis major" or "the act of God." It goes beyond the latter phrases. Any direct legislative or administrative interference would of course come within the term: for example, an embargo. But even such a thing as a breakdown of machinery through accident was deemed ... to come within the words "force majeure."... I conceive that normal bad weather is one thing whereas abnormal tempest, storm or the like may be another thing and might well fall within the "force majeure" clause.

The judge concluded that the clause had no settled meaning. Its meaning has to be constructed within the text of the contract: [Crispin (1920): Page 720].

> I take it that a "force majeure" clause should be construed in each case with a close attention to the words which precede or follow it, and with a due regard to the nature and general terms of the contract. The effect of the clause may vary with each instrument.

Thus, merely that a clause is titled as 'force majeure' or the term is used, does not mean anything. The term has to be constructed in the totality of the text and the context of the contract. The following case is on the doctrine of frustration and not impossibility clauses.

Channel Island Ferries Limited v Sealink UK Limited

Channel Island Ferries Limited (CIF) and Sealink UK Limited (SUKL) operated ferry services between the United Kingdom and the Channel Islands. [Channel Island Ferries Limited v Sealink UK Limited, 1988 WL 622867. Hereafter Channel (1988)] These operations of both the companies were loss making. The companies entered into discussions to combine the two operations and make them profitable. The combined operation was intended to be carried out by Channel Islands' company (BCIF) to be jointly owned by CIF and SUKL. The companies created the new company and entered into an agreement. Clause 7 of the agreement provided: [Channel (1988)].

> BCIF will bareboat charter ships from SUKL and CIF at agreed arm's length commercial rates. The rates agreed for 1987 are £1.1m. per vessel. SUKL will provide two vessels from its existing CI fleet and CIF will provide Corbier.

In a bareboat charter, as the name suggests, just the vessel is given by the owner. The charter organises its own crew. The parties understood that the agreement would create significant redundancies for the crew of SUKL. The intention of the parties was to sign the agreement and announce to the Unions on September 15 and commence operations from October 1. This would have given 15 days of window to negotiate with the Unions. It was, however, later decided to sign the agreement on 30th September, announce the same day and start the operations from October 1. The parties followed this. On October 1, SUKL was to provide two of its vessels, the Earl Granville and the Earl Harold, without the crew. Clause 4(3) of the contract provided: [Channel (1988)].

> No later than the Commencement Date ... SUKL shall make the vessels, the Earl Granville and the Earl Harold available to the Company by bareboat charter ... Provided that if for any reason beyond the control of SUKL either the Earl Granville or the Earl Harold cannot be made so available then SUKL shall make available another vessel or vessels of such sizes and capacity as are suitable to meet the Company's requirements ... at an overall cost to the Company for chartering and operation no greater than the cost envisaged in bareboat chartering the Earl Granville and/or the Earl Harold.

The agreement was announced on September 30. Alongside, SUKL served redundancy notices to the crews and officers involved with the two vessels which was to go on a bareboat charter. There was severe reaction from the employees. The vessels were occupied by the crew who refused to move out. Within a few days, the strike became nationwide. As a result, SUKL could not make available the named vessels. Eventually, SUKL got into an agreement with its Union, within which, it could not have met its commitment to CIF. Following non-fulfilment by SUKL, CIF claimed damages for the breach, which was in the option of purchasing the shares in the new company. SUKL claimed it was not in breach and was saved by the force majeure clause. The force majeure clause read:

> A party shall not be liable in the event of nonfulfillment of any obligation arising under this contract by reason of Act of God, disease, strikes, Lock-Outs, fire, and any accident or incident of any nature beyond the control of the relevant party.

SUKL contended that the strike prevented it from doing a bareboat charter, and subsequently, it was prevented from the agreement with its Union to have complied with clause 4 of the agreement. The Court of Appeal recorded the contention of SUKL: [Channel (1988)].

> The strike, they say, led inevitably to the agreement with the Unions which thereafter prevented compliance; alternatively, if it is not true to say that the strike remained throughout the operative cause of non-compliance, then the agreement was an incident beyond the control of Sealink, and therefore also the case comes within the Force Majeure clause. They say that they were forced to submit ... because they could not support financially a strike any further once that strike had become nation-wide — as it had almost immediately.

The Court of Appeal listed the points to be considered in application of force majeure: [Channel (1988)].

1. that it is for the party relying on a Force Majeure clause to bring himself squarely within that clause;
2. that in most cases that can only be done by showing either legal or physical impossibility;
3. that strikes may collapse suddenly, however adamantly one side may be asserting that it will not give way;
4. a party must not only bring himself within the clause but must show that he has taken all reasonable steps to avoid its operation, or mitigate its results;

The Court of Appeal concluded: [Channel (1988)].

> It is, I think, plain that the strike initially did prevent the tender of the two primary vessels on 1st October and thereafter until the vessels ceased to be occupied. ...In order to succeed in the argument which was advanced, it would be necessary to have shown that had Sealink found alternative vessels and tendered them on bareboat charter, they would have been unable in effect to do so.

There was no evidence that SUK tried to find alternate vessels and tender them. Thus, the Court of Appeal concluded that SUKL 'wholly failed to make out a case that the Force Majeure clause is applicable on the facts' [Channel (1988)].

Aircraft Purchase Fleet Limited V Compagnia Aerea Italiana SPA

Aircraft Purchase Fleet Limited (APFL) had a contract to buy several aircrafts from Airbus and lease them out to Compagnia Aerea Italiana SPA (CAI). [Aircraft Purchase Fleet Limited v Compagnia Aerea Italiana SPA, (2018) EWHC 3315 (Comm). Hereafter APFP (2018)] APFL faced acute difficulties in organising financing for buying the aircrafts. Alongside, the lease contract between CAI and APFL had its own difficulties. Airbus and APFL tried hard to keep the contract going. Airbus made numerous concessions. Eventually, it did not work out and Airbus terminated the sale contract. Parallel to it, without knowing of the termination, CAI refused to take lease of the aircrafts.

Following the breach by CAI to lease aircrafts, APFL claimed $260 million in damages from CAI for the breach. CAI argued that it was not liable for damages as, following the termination by Airbus, it had become impossible for APFL to have leased the aircrafts. The court noted the argument of CAI: [APFP (2018): Para 109].

> CAI argued that this arose by the application of the doctrine of frustration: it had become impossible for either party to perform the Framework Agreement once Airbus had terminated the 2013 and 2014 aircraft deliveries... CAI submitted that, whilst APFL would not be entitled to rely on the doctrine as the frustration was "self-induced" from its perspective, CAI (as the innocent party in this context) was so entitled.

APFL claimed that CAI cannot claim frustration as the Airbus terminated the contract for the reason that CAI was not going ahead with the leasing of the aircrafts. The court concluded that CAI's renunciation did not cause Airbus to terminate the contract. The court ruled in favour of CIA: [APFP (2018): Para 132].

> I ... conclude that, on the evidence, APFL was entirely responsible for rendering itself unable to perform its obligations under the Framework Agreement and that CAI's alleged renunciation was not a factor in such impossibility arising. APFL has not come close to discharging the burden of establishing that Airbus's actions were in any way influenced by CAI's stance ...

CAI succeeded in its claim that the lease contract was frustrated as APFL had no aircrafts to lease.

Seadrill Ghana Operations Ltd v Tullow Ghana Ltd.

Tullow Ghana Limited had two offshore petroleum licences about 60 Kms off the coast of Ghana. [Seadrill Ghana Operations Ltd v Tullow Ghana Ltd., (2018) EWHC 1640 (Comm). Hereafter Seadrill (2018).] One was known as West Cape Three Points and the other as Deepwater Tano. West Cape included an oilfield called Jubilee. Jubilee was in production since December 2010. Deepwater had three oilfields, Tweneboa, Enyenra and Ntomme. Picking up their first letters, the three were known as TEN. Oil was discovered in TEN in 2009 and first produced in August 2016.

Tullow hired from Seadrill Ghana Operations Limited a sixth generation ultra-deepwater semi-submersible rig, West Leo. The contract was entered into on 3 November 2011 and was to last till June 2018. Within the contract, the daily operating charges for the hire were US $600,000. Tullow had decided to use West Leo initially in TEN and then later in the Greater Jubilee Field.

There was a dispute between Ghana and Cote d'Ivoire (Ivory Coast) on the boundary of their territorial waters. In September 2014, the two countries entered into an arbitration under the United Nations Convention on the Law of the Sea (UNCLOS) to resolve the dispute. In this dispute, if Cote d'Ivoire were correct, TEN would lie in the waters belonging to Cote d'Ivoire. In support of the claim, on 25 April 2015, the arbitration tribunal made a Provisional Measures Order (PMO) that 'Ghana shall take all necessary steps to ensure that no new drilling either by Ghana or under its control takes place in the disputed area' [Seadrill (2018): Page 195].

'Spudding' is the drilling a hole in the sea bed. After this, 'completion' of the well is done. Only after this, oil can be pumped out from the well. The implication of the PMO was that the 'completion' of the spudded wells could continue in TEN but new wells could not be spudded. This was fortunate for Tullow because several spudded wells remained to be completed in TEN and West Leo was scheduled to be used for such completions. However, it was expected that the last such well would be completed in September 2016. Thereafter, it was envisaged by Tullow that West Leo would be used in the Greater Jubilee Field.

In February 2016, a technical problem was found with the 'turret' being used in the Jubilee field. In consequence, Ghana was unwilling to approve the Greater Jubilee Plan. Thus, Tullow claimed there was no further work for the West Leo to do as from October 2016. Tullow ceased to pay the daily rate of hire and terminated the contract for the hire of the rig. Tullow justified its refusal to pay hire by reference to the 'force majeure' clause in the contract for the hire of the West Leo. The force majeure clause of the contract read as follows: [Seadrill (2018): Page 200].

> 27.1 Neither COMPANY nor CONTRACTOR shall be responsible for any failure to fulfil any term or condition of the Contract if and to the extent that fulfilment has been delayed or temporarily prevented by an occurrence, as hereunder defined as FORCE MAJEURE, which has been notified in accordance with this Clause 27 and which is beyond the control and without the fault or negligence of the party affected and which, by the exercise of reasonable diligence, the said party is unable to prevent or provide against. Both parties shall use their reasonable endeavours to mitigate, avoid, circumvent, or overcome the circumstances of FORCE MAJEURE.
>
> 27.2 For the purpose of the Contract, Force majeure shall be limited to the following:
>
> ...
>
> (h) Drilling moratorium imposed by the government
>
> ...
>
> 27.5 In the event of force majeure occurrence, the party that is or may be delayed in performing the Contract shall notify the other party without delay giving the full particulars thereof and shall use all reasonable endeavours to remedy the situation without delay.
>
> ...
>
> 27.8 In the event that a FORCE MAJEURE condition prevails for a period of sixty (60) consecutive days then COMPANY may terminate the CONTRACT forthwith by giving notice, or may elect keeping CONTRACTOR under CONTRACT and keep paying the DAILY FORCE MAJEURE RATE.'

Seadrill did not accept that the 'force majeure' clause had any application to the facts of the case. It claimed US$277.4 million in damages due under the contract for the period from September 2016 through to June 2018. Seadrill claimed that Tullow's refusal had to do with the collapse of the oil prices in 2014, which had led to a reduction in demand for rigs such as West Leo. As a result, the hiring charges had dropped from about $600,000 per day to $150,000 per day at the end of 2016. The question which the court had to resolve was if the reliance of Tullow on 'force majeure' was justified.

After detailed examination of the case facts, the court concluded that there was prohibition on a 'drilling moratorium imposed by the government' but this was not the causative factor for not pursuing with the hire of the drill. The court noted: [Seadrill (2018): Page 210].

> Clause 27.1 of the contract requires Tullow to have been prevented from or delayed in fulfilling its obligations by an occurrence which is a force majeure. Thus there is a clear causation requirement between the force majeure and Tullow's failure to provide drilling instructions to Seadrill.

The court commented that the questions of causation are sensitive to the legal context in which these arise. These have to be determined by a 'broad common sense view of the whole position' [Seadrill (2018): Page 210]. In the case before it, the question was 'whether a force majeure was the cause of Tullow being unable to fulfil its obligations' [Seadrill (2018): Page 210]. The court noted: [Seadrill (2018): Page 211].

> It is true that Tullow never had the right to work in the Greater Jubilee Field but Tullow expected that it would obtain approval to do so; that is apparent from the rig schedules. When the Government failed to approve the Greater Jubilee Plan in December 2015 Tullow expected that agreement on terms would be reached. ... Thus it was that Tullow's expectations could not be fulfilled.

The court observed that there were 'two effective causes of Tullow being unable to provide drilling instructions in October 2016, one being a force majeure, and the other not' [Seadrill (2018): Page 212]. It was for Tullow to show that it was 'delayed in or prevented from doing so by a force majeure' [Seadrill (2018): Page 212].

The court presented the factual matrix: [Seadrill (2018): Page 212].

> Tullow had intended to drill and complete wells in the Greater Jubilee Field from October 2016. That intention was not frustrated by a force majeure but by an event which was not a force majeure, namely, the failure of the Government to approve the Greater Jubilee Plan. Tullow's own intention with regard to drilling in the Greater Jubilee Field in October 2016 had also changed.

The court concluded: [Seadrill (2018): Page 212].

> Thus, with regard to the Greater Jubilee Field, a force majeure event did not to any extent delay or prevent Tullow from drilling there in October 2016. Accordingly, in my judgment, Tullow is unable to rely upon the force majeure clause notwithstanding that a force majeure prevented it from using West Leo to complete EN10 in TEN.

Thus, Tullow could not rely on the force majeure clause as it was not 'the effective cause of its failure to perform was not a force majeure within the meaning of the clause' [Seadrill (2018): Page 212].

2 Entertain Video Limited v Sony DADC Europe Limited

2 Entertain Video Limited (2E) is a subsidiary of BBC Studios Limited, the main commercial entity within the British Broadcasting Group (the BBC). [2 Entertain Video Limited v Sony DADC Europe Limited, (2020) EWHC 972 (TCC). Hereafter Sony (2020).] The company is responsible for the BBC's video catalogue and new release stock. The company published, marketed and sold pre-recorded Blu-ray discs, DVDs, CDs and other home entertainment media. The company had entered into a contract with Sony to provide logistics services, including warehouse storage and distribution of home entertainment media. Sony owned and occupied a warehouse from where it provided the logistics and storage service.

There was rioting and violent civil disorder in London and other cities in the UK in 2011. The warehouse was attacked by a group of young men. They gained access to the warehouse by breaking through a fire door or glazed panels. They looted goods and then set the premises on fire by throwing two petrol bombs. The warehouse burned for ten days, causing the total destruction of the building, plant, equipment and stock. The insurance company indemnified the losses. However, the amount received did not fully cover the losses. The parties were in dispute as to who should bear the losses.

2E claimed that Sony had not adequately secured the warehouse but Sony disputed it. The court made a factual determination on the point: [Sony (2020): Para 105].

> It is not in dispute that the riot gave rise to an unprecedented attack on the warehouse. However, criminal attacks on the warehouse and unauthorised entry to the building had occurred before ... The glazed fire door and panels were identified as weak points in security. These matters were sufficient to put Sony on notice that a security review should be carried out, the risks should be assessed, and additional security measures introduced. ...

The judge concluded that Sony had failed to take reasonable measures to secure the warehouse. The judge further concluded that if Sony had taken care, it was likely that the youth would have been 'deterred or delayed in breaking into the warehouse' [Sony (2020): Para 118].

The contract had a force majeure clause. It read: [Sony (2020): Para 206].

> Neither party shall be liable for its failure or delay in performing any of its obligations hereunder if such failure or delay is caused by circumstances beyond the reasonable control of the party affected including but not limited to industrial action (at either party), fire, flood, wars, armed conflict, terrorist act, riot, civil commotion, malicious damage, explosion, unavailability of fuel, pandemic or governmental or other regulatory action.

Sony contended that the destruction of the warehouse was a force majeure event beyond its control. The court ruled on the application of the force majeure clause. It noted that the riots were 'unforeseen and unprecedented' [Sony (2020): Para 207]. However, 'the risk of intruders was foreseeable' [Sony (2020): Para 207]. The court concluded: [Sony (2020): Para 208].

> ... adequate security measures that could have been taken by Sony probably would have deterred or delayed the attack on the warehouse and prevented the youths from gaining

> entry. Reasonable fire precautions, namely, the installation of sprinklers, probably would have suppressed the fire and significantly reduced any damage to the warehouse and its stock. Therefore, the fire and resulting loss did not amount to circumstances beyond the reasonable control of Sony and it is not open to Sony to rely on clause 14.1 as a defence.

Sony could not succeed in its claim as the force majeure clause required it to establish that the loss was beyond its 'reasonable control'.

Financial Difficulties

Financial difficulties or changes in the economic or market conditions are not taken to be impossibilities. In Tennants (Lancashire) Ltd v CS Wilson & Co Ltd (1917) AC 495, the court noted: [Tennants (Lancashire) Ltd v CS Wilson & Co Ltd (1917) AC 495: page 510].

> The argument that a man can be excused from performance of his contract when it becomes "commercially impossible" seems to me to be a dangerous contention which ought not to be admitted unless the parties plainly contracted to that effect.

In Thames Valley Power Ltd. v. Total Gas & Power Ltd. [Thames Valley Power Ltd. v. Total Gas & Power Ltd. (2006) 1 Lloyd's Rep. 441. Hereafter Thames (2006)] 'disapproving the notion that economic circumstances can generally found a claim for force majeure or frustration' [Thames (2006): para 3], the court noted: [Thames (2006): para 3].

> It does not at all follow that the supplier is entitled to rely upon an increase in the market price in comparison to the contract price as a force majeure circumstance. ...This conclusion is consistent with a line of cases, both on force majeure clauses and on frustration, ..., to the effect that the fact that a contract has become expensive to perform, even dramatically more expensive, is not a ground to relieve a party on the grounds of force majeure or frustration.

The following is a judgment on the theme of impossibilities and financial difficulties.

Tandrin Aviation Holdings Limited V Aero Toy Store LLC.,

Tandrin Aviation Holdings Limited got into a sale agreement with Aero Toy Store LLC. to sell a new Bombardier executive jet aircraft. [Tandrin Aviation Holdings Limited v Aero Toy Store LLC., Insured Aircraft Title Service, Inc., (2010) EWHC 40 (Comm). Hereafter Tandrin (2010).] By the time the delivery date came, the 2008 meltdown had happened. The buyer did not take delivery of the aircraft and claimed the 'unanticipated, unforeseeable and cataclysmic downward spiral of the world's financial markets triggered the force majeure clause in the Agreement' [Tandrin (2010): para 38], frustrating the contract. The force majeure clause in the contract read: [Tandrin (2010): para 8].

Force Majeure.

> Neither party shall be liable to the other as a result of any failure of, or delay in the performance of, its obligations hereunder, for the period that such failure or delay is due to: Acts of God or the public enemy; war, insurrection or riots; fires; governmental actions; strikes or labor disputes; inability to obtain aircraft materials, accessories, equipment or parts from vendors; or any other cause beyond Seller's reasonable control. Upon the occurrence of any such event, the time required for performance by such party of its obligations arising under this Agreement, shall be extended by a period equal to the duration of such event.

The court noted the principles of law for the application of force majeure: [Tandrin (2010): para 40].

> It is well established under English law that a change in economic/market circumstances, affecting the profitability of a contract or the ease with which the parties' obligations can be performed, is not regarded as being a force majeure event. Thus a failure of performance due to the provision of insufficient financial resources has been held not to amount to force majeure.

The court noted that the term force majeure 'is not a term of art' [Tandrin (2010): para 43]. The wordings of the clause have to be properly constructed. The court at the outset noted that the force majeure clause in the contract was not 'even remotely connected with economic downturn, market circumstances or the financing of the deal' [Tandrin (2010): para 44]. The buyer contended that the economic meltdown was 'beyond Seller's reasonable control' and therefore it was covered by the force majeure clause. The court dispelled the contention: [Tandrin (2010): para 45].

> The natural and ordinary meaning of such a provision is that it is addressing the position of the seller rather than the purchaser and is a force majeure circumstance that only the seller can rely upon. ... it is the seller who has the principal performance obligations under the Agreement. The purchaser's essential performance obligation is to pay the price and accept delivery, obligations that are far less likely to be affected by force majeure circumstances.

The court concluded that the expression 'any other cause beyond the seller's reasonable control' in the clause cannot 'sensibly be construed to include matters with which the seller was never expected to be concerned' [Tandrin (2010): para 46]. The court noted that the onus was on ATS to establish the cover of force majeure: [Tandrin (2010): para 48].

> Under English law, just as the burden of proof is on the party seeking to rely upon a force majeure clause to prove the facts bringing the case within the clause, so the burden of proof is on ATS to show that this force majeure clause is capable of being construed so as to include any funding difficulties it is encountering.

The court concluded that ATS cannot claim the benefit of the force majeure clause. While changes in the economic context are not an impossibility and a contract cannot be frustrated for it, the parties are free to provide otherwise by contract terms. The contract term can expressly provide that changes in the economic or market situation would be an impossibility.

It is a common law principle that a contract can be frustrated if it becomes impossible to perform. The impossibility can be physical, natural or a prohibition imposed by law. Contract terms have been introduced on the principle of impossibility. A clause states what the parties take to be impossible for them to perform. In this case, the parties can frustrate the contract on the occurrence of the event. However, the parties cannot provide its opposite, that an event is not to be taken to be an impossibility, when it is. The impossibility clause is often written as a force majeure clause. The term 'force majeure' does not have a fixed meaning. The term has to be interpreted within the text of the contract. The applicability of the clause and its interpretation is context and fact specific. The burden of establishing the applicability of a force majeure clause is on the party claiming its benefit. Changes in the economic or make conditions are not taken to be an impossibility.

References

Entertain Video Limited v Sony DADC Europe Limited (2020) EWHC 972 (TCC)
Aircraft Purchase Fleet Limited v Compagnia Aerea Italiana SPA (2018) EWHC 3315 (Comm)
Bunge SA v Nidera BV (2015) UKSC 43.
Channel Island Ferries Limited v Sealink UK Limited, 1988 WL 622867
Lebeaupin v Richard Crispin and Company (1920) 2 K.B. 714
National Carriers Ltd. v. Panalpina (Northern) Ltd, (1981) A.C. 675
Seadrill Ghana Operations Ltd v Tullow Ghana Ltd. (2018) EWHC 1640 (Comm). Hereafter Seadrill (2018)
Tandrin Aviation Holdings Limited v Aero Toy Store LLC., Insured Aircraft Title Service, Inc. (2010) EWHC 40 (Comm)
Tennants (Lancashire) Ltd v CS Wilson & Co Ltd (1917) AC 495
Thames Valley Power Ltd. v. Total Gas & Power Ltd. (2006) 1 Lloyd's Rep. 441

Chapter 8
General Damages

For every breach of a term of a contract, the other party can claim damages for the losses arising from the breach. The principle for award of damages is rudimentary, dating back to the prior centuries. Specific performance of contract is requiring the parties to do what they have undertaken to do. The common law courts award specific performance only in special circumstances, where a monetary award would not do justice. The courts exercise this discretionary remedy typically for sale of land. In all other contracts, the principle for award of damages is to put the parties in a position they would be, by money amount, if the contract had been performed. The principle is formulated in Robinson v Harman (1848) 1 Exch 850: [Robinson v Harman (1848) 1 Exch 850: p 855].

> The rule of the common law is, that where a party sustains a loss by reason of a breach of contract, he is, so far as money can do it, to be placed in the same situation, with respect to damages, as if the contract had been performed.

In introducing a clause to cover the above principle, two interfaces were encountered. The first was, every breach has consequences and implications. However, the consequences are of an uncertain and speculative nature. These leave the parties forever disputing on the damages. A solution has been found by waving a claim of consequential and indirect losses. We will explore the theme of consequential and indirect losses in a subsequent chapter. This leaves only the direct losses arising from the breach to be claimed. The most appropriate solution to claim this would be to specify the damages in the contract. This would save the parties from the labour of undertaking the hypothetical journey of putting the party in a position the party would be if the contract had been performed. Specifying damages as an amount is called liquidated damages. The courts recognise liquidated damages only if it appears to be a genuine pre-estimate of the losses. This significantly limits the specifying the damages in the contract. In a subsequent chapter, we will explore the theme of liquidated damages. For the most breaches, the contract clauses can only elaborate the mechanics of putting the party in a position the party would be if the contract were performed. We will take up the theme in this chapter. Over 150 years, the courts have

A. Pathak, *Contract Terms in International Business*,
https://doi.org/10.1007/978-981-96-8146-4_8

given expression to the principle of award of damages in different kinds of contracts and contexts. A landmark case on the theme is the House of Lords judgment in Ruxley Electronics and Construction Limited v Forsyth, (1996) UKHL 8.

Ruxley Electronics and Construction Limited v. Forsyth

Mr. Stephen Forsyth commissioned Ruxley Electronics & Construction Ltd., trading as Home Counties Swimming Pools, to build a swimming pool for him in his garden. [Ruxley Electronics and Construction Limited v. Forsyth, (1996) AC 344. Hereafter Ruxley (1996).] The depth of the pool at the deep end was to be seven feet six inches. After the pool was completed, it was only six feet nine inches. The pool as constructed was safe for diving. A depth of 6 ft. is adequate, even for a beginner. To increase the depth to the contracted measure, it would have cost £21,560. The second highest court of the United Kingdom, the Court of Appeal reasoned that the only way the contracted depth could be secured was by reconstruction of the pool and awarded £21,560 for cost of cure. The judgment came in appeal before the House of Lords. The House of Lords emphasised that damages were not to penalise the contract breaker but to cover the losses the party sustained due to the breach. It noted: [Ruxley (1996): page 353].

> There is no question of punishing the contract breaker. ... Since the law relating to damages for breach of contract has developed almost exclusively in a commercial context, these criteria normally proceed on the assumption that each contracting party's interest in the bargain was purely commercial and that the loss resulting from a breach of contract is measurable in purely economic terms.

The court explained that in a case where a landlord contract for a building work, the work when completed may serve the practical purpose for which it was built perfectly satisfactorily. But in some minor respects, the work may fall short of the contract specification. In this case, the House of Lords concluded: [Ruxley (1996): page 353].

> The difference in commercial value between the work as built and the work as specified is nil. ... Nevertheless the contractual defect could only be remedied by demolishing the work and starting again from scratch. The cost of doing this would be so great in proportion to any benefit it would confer on the owner that no reasonable owner would think of incurring it.

Similarly, emphasising that damages are 'designed to compensate for an established loss and not to provide a gratuitous benefit,' [Ruxley (1996): page 357] the House of Lords noted: [Ruxley (1996): page 358].

> [Frosyth] ... has acquired a perfectly serviceable swimming pool, albeit one lacking the specified depth. His loss is thus not the lack of a useable pool with consequent need to construct a new one. Indeed were he to receive the cost of building a new one and retain the existing one he would have recovered not compensation for loss but a very substantial gratuitous benefit, something which damages are not intended to provide.

The loss in every case is a question of fact and degree. Undoubtedly, if the completed work is inadequate or not useful, the damages may have to be in reconstruction. The House of Lords noted: [Ruxley (1996): page 358].

> Where the contract breaker has entirely failed to achieve the contractual objective it may not be difficult to conclude that the loss is the necessary cost of achieving that objective. Thus if a building is constructed so defectively that it is of no use for its designed purpose the owner may have little difficulty in establishing that his loss is the necessary cost of re- constructing.

To illustrate, if the swimming pool were for a sporting complex, the pool with the deficient depth would not have met the designated purpose and would have needed to be reconstructed. The House of Lords did not award the cost of reconstruction. A key thing which emerges from the case is award of damages is only to cover the legitimate losses and not penalise the party in breach or profit from it.

Damages: Sale of Goods

The principle for award of damages, by money compensation, put the parties in a situation they would be, if the contract were performed got ready application for sale of goods as there was a market which gave a money equivalent for goods. If the seller breached, the buyer could buy from an alternate source and claim the difference. The market price and the contract price became the reference for the award of damages. The principles developed by the common law courts on sale of goods came to be codified as the Sale of Goods Act, 1897. The act has been re-enacted as the Sale of Goods Act 1979. The provision on the award of damages has been reproduced from the first act into the second one. In the Sale of Goods Act 1979, it reads:

> 51 Damages for non-delivery
>
> (3) Where there is an available market for the goods in question the measure of damages is prima facie to be ascertained by the difference between the contract price and the market or current price of the goods at the time or times when they ought to have been delivered, or (if no time was fixed) then at the time of the refusal to deliver.

The United Kingdom Supreme Court in Bunge SA v Nidera BV (2015) UKSC 43 noted on the statement of the common law principle: [Bunge SA v Nidera BV (2015) UKSC 43. Hereafter Bunge (2015): para 14].

> The fundamental principle of the common law of damages is the compensatory principle, which requires that the injured party is "so far as money can do it to be placed in the same situation with respect to damages as if the contract had been performed": In a contract of sale where there is an available market, this is ordinarily achieved by comparing the contract price with the price that would have been agreed under a notional substitute contract assumed to have been entered into in its place at the market rate but otherwise on the same terms.

Thus, the law on award of damages for sale of goods works on a notional or fictional basis. The party does not actually have to get into a substitute contract. The damages will be awarded with reference to the market price. Further, only the difference in the price will be awarded. The other associated losses do not find a mention in the law. The common law principles, coming from the prior centuries, are rudimentary and do not adequately address contemporary contracts. For this reason, the parties provide contract terms in their contract. The Supreme Court noted on damages: [Bunge (2015): para 26].

> … damages clauses are commonly intended to avoid disputes about damages, either by prescribing a fixed measure of loss (as in the case of a liquidated damages clause) or by a providing a mechanical formula in place of the more nuanced and fact-sensitive approach of the common law.

The damages clauses are of two kinds. The first is liquidated damages, which we will explore in a subsequent chapter. The second is, in the context of the nature of the contract, the clause provides a mechanism or means of putting the parties in a position they would be as if the contract were performed. What then is the relationship between the common law principles and the contract terms. The court noted: [Bunge (2015): para 26].

> In either case, it is inherent in the clause that it may produce a different result from the common law. For that reason, there can be no scope for a presumption that the parties intended the clause to produce the same measure of damages as the compensatory principle would produce at common law. The mere fact that in some cases its application will over- or under-estimate the injured party's loss is nothing to the point. Such clauses necessarily assume that the parties are willing to take the rough with the smooth.

We can illustrate it with the following clause:
Damages.

1. If the buyer terminates the contract for breach of any term by the seller, the buyer may buy goods of the same description from another source. The seller will pay for the price in excess of the contract amount.
2. If the buyer does not buy the goods from an alternate source, the seller will pay the excess price if any, between the market price on the date of default and the contract price.

The clause, thus, creates a mechanism for award of damages for breach of contract by the seller. Within the common law principle, the damages were fixed at the difference between the contract price and the prevailing price on the day of the breach. In the mechanics created in this case, the buyer has a choice. The buyer could actually get in a substitute contract. In this case, the damages will be worked out on the basis of the price difference between the actual price paid and the contracted price. The buyer does not have to get in a substitute contract. In this case, the damages would be excess price between the market price on the date of default and the contract price.

As the principles for award of damages are rudimentary and do not attend to contemporary business practices, contract terms have to be introduced to provide for damages in a meaningful way. Thus, contracts have to create a mechanics for the claim of damages. Better one understands the transaction, and the likely breaches, better the mechanics would be. The boundary rails are the mechanics must not be punitive to the party in breach or give a gratuitous benefit to the innocent party. Thus, there are no standard terms on award of damages. In every case, the contract terms have to create a mechanics for the award of damages. We review below Bunge SA v Nidera BV, [Bunge (2015)] a landmark judgment of the United Kingdom Supreme Court on award of damages.

Bunge v Nidera: The Contract

The case has already been introduced in the chapter on anticipatory breach. To refresh the key facts, Nidera BV entered into a contract with Bunge SA to buy 25,000 Metric tonnes of wheat. The sale was for: '25,000 mt of Russian milling wheat, 2010 crop, f.o.b. Novorossiysk'. The shipment period was from 23 to 30 August 2010. Nidera SA was to arrange for a ship to take the delivery of the goods at the Russian port Novorossiysk from 23 to 30 August 2010. The contract incorporated Grain and Feed Trade Association (GAFTA) form 49.

On 5 August 2010, Russia introduced a legislative embargo on exports of wheat from its territory, which was to run from 15 August to 31 December 2010. On 9 August 2010, the seller sent an email to the buyer informing them of the export embargo and stating that the contract was, therefore, 'cancelled' under Clause 13 of the contract. On 11 August 2010, the buyer responded that the email of the seller was an anticipatory breach which the buyer accepted. Within clause 13 of the contract, the seller could have cancelled the contract when there was an actual 'prohibition of export'. As the legislative embargo could be lifted, on 9 August 2010, there was no prohibition on export. The Supreme Court settled that the seller 'jumped the gun by their unqualified statement that the contract was cancelled' [Bunge (2015): para 41]. The question before the Supreme Court was on the damages that should be awarded to the buyer.

Damages in Anticipatory Breach

The common law principles for damages were developed to address the cases of breach. The principles do not clearly answer its application in the case of anticipatory breach. The acceptance of anticipatory breach gives rise to particular problems of legal analysis on the assessment of damages. The judgment quotes Lord Mustill that ordinary rules of damages cannot be applied to anticipatory breach: [Mustill, "The Golden Victory—Some Reflections" (2008) 124 LQR 569, 571–572.]

> … unlike the position regarding actual breach I do not see how damages for an 'anticipatory' breach can be awarded with any semblance of intellectual rigour without at least an attempt to inquire into what was the breach to which the damages are attached, and what kind of breach it was which could be committed before there was any present obligation to perform.

Lord Mustill laments that the courts have not found a coherent and conceptually sound approach for dealing with the award of damages in the case of anticipatory breach: [Mustill, "The Golden Victory—Some Reflections" (2008) 124 LQR 569, 571–572.]

> … the common law has never succeeded in finding a solution which is both theoretically sound and capable of producing sensible results in practice. The attempt was, to all intents and purposes, given up a long time ago, and the courts have been content to employ that powerful but dangerous weapon of the common law, a fiction.

The fiction was to assume that the breach happened when the anticipatory breach was made and take the prevailing market price on the day, compare it with the contract price and award the damages. In the present case, the Supreme Court raised two questions for the award of damages in the case of anticipatory breach. The first question was the date to be taken into account for settling on the market price. The court, thus, answered it: [Bunge (2015): para 17].

> The answer … is only a prima facie answer, is that where there is an available market for the goods, the market price is determined as at the contractual date of delivery, unless the buyer should have mitigated by going into the market and entering into a substitute contract at some earlier stage. Normally, however, the injured party will be required to mitigate his loss by going into the market for a substitute contract as soon as is reasonable after the original contract was terminated. Damages will then be assessed by reference to the price which he obtained.

What if the buyer chooses not to get into a substitute contract. The court noted on this: [Bunge (2015): para 17].

> If he chooses not to do so, damages will generally be assessed by reference to the market price at the time when he should have done. The result is that in practice where there is a renunciation and an available market, the relevant market price for the purposes of assessing damages will generally be determined not by the prima facie measure but by the principles of mitigation.

Thus, in the case of anticipatory breach 'in practice' the buyer will contract to buy from another source to mitigate the losses. This will be the basis for the award of damages. The buyer not mitigating by buying from another source and claiming damages on the basis of a 'prima facie measure' is 'generally' not done. The second question the court posed was whether the subsequent events, in the case the party does not mitigate by getting into a substitute contract, following the anticipatory breach, be taken into account in settling the damages. The court answered: [Bunge (2015): para 23].

> There is no principled reason why, in order to determine the value of the contractual performance which has been lost by the repudiation, one should not consider what would have happened if the repudiation had not occurred. On the contrary, this seems to be fundamental to any assessment of damages designed to compensate the injured party for the consequences of the breach.

The court, thus, formulated that in the case of an anticipatory breach, the buyer should mitigate by getting into a substitute contract. This would be the means to put the buyer in a position the buyer would be if the seller had not made an anticipatory breach of the contract. However, if the buyer does not get into a substitute contract, the court should consider how things would have developed if the anticipatory breach had not been made.

Bunge v Nidera: Clause 20 of GAFTA 49

We now come to the amount of damages the buyer claimed within the terms of the contract. The contract had a clause on damages. It read: [Bunge (2015): para 38].

> 20. Default —In default of fulfilment of contract by the seller, the following provisions shall apply:
>
> (a) The buyer … at their discretion have the right to purchase, against the defaulter, and such purchase shall establish the default price.
>
> (b) If the seller be dissatisfied with such default price or if the right at (a) above is not exercised … the assessment of damages shall be settled by arbitration.
>
> (c) The damages payable shall be based on, but not limited to the difference between the contract price and either the default price established under (a) above or on the actual or estimated value of the goods on the date of default established under (b) above.

The contract price of the wheat was $160 per metric tonne. The buyer took statements from two brokers for the market price on August 11. The brokers stated the market price to be USD285 and USD280, respectively. The buyer took the average as the market price at USD282.50. Thus, the market price was USD 122.5 in excess of the contract price. On this basis, the buyer claimed USD 3,062,500 in damages before GAFTA tier 1 arbitration tribunal. The seller argued that no loss was suffered by the buyer as the embargo did not get lifted. Agreeing with the seller, the arbitrator reasoned that the contract would have been cancelled in any event when the time came for delivery. Thus, he did not award substantive damages. GAFTA's Board of Appeal noted that clause 20(c) had to be followed for the award of damages. It awarded USD 3,062,500, representing the difference between the contract and the market price on 11 August 2010, the date the repudiation was accepted. Both, the Commercial Court and the Court of Appeal agreed with this view. The dispute was before the Supreme Court to decide on the damages.

Bunge v Nidera: Award of Damages

The seller argued before the Supreme Court that damages clauses in contracts are never intended to depart from the common law principle that the party only can be compensated for the losses suffered. As the buyer had not suffered losses, damages could not be awarded. The court did not accept the proposition. It reasoned that the parties introduce damages clauses as the common law principles are basic and rudimentary. The damages clause 'may produce a different result from the common law' [Bunge (2015): para 26]. There is no presumption for the application of the principles of common law.

The court, however, noted that difficulties arise if the clause is not clearly worded. In such cases, it could not have been intended to 'operate arbitrarily' to award damages 'approximate to the true loss' [Bunge (2015): para 26]. In this context, the court observed that the contractual clauses are not to be regarded as complete codes. The court noted: [Bunge (2015): para 27].

> … such clauses are not necessarily to be regarded as complete codes for the assessment of damages. A damages clause, like any other contractual provision, is conclusive of the matters with which it deals. … But it is a question of construction whether the mere fact that it deals with damages means that it must have been intended to do so exhaustively, thereby impliedly excluding any considerations which it has not expressly addressed. To treat a damages clause as a complete code in this all-embracing sense is to tax the foresight of the draftsman in a way which is rarely appropriate unless the alternative is to undermine the coherence or utility of the clause.

The court then turned to apply the principles to the clause on damages in the contract. The court noted that in GAFTA 'fulfilment' has been used for performance of the contract and 'default of fulfilment' for non-performance. Thus, clause 20 is on non-performance of the contract. This includes all cases of non-performance, whether arising from breach or anticipatory breach. Reading the clause from the vantage of the buyer, once the anticipatory breach was accepted and the contract terminated on August 11, the buyer could have contracted with another party to get the supplies. The seller would have paid the additional amount incurred by the buyer. If the seller disagreed, the parties could take the dispute to the arbitrator. The arbitrator could award damages with reference to the price at which the buyer bought the goods. But the clause is of no help if the buyer does not get into a substitute contract. The court noted that clause 20 was not a complete code on damages. The court noted: [Bunge (2015): para 32].

> Clause 20 is not sufficiently comprehensive to be regarded as a complete code covering the entire field of damages. Sub-clause (c) covers the same territory as sections 50(3) and 51(3) of the Sales of Goods Act, and sub-clauses (a) and (b) cover the territory occupied by the common law principles concerning the mitigation of losses arising from price movements. But this is very far from the entire field. These provisions bring a valuable measure of certainty to issues arising from price movements which have given rise to difficulty and dispute at common law for 150 years.

The court noted that clause 20 was only concerned with determining the market price or the value of goods. It does not deal with the 'effect of subsequent events which would have resulted in the original contract not being performed in any event' [Bunge (2015): para 31]. The court noted: [Bunge (2015): para 32].

> Clause 20 … neither provides nor assumes that assessment will depend only on the difference between the contract price and the relevant market price or value. It provides that the damages payable "shall be based on" that difference. It does not exclude every other consideration which may be relevant to determine the injured party's actual loss. The clause is consistent with a conclusion that because of a subsequent supervening event the contract would never

> have been performed and the same loss would have been suffered even if it had not been renounced.

The court concluded: [Bunge (2015): para 35].

> This result seems to me to be consistent with the principle. The alternative is to allow the clause to operate arbitrarily as a means of recovering what may be very substantial damages in circumstances where there has been no loss at all.

The principle for award of damages comes from the prior centuries and is rudimentary. It simply provides to put the party in a position the party would be if the contract were performed. In GCCs, contract terms provide a mechanics for achieving this result. A contract can identify the possible breaches and provide a mechanics for covering the losses arising from those breaches. The mechanics may create a somewhat different result from the common law principles. This is acceptable. However, the mechanics must not be imposing a penalty on the other party or profit from it. Better one understands the transaction, more effective would be the mechanics. However, the damages clause, like any other clause in the contract, cannot be expected to be a comprehensive code. The result will be that the general principles will interact and interface with the contract terms to provide binding directions.

References

Bunge SA v Nidera BV (2015) UKSC 43
Mustill M (2008) The Golden Victory—Some Reflections. 124 LQR 569:571–572
Robinson v Harman (1848) 1 Exch 850: p 855
Ruxley Electronics and Construction Limited v. Forsyth, (1996) AC 344

Chapter 9
Liquidated Damages

The simplest approach to bring certainty to the award of damages for the parties would be to state the amount to be paid in the case of a breach. The amount to be paid in the case of a breach is called liquidated damages. Stating damages as liquidated damages would take away all the complexities for the parties in creating a mechanics for claiming damages. Liquidated damages, however, have posed conceptual challenges ever since their introduction. The contract is of the contracting parties, not the courts. The courts could award the stated amount in damages as the intention of the parties. But this will leave the stronger party to the contract free to state any amount as damages and effectively impose penalty on the other.

The object of awarding damages is to put the injured party in the same position in which he would have been had the contract been performed. If an aggrieved party were allowed to claim anything more, it would actually amount to a penalty. The only way the courts could decide whether the liquidated damages amounted to a penalty was by assessing the actual losses. This could be done only by requiring the party claiming the liquidated damages to prove the losses. However, the very purpose of stipulating liquidated damages was to save the inconvenience of establishing it before the courts. Insisting on this would amount to requiring the contracting parties not to provide for liquidated damages at all. However, this was not conducive for businesses.

More than 100 years back, in Dunlop Pneumatic Tyre Co. Ltd v. New Garage and Motor Co. Ltd., [Dunlop Pneumatic Tyre Co. Ltd. v. New Garage and Motor Co. Ltd. (1915) A.C. 79. Hereafter Dunlop (1915).] the House of Lords balanced the two contradictory claims by stating that if the liquidated damages appear to be genuine pre-estimates of the losses, these would be awarded without requiring the party to establish the losses. The court formulated: [Dunlop (1915): page 86].

> The essence of a penalty is a payment of money stipulated as in terrorem of the offending party; the essence of liquidated damages is a genuine covenanted pre-estimate of damage.

A. Pathak, *Contract Terms in International Business*,
https://doi.org/10.1007/978-981-96-8146-4_9

The court emphasised that whether a liquidated damages clause was imposing a penalty has to be judged not by the terms employed but the essence of the transaction. The court noted: [Dunlop (1915): page 86].

> Though the parties to a contract, who use the words penalty or liquidated damages, may, prima facie, be supposed to mean what they say, yet the expression used is not conclusive. The court must find out whether the payment stipulated is in truth a penalty or liquidated damages.

The House of Lords elaborated that to judge whether a stated amount is a genuine pre-estimate of the losses or a penalty, the contract has to be constructed and judged in the context of the circumstances 'of as at the time of the making of the contract, not as at the time of the breach' [Dunlop (1915): page 87]. Applying these principles, if the liquidated damages did not appear to be a genuine pre-estimate of the losses, the clause was to be ignored and the party required to establish the losses. Following the Dunlop case, there have been a large number of cases on liquidated damages. The United Kingdom Supreme Court in Cavendish Square Holding BV v. Talal El Makdessi, 2(2015) UKSC 67 [Hereafter Cavendish (2015)] has revisited and consolidated the principles on award of liquidated damages.

Cavendish Square Holding BV v. Talal El Makdessi

The Supreme Court had joined two cases together as they had the same question, on the award of liquidated damages [Cavendish (2015)]. The first case was Cavendish Square Holding BV v. Makdessi. In this case, Mr El Makdessi and Mr Ghoussoub entered into an agreement that 47.4 per cent shareholding in an underlying company should be held between them in the ratio of 53.88 per cent to 46.12 per cent. The price was payable in stages. US$65.5 m was payable on completion of the sale and the group reorganisation. Thereafter, there were to be interim and final payments from the profits of the company in the preceding four years. A clause of the contract prohibited Mr El Makdessi from various competitive or potentially competitive activities. The contract provided that in the event of breach of the clause, he would not be entitled to receive the interim and/or final payments due, and could be required to sell Cavendish the rest of his shares at a "Defaulting Shareholder Option Price". Mr El Makdessi was clearly in breach. However, he claimed that the damages clauses were unenforceable penalty clauses.

The second case was ParkingEye Limited v. Beavis. ParkingEye Limited ran a car park. It had put prominent notices to the entrance of the car park and also inside statements including "2 h maximum stay" and "Parking limited to 2 h". The notices further stated:" Failure to comply … will result in a Parking Charge of £85 … By parking within the car park, motorists agree to comply with the car park regulations". Mr Beavis left his car parked for 56 min over the permitted two-hour period. The company claimed £85 in damages. Mr Beavis argued that the £85 charge demanded of him by ParkingEye Ltd. was an unenforceable penalty.

The Supreme Court reviewed the case law of more than hundred years, starting from the Dunlop Case. The following passages from this very lengthy judgment serve as an overview. Lord Neuberger and Lord Sumption noted: [Cavendish (2015): para 32].

> The true test is whether the impugned provision is a secondary obligation which imposes a detriment on the contract-breaker out of all proportion to any legitimate interest of the innocent party in the enforcement of the primary obligation. The innocent party can have no proper interest in simply punishing the defaulter. His interest is in performance or in some appropriate alternative to performance... But compensation is not necessarily the only legitimate interest that the innocent party may have in the performance of the defaulter's primary obligation.

The court was making a distinction between primary obligation and secondary obligation of the contracting parties. For example, a seller delivering the goods is a primary obligation but giving a receipt may only be a secondary obligation. The damages stipulated in the clause should not be 'out of all proportion', with reference to the primary obligation. Lord Mance, in his judgment, noted: [Cavendish (2015): para 152].

> What is necessary in each case is to consider, first, whether any (and if so what) legitimate business interest is served and protected by the clause, and, second, whether, assuming such an interest to exist, the provision made for the interest is nevertheless in the circumstances extravagant, exorbitant or unconscionable.

Lord Neuberger and Lord Sumption noted: [Cavendish (2015): para 32].

> The penalty rule is an interference with freedom of contract. It undermines the certainty which parties are entitled to expect of the law. ... In a negotiated contract between properly advised parties of comparable bargaining power, the strong initial presumption must be that the parties themselves are the best judges of what is legitimate in a provision dealing with the consequences of breach.

The judges further noted: [Cavendish (2015): para 9].

> The distinction between a clause providing for a genuine pre-estimate of damages and a penalty clause has remained fundamental to the modern law, as it is currently understood. The question whether a damages clause is a penalty falls to be decided as a matter of construction, therefore as at the time that it is agreed.... This is because it depends on the character of the provision, not on the circumstances in which it falls to be enforced.

The judgment recognised that the fundamental approach was to make a determination whether a liquidated damages clause was a genuine pre-estimate of losses or a penalty clause. In doing this, however, it was to be considered whether the breach for which the liquidated damages was claimed was a primary obligation of the contract or a secondary obligation of the contract. The judgment further recognising that at a general level of principles, the penalty rule was 'an interference with freedom of contract'. For this reason, in negotiated contracts (as opposed to standard term contracts), where the bargaining power of the parties was comparable, there should be a strong presumption of the validity of the liquidated damages clause. The judgment has come to find application in the context of the nature of the contract and the breach.

Often, it is not possible for the contracting parties to pre-estimate the losses. Even if the damages could be pre-estimated, there is a risk in settling the amount. If the damages turned out to be higher, the party would be without any remedy. Further, a liquidated damages clause would readily get challenged as punitive. For these reasons, in most GCCs, liquidated damages are used only for delays. A small reasonable percentage of the contract value is stated as the damages for each day's delay. The United Kingdom Supreme Court has noted: [Triple Point Technology, Inc v PTT Public Company Ltd, (2021) UKSC 29. Hereafter Triple Point (SC): Para 74].

> A liquidated damages clause is a clause in a contract which stipulates what amount of money will be payable as damages for loss caused by a breach of the contract irrespective of what loss may actually be suffered if a breach of the relevant kind (typically, delay in performance of the contract) occurs.

The Supreme Court noted that the clause finds much application in construction and engineering projects: [Triple point (SC): para 74].

> Liquidated damages clauses are a standard feature of major construction and engineering contracts and commonly provide for damages to be payable at a specified rate for each week or day of delay in the completion of work by the contractor after the contractual completion date has passed.

We review below the latest and a landmark judgment of the United Kingdom Supreme Court on liquidated damages, Triple Point Technology, Inc v PTT Public Company Ltd, (2021) UKSC 29, on the scope and application of liquidated damages clauses on delay.

The Triple Point Case: The Contract

PTT Public Company Ltd is a company incorporated in Thailand. It was engaged in commodity trading in oil, refined products and petrochemicals. It used a software, TCS system, for its trading business. It expanded its operations into newer commodities. For this, it needed a new software system, commodities trading, risk management and vessel chartering and operations system (a CTRM system). As is evident from the title, the software integrated all aspects of commodity trading. PTT invited tender for the design, development, supply and implementation of a new system on the basis of the Terms of Reference.

Triple Point Technology, Inc. is a company incorporated in the State Delaware, USA. It designs, develops and implements software for use in commodities trading. The software runs on its platforms, Commodity XL (CXL) and Softmar Vessel Chartering and Vessel Operations (VO). Triple Point responded with a bid. PTT was interested in the bid of Triple Point. The parties had a round of discussions on technical details of the project. Following this, Triple Point revised its bid. PTT accepted the revised bid and a contract was formed between the parties. The parties signed a contract document.

The bid provided the contract to be done in two phases. In Phase 1, the existing TCS system was to be replaced. In Phase 2, the development of the system for the new commodities was to be done. Each phase had several stages through which the phase was to be monitored and completed. The bid incorporated detailed terms of contract set by PTT in its Terms of Reference. The contract was subject to UK courts and law. The bid stated the total price for Phase I to be $6.92 million. This comprised $2.6 million for CTRM software; $4.04 million for implementation, including training, testing, initial support and maintenance; and $280,000 for travel and related expenses.

The work on the project proceeded slowly. Triple Point failed to integrate the three software packages, CXL, VO and CR. The system installed by Triple Point did not have the functionality specified in the contract. Triple Point achieved completion of Stages 1 and 2 of Phase 1, but with a delay of 149 days. Triple Point submitted an invoice for $1,038,000 in respect of this work. PTT duly paid the sum.

Triple Point then asked PTT to pay further invoices in respect of other work which was not yet completed. PTT refused to make these payments. Triple Point contended that the payment schedules provided for payment by reference to calendar days. PTT relied on the provisions of the contract to maintain that the payments had to be done on achievements of the milestones. Triple Point was not willing to continue working without receiving further payment. It suspended work and left the site. PTT maintained that Triple Point had wrongfully suspended work and terminated the contract under the terms of the contract. Triple Point commenced proceeding before the High Court (Technology and Construction Division) to recover the outstanding sums claimed in its invoices. [Triple Point Technology, Inc. v PTT Public Company Limited, (2017) EWHC 2178 (TCC). Hereafter Triple Point (HC).] PTT made counterclaims for breach of contract by Triple Point. The court concluded that Triple Point was entitled to receive payment only when it reached the various milestones. Triple Point was in breach of the contract and would have to pay damages to PTT.

The contract clause on damages provided:

> 5.3 If CONTRACTOR fails to deliver work within the time specified and the delay has not been introduced by PTT, CONTRACTOR shall be liable to pay the penalty at the rate of 0.1% (zero point one percent) of undelivered work per day of delay from the due date for delivery up to the date PTT accepts such work …
>
> 12.3 CONTRACTOR shall be liable to PTT for any damage suffered by PTT as a consequence of CONTRACTOR's breach of contract …

The Triple Point Case: Are the Liquidated Damages Punitive?

Article 5.3 was a liquidated damages clause. It required Triple Point to pay damages for delay at the rate of 0.1% of undelivered work per day. Triple Point contended that the amount was a penalty and not enforceable. It claimed that Article 5 itself describes it as a 'penalty'. The High Court judge noted on the contention that it trite law that 'a penalty is unenforceable in English law' [Triple Point (HC): para

265]. The court brought out the 'approach of the Courts to the language used in such clauses': [Triple Point (HC): para 265].

> In a liquidated damages clause (which uses that term) it is clear that the use of that description is not determinative and that the court may nonetheless find that the "liquidated damages" amount to a penalty. By the same token, even though the commonly used term "penalty" appears in the contract, it is open to the Court to conclude that the clause in reality sets a reasonable level of liquidated damages. In this case, that is how I construe Article 5.

The second contention raised by Triple Point was that the liquidated damages were irrespective of the reason or circumstances of the delay. Thus, it was a penalty, as it was 'out of all proportion to any legitimate interest of PTT in enforcement of the primary obligation'. In this phrasing, Triple Point was relying on the principle set by the United Kingdom Supreme Court in Cavendish Square Holdings BV v Makdessi, reviewed above, for distinguishing liquidated damages from penalty. The High Court found the argument 'hopeless given the apparent reasonableness of the amounts specified in Article 5.' [Triple Point (HC): para 266] The breach by Triple Point was not of a secondary obligation but abandoning the primary obligation, of developing the software platform. Further, in the view of the High Court, damages at the rate of 0.1% per day of delay were reasonable. The High Court judge awarded liquidated damages as follows:

1. Delay on Stages 1 and 2 of Phase 1, under clause 5.3, from 13th October 2013 to 19 March 2014, the date of completion: $154,662.
2. Delay on all other elements of the work, under clause 5.3, from the specified completion dates to 15 February 2015, the date when the contract was terminated: $3,304,616.40.
3. PTT was awarded, under clause 12.3, the clause on general damages, the cost of procurement of an alternative system in the sum of US$10,574,756.78.
4. PTT was awarded, under clause 12.3, the clause on general damages, recover wasted costs in the sum of US$630,000.

Triple Point challenged the award of damages before the Court of Appeal.

Before the Court of Appeal, Triple Point challenged the finding of the High Court judge. It asserted that Article 5.3 imposed a detriment on Triple Point 'out of all proportion to any legitimate interest of the innocent party' [Triple Point Technology, Inc. v PTT Public Company Ltd, (2019) EWCA Civ 230. Hereafter Triple Point (CA): para 69]. PPT resisted the argument by claiming that 'the sums generated by the contractual formula are modest, when compared with the financial consequences of delay in installing the software' [Triple Point (CA): para 70]. Triple Point, in employing the term 'legitimate interest' was relying on Cavendish Square Holdings BV v Makdessi, reviewed above. The Court of Appeal dispelling the contention, noted: [Triple Point (CA): para 71].

> The losses flowing from late delivery of the software and its impact on PTT's business could well be much greater than that. Although the contractual formula is not perfect, it is a genuine pre-estimate of the losses likely to flow from delay.

Triple Point raised another argument referencing Articles 12.3 and 5.3 together. Triple Point claimed that Article 12.3 allowed double recovery. The damages for delays could be claimed twice, first under Article 5.3 as liquidated damages and then, as general damages under Article 12.3. As a result, the liquidated damages clause should be held to be punitive. The Court of Appeal disagreed. It noted: [Triple Point (CA): para 72].

> This is a hopeless argument. A liquidated damages clause … operates in substitution for a general assessment of the claimant's losses caused by delay. It does not enable the wronged party to recover compensation for the same losses twice over.

The Court of Appeal brought out the object of a liquidated damages clause is to bring certainty by specifying the amount of damages. The liquidated damages clause will apply first, and the damages for the breach claimed under liquidated damages will not be claimed again under the general assessment. Once liquidated damages are provided for a breach, the damages for the breach have to be claimed only under the liquidated damages clause. The party has no choice of choosing between the two clauses.

The Triple Point Case: The Court of Appeal

Triple Point then raised the contention that Article 5.3 did not apply at all to the uncompleted work. To recall, Article 5.3 reads: 'If CONTRACTOR fails to deliver work … shall be liable to pay the penalty at the rate of 0.1% … from the due date for delivery up to the date PTT accepts such work'. Triple Point claimed the clause applied when there was a delay but subsequent completion and acceptance by PTT. It did not apply in respect of work which the employer never accepted. The Court of Appeal found this to be a 'formidable argument' [Triple Point (CA): para 76] which raised important questions of 'general principle concerning the operation of liquidated damages clauses in termination or abandonment cases' [Triple Point (CA): para 76].

The court reviewed the limited number of cases on the theme in the past 100 years. It found that the courts had taken divergent views. This was compounded by that each judgment was with reference to its own particular wording of the contract terms. The Court of Appeal summarised the divergent views in the cases where a contractor failed to complete the contract and a second contractor stepped in: [Triple Point (CA): para 106].

1. The liquidated damages clause does not apply.
2. The liquidated damages clause only applies up to the termination of the contract.
3. The liquidated damages clause continues to apply until the second contractor achieves completion.

The Court of Appeal commented on the three views: [Triple Point (CA): para 108].

> Much will turn on the precise wording of the liquidated damages clause in question. … I have my doubts about the cases in category (iii). If they are correct, it means that the employer and the second contractor can control the period for which liquidated damages will run.

Thus, option 3 was not a plausible one. The Court of Appeal saw 'much force' [Triple Point (CA): para 109] in the reasoning of 1, that is, the liquidated damages clause does not apply if the contract is terminated. The Court of Appeal appraised the second category, where the liquidated damages was to run till the contract was terminated. It noted that the 'approach is not free from difficulty' [Triple Point (CA): para 110]. It elaborated: [Triple Point (CA): para 110].

> If a construction contract is abandoned or terminated, the employer is in new territory for which the liquidated damages clause may not have made provision. Although accrued rights must be protected, it may sometimes be artificial and inconsistent with the parties' agreement to categorise the employer's losses as £x per week up to a specified date and then general damages thereafter.

The Court of Appeal found it 'more logical' to assess the total loss 'applying the ordinary rules for assessing damages for breach of contract' [Triple Point (CA): para 110]. The court concluded the discussion: [Triple Point (CA): para 110].

> In my view, the question whether the liquidated damages clause (a) ceases to apply or (b) continues to apply up to termination/abandonment, or even conceivably beyond that date, must depend upon the wording of the clause itself. There is no invariable rule that liquidated damages must be used as a formula for compensating the employer for part of its loss.

The court, reviewing the liquidated damages clause (5.3) of the contract, noted: [Triple Point (CA): para 112].

> This clause … seems to be focused specifically on delay between the contractual completion date and the date when Triple Point actually achieves completion. The phrase in article 5.3 'up to the date PTT accepts such work' means 'up to the date when PTT accepts completed work from Triple Point'. In my view Article 5.3 in this case … has no application in a situation where the contractor never hands over completed work to the employer.

Triple Point had completed stages 1 and 2 of Phase 1 with delays. It had abandoned the rest of the contract. The Court continued: [Triple Point (CA): para 113].

> The consequence of this analysis is that PTT is entitled to recover liquidated damages of $154,662 in respect of Triple Point's delay of 149 days in completing stages 1 and 2 of Phase 1. PTT is not entitled to recover liquidated damages for any of the other delays. That is because Triple Point did not complete any other sections of the work.

Did this then mean that PTT could not claim damages for the stages which did not get completed? The court gave the answer: [Triple Point (CA): para 113].

> The fact that PTT cannot recover liquidated damages in respect of any other sections of the work does not mean that it is left without a remedy for non-completion. Such damages are at large, rather than fixed in advance. PTT is entitled to recover damages for breach of Articles 5 and 12 of the CTRM contract, assessed on ordinary principles.

Thus, PTT would claim damages for the remaining stages of Phase 1 and the entire Phase 2 on the general principles of damages, contained in clause 12.3 that Triple Point shall be liable to PTT 'for any damage suffered by PTT as a consequence of CONTRACTOR's breach of contract' [Triple Point (CA): para 16].

The Triple Point Case: The Supreme Court

PTT came in appeal before the United Kingdom Supreme Court on the decision that it could not claim liquidated damages on the work which Triple Point never completed. If the liquidated damages clause did not apply to the unfinished work, the onus would be on PTT to establish the losses it suffered due to the delays. The Supreme Court stated that liquidated damages clauses are introduced to bring certainty: [Triple Point (SC): Para 35].

> Parties agree a liquidated damages clause so as to provide a remedy that is predictable and certain for a particular event (here, as often, that event is a delay in completion). The employer does not then have to quantify its loss, which may be difficult and time-consuming for it to do.

On termination of a contract, the parties are discharged from their obligations under the contract. The innocent party claims damages from the other party. In this context, the Supreme Court noted: [Triple Point (SC): Para 35].

> Parties must be taken to know the general law, namely that the accrual of liquidated damages comes to an end on termination of the contract. After that event, the parties' contract is at an end and the parties must seek damages for breach of contract under the general law. That is well-understood. Parties do not have to provide specifically for the effect of the termination of their contract. They can take that consequence as read.

The Supreme Court brought together the principles of termination and damages. The moment a contract is terminated, both the parties are freed from further performance of the contract. There can be no further delays. The delays have already happened and the damages on this account accrued. After the termination, the party will claim damages for the loss of the contract under the other clauses on damages in the contract. The court clarified that the parties out of prudence provided that the liquidated damages would run till the work is completed, and not thereafter. However, this cannot be read to mean that 'if that event does not occur the contractor is free from all liability for liquidated damages, and that the employer's accrued right to liquidated damages simply disappears' [Triple Point (SC): Para 36]. The court noted: [Triple Point (SC): Para 36].

> It is much more probable that they will have intended the provision for liquidated damages to cease on completion and acceptance of the works to stand in addition to and not in substitution for the right to liquidated damages down to termination. Reading the clause in that way meets commercial common sense and prevents the unlikely elimination of accrued rights.

The Supreme Court applied the principle to the Triple Point Case and noted that there was no commercial reason for the parties to agree for the liquidated damages, only in one case, where the work is delivered. There is no reason for the parties to not want liquidated damages in other cases, that is, where the work is not delivered. The court noted: [Triple Point (SC): Para 38].

If their purpose was to achieve a certain and quick resolution of the employer's claim for loss for the potential benefit of both parties, in the event of delay, then it would not be achieved by limiting article 5.3 to the situation where the work is ultimately done and accepted. … In my judgment, additional wording is not needed. It would be sufficient to interpret the words "up to the date PTT accepts such work" as meaning "up to the date (if any) PTT accepts such work".

The Supreme Concluded that the clause 'on its true construction' applied whether PTT the work or not. [Triple Point (SC): Para 48].

> The function of the words … was to provide an end date for liquidated damages on acceptance of the works by PTT to ensure that in that event there was no further claim for liquidated damages in respect of the relevant delay. But it did not follow that there were to be no liquidated damages if there was no such acceptance. To reach that conclusion would be to render the liquidated damages clause of little value in a commercial contract.

The Supreme Court, thus, recognised the award made by the High Court for the part of the work which was never delivered.

The damages terms in GCCs have clause(s) on liquidated damages. The liquidated damages are assessed by the courts and awarded only if the amount is a genuine pre-estimate of the losses suffered by the breach. In deciding this, the words and phrases employed are not decisive. The courts go with the substance of it, that is, the nature of the breach and the amount, and not the words employed. The liquidated damages clause invariably a small percentage of the contract value. In this context, a further development has been to explore the nature of the breach, whether it is a primary obligation of the contract, affecting the transaction itself, or a secondary obligation. The Triple Point Case has reiterated these principles and cleared the doubt on its applicability in relation to undelivered work. This has been secured by unifying the principles of termination and damages. Once a contract is terminated, the party cannot delay any further as the parties are discharged from further performance. The suffering party will claim damage for the loss of the contract. The measure for the delay till the termination is in the liquidated damages clause.

References

Cavendish Square Holding BV v. Makdessi, 2(2015) UKSC 67
Dunlop Pneumatic Tyre Co. Ltd. v. New Garage and Motor Co. Ltd. (1915) A.C. 79
Triple Point Technology, Inc v PTT Public Company Ltd, (2021) UKSC 29
Triple Point Technology, Inc. v PTT Public Company Limited, (2017) EWHC 2178 (TCC)
Triple Point Technology, Inc. v PTT Public Company Ltd, (2019) EWCA Civ 230

Chapter 10
Consequential and Indirect Losses

A breach is like a pebble being dropped in a pond, it leads to consequences like ripples. How far does one follow the consequences in making the party in breach liable for the losses? The answer is, one goes as far as the parties intend to go as the contract is theirs. If the parties are certain on the consequences of a breach and provide for it, effect should be given to it. However, consequences of a breach are often open ended and making a claim for them push the contracting parties in a speculative uncertain domain. To void the uncertainties, GCCs have a clause excluding the parties from making a claim for consequential losses. The clause may read like:

> Neither party shall be liable to the other party for any indirect and consequential damages or for any loss of profits or loss of production.

Another clause is:

> Neither Party shall be liable to the other Party for loss of use of any Works, loss of profit, loss of any contract or for any indirect or consequential loss or damage which may be suffered by the other Party in connection with the Contract.

The clauses excluding indirect and consequential losses have come to be interpreted in relation to a landmark judgment of the House of Lords on the theme of direct and indirect losses, Hadley v. Baxendale [Hadley v Baxendale (1854) 9 Ex. 341]. In this 1854 judgment, the House of Lords formulated: [Hadley v Baxendale (1854) 9 Ex. 341: page 354].

> Where two parties have made a contract which one of them has broken, the damages which the other party ought to receive in respect of such breach of contract should be such as may fairly and reasonably be considered either arising naturally, i.e., according to the usual course of things, from such breach of contract itself, or such as may reasonably be supposed to have been in the contemplation of both parties, at the time they made the contract, as the probable result of the breach of it.

The damages arising naturally from a breach are known as the first limb of Hadley v Baxendale rule. It is a direct loss arising from the breach. And what is supposed to

A. Pathak, *Contract Terms in International Business*,
https://doi.org/10.1007/978-981-96-8146-4_10

be in the contemplation of the parties has been known as the second limb of Hadley v Baxendale rule. This is an indirect loss arising from a breach of the contract. The judgment deals with direct and indirect losses arising from a breach. The clauses excluding indirect and consequential losses overlap with the judgment. For this reason, the clauses have been interpreted with reference to the judgment. The evolution of the clauses has also been with reference to the judgment and the changing business practices.

The clauses started out by using the term 'indirect or consequential' losses. In Saint Line Ltd v Richardsons, Westgarth and Co Ltd, the court noted: [Saint Line Ltd v Richardsons, Westgarth and Co Ltd (1940) 2 KB 99: page 103].

> Direct damage is that which flows naturally from the breach without other intervening cause and independently of special circumstances, while indirect damage does not so flow. ... The word 'consequential' is not very illuminating, as all damage is in a sense consequential.

The question in the case was if loss of profit was a consequential loss. The court noted: [Saint Line Ltd v Richardsons, Westgarth and Co Ltd (1940) 2 KB 99: page 104].

> In my judgment the words 'indirect or consequential' do not exclude liability for damages which are the natural result of the breaches complained of. ... If one takes loss of profit, it is quite clear that such a claim may very well arise directly and naturally from the breach based on delay.

Thus, as the very reason for a contract is to profit from it, loss of profit would be contended to be a direct loss. In Deepak Fertilisers Ltd v ICI Chemicals and Polymers Ltd, the clause excluded liability 'by reason of its performance or obligation under this contract, be liable in tort or for loss of anticipated profits, catalyst, raw material and products or for indirect or consequential damages' [Deepak Fertilisers Ltd v ICI Chemicals and Polymers Ltd, (1999) 1 T.C.L.R. 200: page 227]. A methanol plant, which was a subject matter of the contract had got destroyed. The Court of Appeal noted: [Deepak Fertilisers Ltd v ICI Chemicals and Polymers Ltd, (1999) 1 T.C.L.R. 200: page 228].

> The direct and natural result of the destruction of the plant was that Deepak was left without a methanol plant, the reconstruction of which would cost money and take time, losing for Deepak any methanol production in the meantime. Wasted overheads incurred during the reconstruction of the plant, as well as profits lost during that period, are no more remote as losses than the cost of reconstruction. Lost profits cannot be recovered because they are excluded in terms, not because they are too remote.

Thus, exclusion of indirect and consequential losses may not exclude loss of profit. However, if loss of profit is expressly excluded, the party would not be able to claim it.

The Minibar Case

By the 1990s, hotels had come to put minibars in the hotel rooms for the customers to use the items and pay for them. But this had led to dishonesty by the customers, ranging from leaving the hotel without paying or refilling bottles with water. Hotel Services Limited (HSL) came up with a solution to the problem. [Hotel Services Ltd. v Hilton International Hotels (UK) Ltd., 2000 WL 191222. Hereafter Hilton (2000)] It developed a device named Robobar, which electronically registered any withdrawals of the items from the device and registered it in the name of the customer. HSL represented to Hilton hotel that by using it, the hotel could increase its profit: [Hilton (2000): para 7].

> We believe Robobar presents a very viable opportunity for your Hotel to increase it's Food and Beverage profit as is already the case at many Hotels throughout the World.

Hilton International Hotels (UK) Ltd entered into a contract to put the Robobar in all the rooms in two of its hotels in London. Within the contract, HSL was to lease the Robobars for ten years. The Robobar itself had a problem. The chiller leaked ammonia which corroded the equipment. The leakage also created a risk of injury to the customers. HSL could not correct the defect in the Robobars. Following this, Hilton terminated the contract and the Robobars were dismantled and removed from the hotel rooms. Hilton claimed damages including loss of profit on the minibars amounting to £127,000. The contract had a limitations clause which read:[Hilton (2000): para 4].

> The Company [HSL] will not in any circumstances be liable for any indirect or consequential loss, damage or liability arising from any defect in or failure of the System or any part thereof or the performance of this Agreement or any breach hereof by the Company or its employees.

Following the clause, HSL disclaimed any liability. The court took a preliminary view that Hilton had rented the Robobar to make a profit. Thus, the court noted:[Hilton (2000): para 8].

> In this situation we see nothing wrong with the simple conclusion that … the loss of any profits which it would otherwise have been earning were direct or natural consequences of the dangerous unserviceability of the equipment and therefore untouched by an exemption clause which (since all recoverable loss is literally consequential) plainly uses "consequential" as a synonym of "indirect".

The court, however, noted that in the light of the case law that has developed over the decades on the clauses, a resolution was not 'so simple'[Hilton (2000): para 9]. The court noted that it was a question of the distribution of the losses between normal and consequential:[Hilton (2000): para 11].

> One would like to say simply that all consequential losses are recoverable provided they were either objectively or subjectively foreseeable by the parties; but to do this is to restore to the word "consequential" the natural meaning of which commercial and legal usage in exclusion clauses has long since robbed it. Instead one has to go back to the language of the clause in its documentary and factual context and try to see what it means.

To the argument that profit is a consequential loss, the court reasoned:[Hilton (2000): para 13].

> But where the contract is one of hire, the "thing itself" is not the equipment but the use of the equipment, and if through breach of contract it becomes unusable and dangerous the natural or immediate loss is, it seems to us, the profit (if any) which it would otherwise be yielding and the cost of neutralising the danger.

In conclusion, the court decided:[Hilton (2000): para 20].

> We prefer therefore to decide this case … on the direct ground that if equipment rented out for selling drinks without defalcations turns out to be unusable and possibly dangerous, it requires no special mutually known fact to establish the immediacy both of the consequent cost of putting it where it can do no harm and—if when in use it was showing a direct profit—of the consequent loss of profit. Such losses are not embraced by the exclusion clause, read in its documentary and commercial context.

Thus, Hilton was awarded the loss of profit as it was not a consequential loss but a direct loss arising from the breach of the lease of the Robobars.

Exclusion of Loss of Profit

In a recent case, The Star Polaris [The Star Polaris [2016] EWHC 2941] (2016) EWHC 2941, the High Court has emphasised on textual and contextual interpretation of the contracts to give a meaning to the term 'consequential or special losses' than confining it to the second limb of Hadley v Baxendale. The High Court noted: [The Star Polaris (2016) EWHC 2941: para 39].

> In my judgment therefore … "consequential or special losses, damages or expenses" does not mean such losses, damages or expenses as fall within the second limb of Hadley v Baxendale but does have the wider meaning of financial losses caused by guaranteed defects, above and beyond the cost of replacement and repair of physical damage.

As a result of the case law, it can be contended that loss of profit is a direct loss and claimable, even if the exclusion clause excludes indirect and consequential losses. However, a claim of loss of profit is highly fact sensitive. It requires establishing facts like the benefits that would have arisen if the contract had been performed. The savings that would have been made if the contract had been performed. The efficiencies that would have been brought if the contract had been performed. The additional businesses and revenues that would have been secured if the contract had been performed. These are all hypothetical questions, the party claiming loss of profit has to establish. This inevitably involves a degree of speculation and is not free from uncertainties. [Soteria Insurance Limited (formerly Cis General Insurance Limited) v IBM United Kingdom Limited, (2022) EWCA Civ 440. Hereafter IBM (2022): Para 66.] As it is difficult for the parties to establish the losses, often 'loss of profit' is expressly excluded along with indirect and consequential losses. The Court of Appeal in the IBM Case noted: [IBM (2022): Para 68].

> All loss of profit/revenue/savings claims are difficult for the potential contract-breaker to estimate in advance. They can be notoriously open-ended. Claims for loss of profit, revenue and savings are therefore types of potential loss which, because of those problems of speculation and ascertainment, are routinely excluded by clauses.

Thus, exclusion clauses have expressly come to exclude indirect and consequential losses; and loss of profit. However, there are other kind of losses which arise in a contract which makes still not get covered. We will need to turn to the founding principle of award of damages to explore them.

Reliance Losses

The founding principle for award of damages is Robinson v. Harman, which states the principle as to put the party in a position 'so far as money can do it, to be placed in the same situation with respect to damages, as if the contract had been performed. [Robinson v. Harman (1848) 1 Exch 850.] To give effect to it, we would ask, what interest or gains the parties would have made, if the contract had been performed. This is called the performance interest for the award of contracts. In some cases, however, it may not be possible to estimate the interest or gains if the contract had been performed.

In Anglia Television Limited v. Reed [Anglia Television Ltd. v Reed, (1972) 1 Q.B. 60.], Anglia Television Limited entered into a contract with an actor, Reed, to act in a television play. The actor breached the contract and the production had to be abandoned. The television company could not 'say what their profit would have been on this contract if Mr Reed had come here and performed it' [Anglia Television Ltd. v Reed, (1972) 1 Q.B. 60: page 63]. The company, thus, instead of claim for loss of profits, claimed for wasted expenditure. It had incurred expenditure for arranging for the production which got wasted. The Court of Appeal, allowing the claim of wasted resources, noted: [Anglia Television Ltd. v Reed, (1972) 1 Q.B. 60: page 63].

> It seems to me that a plaintiff in such a case as this had an election: he can either claim for his loss of profit; or for his wasted expenditure. But he must elect between them. He cannot claim both. If he has not suffered any loss of profits-or if he cannot prove what his profits would have been-he can claim in the alternative the expenditure which has been thrown away, that is, wasted, by reason of the breach. .... He must pay damages for all the expenditure so wasted and thrown away.

This alternate basis for a claim for damages came to be known as the reliance interest. Both, expectation interest and reliance interest, are founded on the same starting principle for award of damages. In Surrey County Council and Another v Bredero Homes Ltd., it was explained: [Surrey County Council and Another v Bredero Homes Ltd., (1993) 1 W.L.R. 1361: page 1369].

> The starting principle ... the object is to put the aggrieved party in the same financial position as if the contract had been fully performed. But the law also protects the negative interest of the aggrieved party. If the aggrieved party is unable to establish the value of a loss of bargain

> he may seek compensation in respect of his reliance losses. The object of such an award is to compensate the aggrieved party for expenses incurred and losses suffered in reliance on the contract.

In Surrey Case, the party had not suffered any loss due to the breach. The judge noted: [Surrey County Council and Another v Bredero Homes Ltd., (1993) 1 W.L.R. 1361: page 1369].

> These two complementary principles share one feature. Both are pure compensatory principles. If the aggrieved party has suffered no loss he is not entitled to be compensated by invoking these principles. The application of these principles to the present case would result in an award of nominal damages only."

In Omak Maritime Ltd. v Mamola Challenger Shipping Co. [Omak Maritime Ltd. v Mamola Challenger Shipping Co. (2010) EWHC 2026 (Comm)], the breach had put the party in a better position. The party sought to claim for wasted expenditure. The court noted:[Omak Maritime Ltd. v Mamola Challenger Shipping Co. (2010) EWHC 2026 (Comm): para 36].

> I am not therefore persuaded that the right to choose or elect between claiming damages on an expectancy basis or on a reliance basis indicates that there are two different principles at work. Both bases of damages are founded on, and are illustrations of, the fundamental principle in Robinson v Harman.

In this context, where the party had recuperated more than the losses, it would be 'wrong in principle' to award substantial damages. The court noted: [Omak Maritime Ltd. v Mamola Challenger Shipping Co. (2010) EWHC 2026 (Comm): para 59].

> Such an award would place the Owners in a better position than they would have been in had the contract been performed. Moreover, damages for breach of contract are intended to compensate for loss suffered and the Owners have, as a result of their own efforts to mitigate their loss, suffered no loss.

The following judgment comprehensively deals with exclusion clauses and a claim of wasted resources arising from a breach.

The Soteria Case

CIS General Insurance Limited was in the business of underwriting and distribution of general insurance products [IBM (2022)]. It decided to get a new IT solution for its business. The initiative was known as Project Cobalt. Towards this, CIS entered into a contract with IBM United Kingdom Limited to supply the new IT system for CIS's insurance business and for the management of the system for a term of ten years. The contract comprised a Master Services Agreement (MSA), with two associated documents. The Implementation Statement of Work set out the cost of supply and implementation of the new IT system in the total sum of £50.2 m. The Management SOW identified the total figure for the management services over the 10-year period at £125.6 m. The contract provided various stages for the completion of the project with completion dates.

IBM caused serious delays in the project from the beginning itself. IBM submitted an invoice in the sum of £2.9 m in respect of milestone reflecting payments due in respect of software licences and, under the Implementation SOW, became due in January 2017. CISGIL considered that the sum was not payable because of the significant delays to the contract. Following the non-payment, IBM claimed it had right under the contract to terminate it for the breach of non-payment. CIS disputed that IBM did not have the right to terminate and it would be in repudiatory breach if it terminated the contract. IBM claimed otherwise and terminated the contract.

CISGIL initiated proceedings against IBM for wrongfully terminating the contract and claimed damages in the sum of £132 million in respect of their wasted expenditure. IBM defended the claim that they were entitled to terminate the contract and made a counterclaim for £2.9 m for the unpaid invoice. The High Court held that IBM had wrongfully terminated the contract. CIS established a claim for wasted expenditure, arising from the wrongful termination at £122 million. However, the High Court ruled that the claim for wasted expenditure was excluded in its entirety by clause 23.3 of the contract. The clause read: [IBM (2022): para 23].

> Subject to clause 23.2 and 23.4, neither party shall be liable to the other or any third party for any Losses arising under and/or in connection with this Agreement (whether in contract, tort (including negligence), breach of statutory or otherwise) which are indirect or consequential Losses, or for loss of profit, revenue, savings…, data…, goodwill , reputation… even if such Losses were foreseeable and notwithstanding that a party had been advised of the possibility that such Losses were in the contemplation of the other party or any third party.

The dispute came before the Court of Appeal for an interpretation of the clause.

Interpretation of Contract Terms

The court started out with well-established principles for interpretation of terms of contracts. The court drew from Rainy Sky SA v Kookmin Bank, where the Supreme Court had stated: [Rainy Sky SA v Kookmin Bank (2011) UKSC 50: para 14].

> The ultimate aim of interpreting a provision in a contract, especially a commercial contract, is to determine what the parties meant by the language used, which involves ascertaining what a reasonable person would have understood the parties to have meant."

In the Rainy Sky SA v Kookmin Bank, the Supreme Court elaborated the principles for interpreting contract terms: [Rainy Sky SA v Kookmin Bank (2011) UKSC 50: para 21].

> The exercise of construction is essentially one unitary exercise in which the court must consider the language used and ascertain what a reasonable person, that is a person who has all the background knowledge which would reasonably be available to the parties in the situation in which they were at the time of the contract, would have understood the parties to have meant. In doing so, the court must have regard to all the relevant surrounding circumstances. If there are two possible constructions, the court is entitled to prefer the construction which is consistent with business common sense and to reject the other…where the parties have used unambiguous language, the court must apply it."

In the present case, the Court of Appeal applying the principle simply noted: [IBM (2022): para 57].

> The short point is whether, as a matter of language, the description of the types of losses being excluded, namely "loss of profit, revenue, savings" is apt to cover or include "wasted expenditure". In my view, the fundamental difficulty, which IBM never addressed, let alone surmounted, is that claims for "wasted expenditure" were not excluded by the terms of clause 23.3 because those words are simply not there.

The court constructed 'the objective meaning' of the exclusion clause 'as understood by a reasonable person in the position of these parties' [IBM (2022): para 58] to not exclude wasted resources. The expression "loss of profit, revenue [or] savings" cannot be taken to exclude wasted resources on the 'natural and ordinary meaning of the words'[IBM (2022): para 58]. The principles of construction of the contract terms 'lead inexorably to that conclusion'[IBM (2022): para 58]. A further support for the construction came in the clause giving 'a good deal of particularity as to what types of loss were being excluded'. This included not only loss of profit, revenue or savings, but also loss of data, goodwill and reputation. The court noted that 'in the light of that specificity the parties' decision not to exclude claims for wasted expenditure is telling' [IBM (2022): para 59].

Construction of Exclusion Clauses

The court recognised that the clause was an exclusion clause. It excluded the right of a party to be awarded the damages. There are, the court recognised 'general rules applicable to the construction of exclusion clauses and other clauses which might reduce the remedies ordinarily available to the victim of a breach of contract'[IBM (2022): para 34]. In Gilbert-Ash (Northern) Limited v Modern Engineering (Bristol) Limited, the House of Lords had stated: [Gilbert-Ash (Northern) Limited v Modern Engineering (Bristol) Limited (1974) AC 689: page 718].

> ... one starts with the presumption that neither party intends to abandon any remedies for its breach arising by operation of law, and clear express words must be used in order to rebut the presumption."

In Stocznia Gdynia SA v Gearbulk Holdings Limited (2010) QB 27, the court stated: [Stocznia Gdynia SA v Gearbulk Holdings Limited, (2009) EWCA Civ 75: para 23].

> The court is unlikely to be satisfied that a party to a contract has abandoned valuable rights arising by operation of law unless the terms of the contract make it sufficiently clear that that was intended. The more valuable the right the clearer the language will need to be.

In BHP Petroleum Limited v British Steel PLC (2000) 2 Lloyd's Rep 277. The court noted: [BHP Petroleum Limited v British Steel PLC, 2000 WL 362480: para 47].

> … a general rule that the more extreme the consequences are, in terms of excluding or modifying the liability that would otherwise arise, then the more stringent the court's approach should be in requiring that the exclusion or limit should be clearly and unambiguously expressed.

The Court of Appeal summarised the principles for interpreting exclusion clauses: [IBM (2022): para 60].

> The more valuable the right, the clearer the language of any exclusion clause will need to be; the more extreme the consequences, the more stringent the court must be before construing the clause in a way which allows the contract-breaker to avoid liability for what may be his catastrophic non-performance.

The court, thus, applied the principle to the exclusion clause: [IBM (2022): para 60].

> In my view, there was nothing in clause 23.3 to suggest that the costs, which CISGIL inevitably incurred in the expectation that Project Cobalt would be completed satisfactorily, would somehow be irrecoverable if IBM repudiated that contract.

The court illustrated it. CISGIL paid £34.1 million to IBM. This money was wasted because a new IT system did not get delivered. It was money spent in expectation of contractual benefits. Applying the principles for award of damages, the loss would be recoverable as damages. For excluding the claim, 'the exclusion must be clear and obvious' [IBM (2022): para 61]. But in the clause, 'there were no relevant exclusionary words, let alone clear and obvious ones' [IBM (2022): para 61]. The court noted: [IBM (2022): para 62].

> The parties cannot be taken to have excluded this obvious and common type of damages in circumstances where they have not made any reference in the relevant clause to wasted expenditure at all.

The court at this stage contrasted between two kinds of losses, loss of profit and loss by waste from breach. The loss of profit and other commercial losses are often unascertainable and speculative. For these reasons, these are excluded from the while the other kind of losses are certain and specific. The Court noted: [IBM (2022): para 70].

> Accordingly, it is unsurprising from a commercial perspective that, whilst speculative and uncertain types of loss were excluded by clause 23.3, at least one kind of easily-ascertainable type of loss—wasted expenditure—was not. In this way the clause, construed in the way that I have construed it, makes commercial sense. The claims that would have compensated CISGIL for being better off as a result of the new IT system were excluded; the claims to compensate them for being worse off as a result of the non-provision of the IT system were not. … the exclusion of loss of profits/revenue/savings, but not wasted expenditure, struck a fair commercial balance between the parties.

The court emphasised that this was consistent with the principle for award of damages. When a contract is breach, the party can claim either the loss of profit or the expenditure but not both. For this reason, clause 23.3 expressly excludes loss of profit but not wasted expenditure. The court further noted that contracts do have clauses excluding wasted expenditure, 'it is not only possible, but it is not uncommon for claims for wasted expenditure to be the subject of an exclusion clause of this type'[IBM (2022): para 72]. With this reference, the court noted that if the parties intended to exclude it: [IBM (2022): para 72].

> ... a prudent drafter would have sought expressly to exclude wasted expenditure, and should not have been content to rely on a clause referring only to loss of profit/revenue/savings. ... But such claims were not excluded here.

The court explained that the clause was seeking to exclude some of the losses which flow from an underlying loss of the bargain, but not to exclude other types of loss which arise from that same lost bargain. It concluded: [IBM (2022): para 82].

> Some types of loss of bargain damages, like loss of profit, revenue or savings, were excluded by clause 23.3. Other types, such as re-procurement costs and wasted expenditure, were not. ... the contract excluded what he called the aggrieved party's positive interests; it did not exclude his negative interest, namely "expenses incurred and losses suffered in reliance on the contract".

The Court of Appeal thus allowed for the wasted expenditure as losses.

The founding principle for award of damages arising from a breach is, by paying money, to put the party in a position the party would be if the contract were performed. This is affected by going forward and establishing what the gains and profits would have been if the contract had been performed. However, if this is not possible for the party to establish, in the alternative, the party can claim wasted expenditure arising from the breach. Every breach has consequences. The contracting parties have disputes for long as to how far do they go in awarding the damages. In most cases, it is uncertain and speculative for the parties to work out what would have happened if the contract had been performed. To bring certainly, clauses were introduced to exclude indirect and consequential losses and loss of profit. As the IBM Case has brought out, a clause of this kind is a choice of the party to elect to claim wasted expenditure and would be awarded. Only an express clause excluding wasted expenditure would disallow it.

References

Anglia Television Ltd. v Reed, (1972) 1 Q.B. 60
BHP Petroleum Limited v British Steel PLC, 2000 WL 362480
Deepak Fertilisers Ltd v ICI Chemicals and Polymers Ltd, (1999) 1 T.C.L.R. 200
Gilbert-Ash (Northern) Limited v Modern Engineering (Bristol) Limited (1974) AC 689
Hadley v Baxendale (1854) 9 Ex. 341
Hotel Services Ltd. v Hilton International Hotels (UK) Ltd., 2000 WL 191222
Omak Maritime Ltd. v Mamola Challenger Shipping Co. (2010) EWHC 2026 (Comm)
Rainy Sky SA v Kookmin Bank (2011) UKSC 50
Robinson v. Harman (1848) 1 Exch 850
Saint Line Ltd v Richardsons, Westgarth and Co Ltd (1940) 2 KB 99
Soteria Insurance Limited (formerly Cis General Insurance Limited) v IBM United Kingdom Limited, (2022) EWCA Civ 440

Stocznia Gdynia SA v Gearbulk Holdings Limited, (2009) EWCA Civ 75
Surrey County Council and Another v Bredero Homes Ltd., (1993) 1 W.L.R. 1361
The Star Polaris (2016) EWHC 2941

Chapter 11
Exclusion Clauses: Negligence and Liabilities in Torts

Contract terms have clauses excluding liabilities for indirect and consequential losses. This is to bring certainty in the claim of damages in the event of a breach. In addition, in the past two decades, contract terms have come to have terms excluding liabilities for negligence or liabilities arising in torts. At times, the terms can specifically state to claim liabilities arising for negligence or in torts. The clause could read as:

> **Liability: X Limited** shall not be liable in contract or in tort for any loss or damage suffered and X Limited's liability is limited to those set out in the Agreement and under statute. Neither party excludes or limits liability to the other party for (1) death or personal injury resulting from negligence, (2) fraud or (3) fraudulent misrepresentation or (4) any other liability that cannot be excluded by law.

Another illustration of a clause on negligence is:

> Supplier will indemnify X Limited against any and all damages, losses, costs, actions, claims, liabilities or expenses suffered or incurred by X Limited whether in contract, tort (including negligence) breach of statutory duty or otherwise, arising out of or in connection with any breach by the supplier.

In the earlier chapter, we reviewed the theme of exclusion of indirect and consequential losses. The exclusion clause in the IBM Case read as follows: [Soteria Insurance Limited (formerly Cis General Insurance Limited) v IBM United Kingdom Limited, (2022) EWCA Civ 440].

> Subject to clause 23.2 and 23.4, neither party shall be liable to the other or any third party for any Losses arising under and/or in connection with this Agreement (whether in contract, tort (including negligence), breach of statutory or otherwise) which are indirect or consequential Losses, or for loss of profit, revenue, savings..., data..., goodwill, reputation... even if such Losses were foreseeable and notwithstanding that a party had been advised of the possibility that such Losses were in the contemplation of the other party or any third party.

To explore the meaning and scope of the clause, we would need to get introduced to negligence and tort, which is a separate subject from contracts.

A. Pathak, *Contract Terms in International Business*,
https://doi.org/10.1007/978-981-96-8146-4_11

Torts and Negligence

Both remedies against negligence and torts are fields developed by the courts in the nineteenth century. The field rapidly developed in the twentieth century. A person can violate a criminal law and cause harm to another person. In this case, the criminal wrong will be punishable by the state. A contracting party may cause harm or loss to another person by not doing his contractual duty. In this case, damages would be awarded within the terms of the contract. The basis for this would be the rights and obligations created by the contract. Tort law covers all other civil wrong, that is, other than contracts, that cause a person loss or harm. The courts over the centuries, have developed different fields where a legal liability arises for a person who causes a loss or harm to another person. There are several subjects under torts including negligence, defamation and nuisance.

The House of Lords decision in Donoghue v Stevenson (1932) AC 562 became the foundation of modern law of negligence for the whole common law jurisdiction worldwide. Mrs. May Donoghue went with a friend to a café where the friend bought a bottle of ginger beer and both consumed it. When the friend poured out the last remaining bit of the ginger beer, a decomposed snail came out. Donoghue suffered shock and gastro-enteritis. She claimed £ 500 in damages from the manufacturer of the ginger beer on the grounds that the manufacturer of a product was liable in negligence to a person injured by the product. Lord Atkin developed the principle based on common sense: [Donoghue v Stevenson (1932) AC 562: page 580].

> The liability for negligence ... is no doubt based upon a general public sentiment of moral wrongdoing for which the offender must pay. ... The rule that you are to love your neighbour becomes in law, you must not injure your neighbour; and the lawyer's question, Who is my neighbour? receives a restricted reply. You must take reasonable care to avoid acts or omissions which you can reasonably foresee would be likely to injure your neighbour. Who, then, in law is my neighbour? The answer seems to be—persons who are so closely and directly affected by my act that I ought reasonably to have them in contemplation as being so affected when I am directing my mind to the acts or omissions which are called in question.

With the judgment it came to be that a person who was proximate to another owed a duty to the other to not cause harm. The duty was of a level of care a reasonable person would have exercised under the same circumstances. The duty could be in not doing certain actions or doing certain actions. In the beginning, the field of negligence was confined to physical actions as opposed to words and loss being in physical injury. The field rapidly developed to spread from physical action to words and loss covering economic loss to include all professional fields like solicitors, directors, auditors and financial analysts. The House of Lords judgment, Hedley Byrne & Co. Ltd. v Heller & Partners Ltd., (1964) A.C. 465, is a landmark, where the court formulated: [Hedley Byrne & Co. Ltd. v Heller & Partners Ltd., (1964) A.C. 465: page 502].

> I consider that it follows and that it should now be regarded as settled that if someone possessed of a special skill undertakes, quite irrespective of contract, to apply that skill for the assistance of another person who relies upon such skill, a duty of care will arise. The

> fact that the service is to be given by means of or by the instrumentality of words can make no difference. Furthermore, if in a sphere in which a person is so placed that others could reasonably rely upon his judgment or his skill or upon his ability to make careful inquiry, a person takes it upon himself to give information or advice to, or allows his information or advice to be passed on to, another person who, as he knows or should know, will place reliance upon it, then a duty of care will arise.

Following the formulation, the field further accelerated to take diverse professions and actions in its fold. Now comes the connection with contracts. A person who contracts with another certainly has proximity to the other. The parties also have duties to one another within the terms of the contract. As the parties are proximate, they may come to have duties to each other. The question then arises would the duties under contract and negligence run concurrently or only the duty under the contract would apply. The House of Lords answered this question in Henderson v Merrett Syndicates Ltd (1995) 2 A.C. 145. In the case, underwriting members brought action against member agents and managing agents at Lloyd's for causing massive losses. The House of Lords held: [Henderson v Merrett Syndicates Ltd (1995) 2 A.C. 145: page 154].

> … in addition to their various contractual duties, managing agents owed a duty of care in tort both to direct and indirect Names to carry out their functions with reasonable skill and care.

The House of Lords held that the governing principle was Hedley Byrne which established liability for words as well as deeds, and for pure economic loss as well as physical damage. The House of Lords ruled: [Henderson v Merrett Syndicates Ltd (1995) 2 A.C. 145: page 194].

> … an assumption of responsibility coupled with the concomitant reliance may give rise to a tortious duty of care irrespective of whether there is a contractual relationship between the parties, and in consequence, unless his contract precludes him from doing so, the plaintiff, who has available to him concurrent remedies in contract and tort, may choose that remedy which appears to him to be the most advantageous."

The House of Lords formulated that the rights under torts run concurrently with the rights under the contract and a party is free to choose the most advantageous remedy. The question then was could the rights under tort be ousted by contract terms. The answer to this was, as a remedy in torts is a civil remedy, developed by common law, the contracting parties are free to oust them by contract terms. The implications of this are three-fold. A contract must not omit to engage with the implications in negligence or torts as the rights under negligence run concurrently. Two, in the case of losses caused to a party, a determination will need to be made on the rights under the contract and negligence. The party would be free to choose the more advantageous right to make a claim for the losses. Three, at this stage, one would appraise the contract terms to see if it has excluded the right itself or a claim for the right. The following case has developed the principles.

The Robinson Case

In James Andrew Robinson v P.E.Jones (Contractors) Limited, [James Andrew Robinson v P.E.Jones (Contractors) Limited, (2011) EWCA Civ 9. Hereafter Robinson (2011).] a buyer of a building discovered 12 years later that the gas fire developed by the builder was not in accordance with good building practices and also building regulations in place then. The cost of remedial work would be very significant. The contract was made under National House-Building Council's standard form of Agreement No. HB5 (1986). Clause 10 of the contract provided: [Robinson (2011): para 11].

> The Vendor shall not be liable to the Purchaser or any successor in title of the Purchaser under the Agreement or any document incorporated therein in respect of any defect error or omission in the execution or the completion of the work save to the extent and for the period that it is liable under the provisions of the N.H.B.C. Agreement on which alone his rights and remedies are founded.

The court explored whether the builder owed a duty of care in tort to the buyer. The Court of Appeal noted: [Robinson (2011): para 67].

> … the relationship between (a) the manufacturer of a product or the builder of a building and (b) the immediate client is primarily governed by the contract between those two parties. Long established principles of freedom of contract enable those parties to allocate risk between themselves as they see fit.

The court proceeded: [Robinson (2011): para 68].

> Absent any assumption of responsibility, there do not spring up between the parties duties of care co-extensive with their contractual obligations. The law of tort imposes a different and more limited duty upon the manufacturer or builder. That more limited duty is to take reasonable care to protect the client against suffering personal injury or damage to other property. The law of tort imposes this duty, not only towards the first person to acquire the chattel or the building, but also towards others who foreseeably own or use it.

The court of appeal elaborated on the principle of assumption of responsibility. It highlighted that the leading cases expanding concurrent liabilities have been on professional negligence. It noted: [Robinson (2011): para 75].

> It is perhaps understandable that professional persons are taken to assume responsibility for economic loss to their clients. Typically, they give advice, prepare reports, draw up accounts, produce plans and so forth. They expect their clients and possibly others to act in reliance upon their work product, often with financial or economic consequences.

The court contrasted professional fields with the other areas and observed that in them there was often no assumption of responsibility. It noted: [Robinson (2011): para 76].

> When one moves beyond the realm of professional retainers, it by no means follows that every contracting party assumes responsibilities (in the Hedley Byrne sense) to the other parties co-extensive with the contractual obligations. Such an analysis would be nonsensical. Contractual and tortious duties have different origins and different functions. Contractual obligations spring from the consent of the parties and the common law principle that contracts

should be enforced. Tortious duties are imposed by law, as a matter of policy, in specific situations. Sometimes a particular set of facts may give rise to identical contractual and tortious duties, but self-evidently that is not always the case.

The court explained the two distinct fields of contracts and torts: [Robinson (2011): para 79].

... it remains the case that (a) contracts and (b) the law of tort are separate sources of obligations. Contractual obligations are negotiated by the parties and then enforced by law because the performance of contracts is vital to the functioning of society. Tortious duties are imposed by law (without any need for agreement by the parties) because society demands certain standards of conduct. There is no reason why the law of tort should impose duties which are identical to the obligations negotiated by the parties.

Following the elaborations, the court 'distilled' the 'essential points' of The Henderson Case as follows: [Robinson (2011): para 80].

(i) When A assumes responsibility to B in the Hedley Byrne sense, A comes under a tortious duty to B, which may extend to protecting B against economic loss.
(ii) The existence of a contract between A and B does not prevent such a duty from arising.
(iii) In contracts of professional retainer, there is commonly an assumption of responsibility which generates a duty of care to protect the client against economic loss.

In the context of building contracts, the court noted: [Robinson (2011): para 81].

Building contracts come in all shapes and sizes from the simple house building contract to the suite of JCT, NEC or FIDIC contracts. The law does not automatically impose upon every contractor or sub-contractor tortious duties of care co-extensive with the contractual terms and carrying liability for economic loss. Such an approach would involve wholesale subordination of the law of tort to the law of contract.

In a building contract too, however, the parties may have 'assumed responsibility' to give rise to 'so as to give rise to Hedley Byrne duties'. But this was not the case here. The parties had a normal contract for construction of a house to certain specifications. The court concluded that 'it is not possible for the claimant to invoke the law of tort in order to impose liabilities upon the defendant which are inconsistent with the contract' [Robinson (2011): para 88].

At this stage, we need to bring a qualification imposed by law. Section 2(1) of the Unfair Contract Terms Act states:

2(1) A person cannot by reference to any contract term or to a notice given to persons generally or to particular persons exclude or restrict his liability for death or personal injury resulting from negligence.

Thus, contract terms cannot exclude liability for death and personal injury. The court noted: [Robinson (2011): para 63].

I now turn to the effect of section 2 of UCTA. Clearly clauses 8 and 10 of the building conditions cannot exclude the defendant's liability in tort for any personal injury caused by negligence in construction. For example, if the claimant suffered gas poisoning as a result

> of the defective flues, the defendant's liability in that regard could not be excluded by any contractual provision. Different considerations arise, however, in relation to tortious liability for economic loss.

The court made distinction between personal injury due to the defect or damage to other property. The court noted: [Robinson (2011): para 65].

> The first and crucial feature of this litigation is that, fortunately, the defective flues did not cause personal injury. Nor did they, or could they, cause damage to other property. The claimant's claim is for economic loss consequential upon defects in a house which the defendant constructed and the claimant purchased.

The following case is also on exclusion of liabilities arising from negligence in building contracts.

The Sheffield Case

In the latest case on the theme of negligence in relation to building, the Sheffield Case, the court abstracted the following principles from a review of the case law: [Sheffield Teaching Hospital Foundation Trust v Hadfield Healthcare Partnerships Limited, Kajima Construction Europe (UK) Limited, Veolia Energy & Utility Services UK PLC, (2023) EWHC 644 (TCC). Hereafter Sheffield (2023): para 71].

(i) When A assumes responsibility to B in the *Hedley Byrne* sense, A comes under a tortious duty to B, which may extend to protecting B against economic loss.
(ii) The existence of a contract between A and B does not prevent such a duty from arising.
(iii) The existence of a contract between A and B does not automatically give rise to such a duty of care in tort co-extensive with the contractual terms and carrying liability for economic loss.
(iv) It is necessary to consider the relationship between the parties, together with the factual and any contractual matrix, in order to ascertain in any given case whether A assumed responsibility to B in the *Hedley Byrne* sense, so as to give rise to a concurrent duty of care in tort.
(v) The allocation of risk in the contract between A and B, including any exclusion or limitation of liability, on a proper construction, may preclude the imposition of any duty of care in tort.

The High Court judge concluded: [Sheffield (2023): para 78].

> [It] is right to question, as a matter of law, whether there is any basis on which building contractors should be distinguished from other professionals when ascertaining whether there has been any *Hedley Byrne* assumption of responsibility. The range of recognisable professions generally has expanded since *Hedley Byrne* and *Henderson*, with the introduction of new technologies and industries, greater research and understanding, and improvements in the training and standards of specialist areas of work. In particular, within the construction industry today there are many disciplines of special skill and expertise which could be described as professional.

The case was a summary trial. Applying the diversity of disciplines in the construction industry, the judge recognised that there 'may be a fine line between design and workmanship responsibility in respect of the fire protection issues' and decided to proceed with a full trial noting that it was 'a matter on which factual and expert opinion evidence will be required' [Sheffield (2023): para 79]. We explore the theme further with the Triple Point Case, [Triple Point Technology, Inc v PTT Public Company Ltd, (2021) UKSC 29. Hereafter Triple Point (SC).] a judgment of the United Kingdom Supreme Court. The judgment dealt with several important aspects of award of damages. We have already reviewed the case on the scope and application of liquidated damages.

The Triple Point Case: Court of Appeal

In the Triple Point Case, the contract terms had limited the liability of the contractor to a cap of the total amount of money the contractor had received following the works delivered by it. The damages clause, however, had the following further stipulation: [Triple Point (SC): para 51].

> 12.3 (Sentence 4): This limitation of liability shall not apply to CONTRACTOR's liability resulting from fraud, negligence, gross negligence or wilful misconduct of CONTRACTOR or any of its officers, employees or agents.

The contractor had abandoned the work as PTT had not paid it on a calendar basis. The demand for a payment without completion of work, as the court determined, had no basis in the contract. The High Court judge had held that "negligence" in sentence 4 of Article 12.3 meant the tort of negligence. It did not include breach of the contractual duty of skill and care. The High Court noted that if "negligence" had that broader meaning, sentence 4 would take away almost the entire protection afforded by the cap. [Triple Point Technology, Inc. v PTT Public Company Limited, (2017) EWHC 2178 (TCC): para 261- 262] The Court of Appeal, thus, read the clause: [Triple Point Technology, Inc. v PTT Public Company Ltd, (2019) EWCA Civ 230. Hereafter Triple Point (CA): para 119].

> The word "negligence" must be read in context. The phrase "fraud, negligence, gross negligence, or wilful misconduct" is describing unusual or extreme conduct, such that Triple Point should forfeit the protection of the cap. It is talking about breaches of contract which are also freestanding torts or deliberate wrongdoing. In my view, "negligence" in this context means the freestanding tort of negligence.

The Court of Appeal illustrated how Triple Point could have been in the freestanding torts of negligence: [Triple Point (CA): para 119].

> For example, if Triple Point's engineers carelessly left electrical wiring exposed which caused personal injury, that would be both a breach of contract and the freestanding tort of negligence. If the engineers did so deliberately, that would be both a breach of contract and wilful misconduct. In those two examples Triple Point would be liable for the full consequences of the engineers' negligent conduct, alternatively their wilful misconduct, without the Article 12.3 cap limiting the financial liability.

The Court of Appeal concluded that the High Court judge's interpretation of the term was 'obviously correct' [Triple Point (CA): para 120]. An alternate view would deprive the contractor of the cap on liability and 'does not fit with the language used or make commercial sense' as it would 'deprive the Article 12.3 cap of any practical effect' [Triple Point (CA): para 121].

The Triple Point Case: The Supreme Court

The interpretation of the clause came up before the UK Supreme Court for resolution. The Supreme Court explained the meaning of the word negligence: [Triple Point (SC): para 52].

> ... the word "negligence" has an accepted meaning in English law... It covers both the separate tort of failing to use due care and also breach of a contractual provision to exercise skill and care. Unless, therefore, some strained meaning can be given to the word "negligence" in the context of the final sentence of article 12.3 the effect of that clause is that liability for negligence does not exclude the breach of a contractual duty of care.

The Court explained in alternate language: [Triple Point (SC): para 100].

> The starting point must be that ... any breach of an obligation to exercise reasonable care and skill would, in common legal language, be called "negligence", whether the source of the obligation is a term of the contract or the law of tort. On a straightforward reading of article 12.3, therefore, liability resulting from breach of a contractual duty of care falls within the exception for "liability resulting from ... negligence".

Another compelling reason the court found was the entire clause 12 'only deals with liability for breach of the CTRM Contract and does not deal with liability in tort at all' [Triple Point (SC): para 101]. Therefore, it 'makes no sense to interpret the word "negligence" in sentence 4 as referring to a basis of liability which is not part of the subject matter of the clause' [Triple Point (SC): para 101].

The law of tort has a category of only negligence. In this context, the court further noted that the terms 'gross negligence' and 'wilful misconduct' are not separate torts. These terms 'must be intended to describe, or at the very least to include, conduct which amounts to a breach of the contract' [Triple Point (SC): para 102]. Similarly, 'fraud' is not a term of tort but finds readily application in contract, where the innocent party can set aside the contract on the grounds of fraud. On the basis of this, the court made an observation: [Triple Point (SC): para 102].

> It is anomalous to treat the term "negligence" as excluding negligent conduct which amounts to a breach of the contract when there is no similar restriction on the scope of the other terms in the list.

If 'negligence' meant the tort of negligence, this would not be good enough for Triple Point and it would produce illogical results. The court noted: [Triple Point (SC): para 103].

> The reason is that … someone who provides services to another person generally owes that person a duty of care in tort whether or not the relationship between them is contractual and even if such a duty of care is also owed under the contract.

Applying it to the clause, the court noted that Triple Point being negligent in 'the performance of the 'Services' … would give rise to a concurrent liability in tort as well as under the contract' [Triple Point (SC): para 103]. The implication is: [Triple Point (SC): para 103].

If the intention were to cap Triple Point's liability to PTT resulting from negligence in the performance of the contract, it would potentially defeat that intention to create an exception from the cap for liability for negligence in tort which arises concurrently with liability for breach of a contractual duty of care.

Triple Point contended that the meaning of the term 'negligence' was confined to 'a negligent act or omission which is a breach of a duty of care owed in tort but is not also a breach of a duty of care arising under the contract' [Triple Point (SC): para 104]. On the contention, the Supreme Court observed that the approach sought to give a convoluted meaning to the term negligence. The Court explained: [Triple Point (SC): para 105].

> No reasonable person would understand the word "negligence" to mean negligence which is neither a breach of a contractual duty of care nor of a concurrent duty of care in tort. Still less is that a possible meaning when, … the context in which the word is used is a clause dealing only with liability for breach of the contract and not with liability in tort at all—let alone with liability in tort which arises altogether outside the scope of the contract.

Exclusion Clauses and Clear Terms

Modern-day contracts are made in the settings of common law and laws made by the legislature. The court set the context of the contracts: [Triple Point (SC): para 108].

> … a vital part of the setting in which parties contract is a framework of rights and obligations established by the common law (and often now codified in statute). These comprise duties imposed by the law of tort and also norms of commerce which have come to be recognised as ordinary incidents of particular types of contract or relationship and which often take the form of terms implied in the contract by law.

The parties may have the freedom to oust the rights given by law but 'clear words are necessary before the court will hold that a contract has taken away valuable rights or remedies which one of the parties to it would have had at common law' [Triple Point (SC): para 106]. The court reviewed the development of the principles for interpretation of the exclusion clauses. It noted that the 'first and still perhaps the leading statement of this principle is that in Modern Engineering (Bristol)Ltd v Gilbert-Ash (Northern) Ltd (1974) AC 689' [Triple Point (SC): para 109]. In the judgment, the court had noted: [Modern Engineering (Bristol)Ltd v Gilbert-Ash (Northern) Ltd (1974) AC 689: p 717].

> It is, of course, open to parties to a contract for sale of goods or for work and labour or for both to exclude by express agreement a remedy for its breach which would otherwise arise by operation of law … But in construing such a contract one starts with the presumption that neither party intends to abandon any remedies for its breach arising by operation of law, and clear express words must be used in order to rebut this presumption.

In Stocznia Gdynia SA v Gearbulk Holdings Ltd (2009) EWCA Civ 75, para 23, the court emphasised: [Stocznia Gdynia SA v Gearbulk Holdings Ltd (2009) EWCA Civ 75: para 23].

> The court is unlikely to be satisfied that a party to a contract has abandoned valuable rights arising by operation of law unless the terms of the contract make it sufficiently clear that that was intended. The more valuable the right, the clearer the language will need to be.

In Federal Republic of Nigeria v JP Morgan Chase Bank NA (2019) EWHC 347 (Comm), the court noted: [Federal Republic of Nigeria v JP Morgan Chase Bank NA (2019) EWHC 347 (Comm): para 34].

> Applying the modern approach … a party is unlikely to have agreed to give up a valuable right that it would otherwise have had without clear words. … So, for example, clear words will generally be needed before a court will conclude that the agreement excludes a party's liability for its own negligence.

It has been a principle of common law that in a contract of service, the supplier will carry out the service with reasonable care and skill. The right has also got codified in Section 13 of the Supply of Goods and Services Act 1982. Applying it, the court noted that in the present case it was: [Triple Point (SC): para 113].

> … an obligation implied by law in the CTRM Contract, in so far as it involved the supply of services, that Triple Point should carry out those services with reasonable care and skill. The parties have not sought to exclude that obligation from arising. Indeed, they have positively reinforced it by article 12.1.

Thus, applying the principle of interpreting exclusion clause, PTT succeeded in its claim.

Liability in negligence arise when a person is proximate to another and owes the person a duty of care. As the contracting parties are proximate, a concurrent duty in negligence may arise. This duty would be concurrent to the duties under the contract. A party who has suffered losses can elect to pursue the dames under the contract terms or under negligence. Further, as a liability under negligence is only a civil right, recognised by common law, the contract terms can exclude the liabilities under negligence. Thus, the exclusion clauses in contracts must take care to refer to torts and negligence and exclude liabilities arising under them. As the Triple Point Case has brought out, a contract term excluding or limiting liabilities for negligence is an exclusion clause. Clear and certain words must be used to make it sufficiently clear the intention of the parties to exclude the right against negligence.

References

Donoghue v Stevenson (1932) AC 562
Federal Republic of Nigeria v JP Morgan Chase Bank NA (2019) EWHC 347 (Comm)
Hedley Byrne & Co. Ltd. v Heller & Partners Ltd., (1964) A.C. 465
Henderson v Merrett Syndicates Ltd (1995) 2 A.C. 145
James Andrew Robinson v P.E.Jones (Contractors) Limited, (2011) EWCA Civ 9
Modern Engineering (Bristol)Ltd v Gilbert-Ash (Northern) Ltd (1974) AC 689
Sheffield Teaching Hospital Foundation Trust v Hadfield Healthcare Partnerships Limited, Kajima Construction Europe (UK) Limited, Veolia Energy & Utility Services UK PLC, (2023) EWHC 644 (TCC)
Soteria Insurance Limited (formerly Cis General Insurance Limited) v IBM United Kingdom Limited, (2022) EWCA Civ 440
Stocznia Gdynia SA v Gearbulk Holdings Ltd (2009) EWCA Civ 75
Triple Point Technology, Inc v PTT Public Company Ltd, (2021) UKSC 29
Triple Point Technology, Inc. v PTT Public Company Limited, (2017) EWHC 2178 (TCC)
Triple Point Technology, Inc. v PTT Public Company Ltd, (2019) EWCA Civ 230

Chapter 12
Ownership Retention Clause

A sale of goods is a specific form of contract. In a contract of sale of goods, the seller agrees to transfer the ownership in the goods for a price in money. In the performance of the contract, when the seller transfers the ownership, it becomes a sale of goods. The transfer of ownership from the seller to the buyer is a defining moment in the relationship between the parties. The risk of the goods getting damaged or lost now falls on the buyer. Buyer gets the right to sell the goods further or consume it. Till the ownership transferred, the buyer, even if he had the possession, did not have these rights. No one can divest a person of his ownership in the goods. Thus, even if the buyer breaches the contract by not paying, the seller cannot claim to revest the ownership in himself. The seller can only claim the price. For all these reasons, the point of time at which the ownership transfers in a sale of goods contract is a crucial event.

Title Retention Clause

So, when does the ownership transfer in a contract of sale of goods? Contracts are voluntarily made. It is for the contracting parties to decide when the ownership would transfer. Thus, the ownership transfers as the parties provide in the contract in express terms. If the contract does not provide in express terms, it is to be implied from the other terms. If the terms on ownership cannot even be implied, the default principles developed by the common law courts, later codified in the sale of goods statute apply.

A seller, who has transferred the ownership to the buyer but is not paid, is at risk. To protect the seller, a clause was introduced in sale of goods contracts stating that the ownership would not transfer till the seller was fully paid. The clause was negatively worded. It did not provide when the ownership would transfer. It provided that, no matter what, even if the buyer was delivered the goods and had the possession of it, the ownership would not transfer till the buyer was fully paid. This came to be

A. Pathak, *Contract Terms in International Business*,
https://doi.org/10.1007/978-981-96-8146-4_12

called 'title retention' clause. Title is another term for ownership. The title retention clause also came to be called 'Romalpa Clause' as it got first explored in Aluminium Industrie Vaassen BV v Romalpa Aluminium Ltd. [Aluminium Industrie Vaassen BV v Romalpa Aluminium Ltd., (1976) 1 WLR 676.] A title retention clause can take a simple form and read:

> Title to the goods shall not pass to the buyer until the purchase price for the goods has been paid in full and received by the seller.

Take the case where the goods are delivered to the buyer and are stored in his warehouse but the seller is not paid. At this stage, the ownership in the goods has not transferred to the buyer. The seller is free to abandon the contract and have his goods restored to him. In this case, the seller will have to pay damages for the breach of the contract but the buyer cannot claim any interest in the goods. The seller could also decide to retrieve his goods for whatever reasons and substitute the goods. The buyer must not mix up the goods of the seller with his own till he pays as this would be conversion of goods within torts. Similarly, the buyer cannot resell or consume the goods as he is not the owner. At the same time, as the seller has the possession of the goods, he has become a bailee of the goods and must take reasonable care of the goods. However, if the goods get damages, eventually, the residual risk is of the seller as the seller continues to be the owner of the goods. Making these implications express, and working with these points, a comprehensive title retention clause may read:

> Title to the goods shall remain vested in the seller and shall not pass to the buyer until the purchase price for the goods has been paid in full and received by the seller. Until title to the goods passes:
>
> the Seller shall have authority to retake, sell or otherwise deal with and/or dispose of all or any part of the Goods;
>
> the seller and its agents and employees shall be entitled at any time and without the need to give notice enter upon any property upon which the goods or any part are stored, or upon which the seller reasonably believes them to be kept;
>
> the buyer shall store or mark the goods in a manner reasonably satisfactory to the seller indicating that title to the goods remains vested in the seller; and
>
> the buyer shall insure the goods to their full replacement value, and arrange for the seller to be noted on the policy of insurance as the loss payee.
>
> Irrespective of whether title to the goods remains vested in the seller, risk in the goods shall pass to the buyer upon delivery.

We explore the working of the title retention clause with the following two cases.

The Caterpillar Case: The Contract

FG Wilson (Engineering) Limited (Wilson) was a Northern Ireland company engaged in manufacturing and selling generator sets and spare parts worldwide. [FG Wilson (Engineering) Ltd v John Holt & Co (Liverpool) Ltd, (2014) 1 W.L.R. 2365. Hereafter Wilson (2014).] It was a wholly owned subsidiary of an American company, Caterpillar Inc. John Holt & Company (Liverpool) Limited was an English company. Its business was predominantly buying generator sets from Wilson for export to Nigeria. We will call the company Holt (Liverpool). The company had incorporated a subsidiary company in Nigeria, John Holt plc (Holt Nigeria) for making sales in Nigeria.

Holt (Liverpool) had been an exclusive distributor of Wilson for Nigeria since 1998. The exclusive distributorship agreement between Wilson and Holt (Liverpool), dated 16 July 1998, appointed Holt (Liverpool) and its subsidiaries as the exclusive distributors of the products of Wilson in Nigeria. The distributorship agreement had the following terms: [Wilson (2014): page 2371].

> Title and risk of loss: Unless seller specifically agrees otherwise in writing, delivery of products sold by seller shall be ex-works (EXW), seller's designated facility and risk of loss and damage to such products shall pass to buyer at such EXW place … … All delivery terms referred to are INCOTERMS 2000 …

As the contract terms were ex-works, the buyer took delivery at the premises of the seller. The risk in the goods passed to the buyer at the time of the delivery at the premises of the seller. The contract had a title retention clause. It read: [Wilson (2014): page 2371].

> Notwithstanding delivery and the passing of risk in the products, title shall not pass to buyer until seller has received payment in full for the products and all other goods … agreed to be sold by seller to buyer for which payment is then due. Until such time as title passes, buyer shall hold the products as seller's fiduciary agent and shall keep them separate from buyer's other goods. Prior to title passing buyer shall be entitled to resell or use the products in the ordinary course of business and shall account to the seller for the proceeds of sale. If the buyer fails to comply with a demand from the seller to return products to which title has not passed, seller may forthwith enter any premises where the products are stored and repossess them …

The contract gave a period of 30 days of the invoice date for the buyer to pay the seller.

The Caterpillar Case: Payment Default

The parties transacted seamlessly. The seller would deliver goods and raise invoices. The buyer would avail the 30-day credit facility and pay. The buyer, alongside, would place fresh orders. The chain of receiving goods and paying the price broke: the buyer failed to pay the seller. The parties attempted to work it out but the invoices remained unpaid. The contract was subject to the jurisdiction of the UK courts. Following the non-payment, the seller made a claim for USD 12 million in dues for the price along with interests before the Commercial Court. Much was brewing between the parties. The buyer had his own grievances that Holt was breaching the agreement. In a counterclaim before the Commercial Court, Holt claimed that Wilson had been supplying generator sets to others in Nigeria over a number of years. Holt demanded USD 53 million in damages. Holt set-off the unpaid invoices against its claims of damages for the breach of the distribution agreement by Wilson. Thus, in net terms, it was Wilson who had to be paying Holt for breaching the contract. The dealership agreement, however, had the following clause: [Wilson (2014): page 2371].

> Buyer shall not apply any set-off to the price of seller's products without prior written agreement by the seller.

Wilson contended that Holt cannot set-off its claim against the price. It must pay the invoices and separately pursue whatever claims of breach it may have against Wilson. Holt countered that following the set-off clause itself, it was fully justified in setting-off the unpaid invoices. The seller could have a claim of 'price' only if the ownership had transferred to buyer. Within the law on sale of goods and the contract terms, an unpaid amount becomes price only when the ownership transfers to the buyer. The crucial question was whether the ownership had transferred to the buyer.

The Caterpillar Case: Title Retention Clause

The title retention clause used the term 'fiduciary agent'. A fiduciary relationship arises as follows. B owns a property. B transfers the ownership in the property to C with the terms that C will manage the property for the benefit of others. The others can be specific individuals or a segment of the public. In this arrangement, B and C have a relationship of trust. When a person has to manage a property for the benefit of others, he is a trustee of the property. A relationship of trust is also called 'fiduciary'. Patten LJ constructed the title retention clause line by line. He noted: [Wilson (2014): page 2383].

> … the first sentence … operates to preserve title in the goods in the seller until payment of the price. Consistently with this, the next sentence 'Until such time as title passes, buyer shall hold the products as seller's fiduciary agent and shall keep them separate from buyer's other goods' requires the buyer to keep the relevant goods separate. Although the buyer is described as a fiduciary agent, it is not at that stage a trustee of the goods in the conventional sense because it has no title to the property on which any trust can be impressed.

Thus, the first two lines only bring out that the ownership would not pass to the buyer till the seller was paid. Till this time, the buyer was not to mix the goods with his own goods. Within the first two lines, use of the term fiduciary agent was not significant. The term became significant in the subsequent lines where the buyer was allowed to sell the goods even before paying. The court proceeded: [Wilson (2014): page 2383].

> But when it then disposes of the goods, it does acquire a title to the moneys paid into its account by the sub-purchaser. And, as the next sentence makes clear 'Prior to title passing buyer shall be entitled to resell or use the products in the ordinary course of business and shall account to the seller for the proceeds of sale', it is required to account for the proceeds of sale and not simply for such of the proceeds as are required to satisfy its liability for the price under the contract with FG Wilson.

In several situations, a person becomes fiduciary, even when, technically, he has not been given the ownership. For example, an agent does not get the ownership in the goods but has the fiduciary duty in relation to the property. Transfer of ownership is not necessary for a person to become in a fiduciary position. The judge noted: [Wilson (2014): page 2383].

> An obligation to account for the entire proceeds of sale is, in my view, only consistent with the buyer remaining a fiduciary agent throughout the process of the sub-sale. .... A natural construction of the clause as a whole is that its purpose is set out in the first of the three sentences I have quoted and that the second and third sentences are merely sub-provisions spelling out the obligations of the buyer in circumstances where title has not yet passed. The paragraph of the terms and conditions headed 'Title and risk of loss' begins with the unequivocal statement that title shall not pass to the buyer until the seller has received payment in full and the second and third sentences are both concerned with that same intervening period: 'until such time as title passes' and 'prior to title passing'. ... This is consistent with the clause as a whole having been drafted by the claimant to be an effective retention of title provision. ... there are dangers as well as benefits in such a provision.

Reading the clause as a whole, the judge constructed that the ownership could never transfer till the seller was paid. In this period, Holt could sell as an agent of Wilson. Thus, the transactions Holt made to its subsidiary company in Nigeria, was a contract between Wilson and Holt (Nigeria). Holt (Liverpool) was only an agent in the transaction. Holt (Liverpool) was a fiduciary agent for the sale. It was accountable for the sums it received from Holt (Nigeria). But at no point of time, ownership transferred to Holt (Liverpool). Thus, within the title retention clause, the ownership in the goods had not transferred to the buyer Holt (Liverpool). Holt (Liverpool) had sub-sold the generators to Holt (Nigeria) as an agent of Wilson. Wilson was certainly entitled to claim the money sold on its behalf to Holt (Nigeria). Holt (Liverpool) was a trustee of the money it had received from the sale. But this was not a 'price'. The court ruled that the seller could not maintain its claim for payment of the price. As a result, Holt could set-off the claim of the seller. We next move to the PST case. [PST Energy 7 Shipping LLC, Product Shipping and Trading S.A. v O.W. Bunker Malta Limited, (2015) EWHC 2022 (Comm), hereafter PST(HC).]

The PST Case: The OWBM Contract

A ship owner, PST Energy 7 Shipping LLC, procured fuel for the ship, and used it up within the credit period without getting the ownership in the fuel. The ship owner ended up with two claimants for the price, as the seller went insolvent and could not pay up the supply chain.

PST Energy 7 Shipping LLC are the owners of the ship 'Res Cogitans'. On 4 November 2014, the ship was supplied 110 metric tons of gasoil and 1,000 metric tons of fuel oil at the Russian port Tuapse, by a company, OW Bunker Malta Ltd. The delivery happened under a contract the parties had entered into on 31 October 2014. Ships require large quantities of fuel for their journeys and there are companies which specialise in distributing and delivering this fuel. The shipping fuel is called 'bunker' in the shipping business. OW Bunker & Trading A.S. (OWBAS), a Dutch company, is one of the large companies in the business of supplying bunker. It has several subsidiaries world over, including OW Bunker Malta Ltd (OWBM). The companies together make OW Bunker Group. The group has its general conditions of contract, Bunker Group's 2013 Terms and Conditions of sale for Marine Bunkers on which the group companies supply bunker. We will call it the OWB terms.

The contract between the parties was on Bunker Group's 2013 Terms and Conditions of sale. It was titled 'Terms and Conditions of sale' and the parties involved were described as 'Seller' and 'Buyer'. The contract was for the delivery of 110 metric tons of gasoil at the rate of US $848 per metric ton and 1,000 metric tons of fuel oil at the rate of US $359 per metric ton. The contract provided for it to be governed by English law with arbitration in London. The contract also stated that the ship owners were to make their payment within 60 days from the date of delivery of the bunkers. The relevant part of the title retention clause reads like the below: [PST (HC): para 11].

H. Title.

> H.1 Title in and to the Bunkers delivered and/or property rights in and to such Bunkers shall remain vested in the Seller until full payment has been received by the Seller of all amounts due in connection with the respective delivery. …
>
> H.2 Until full payment of the full amount due to the Seller has been made … the Buyer agreed that it is in possession of the Bunkers solely as Bailee for the Seller, and shall not be entitled to use the Bunkers other than for the propulsion of the Vessel, nor mix, blend, sell, encumber, pledge, alienate, or surrender the Bunkers to any third party or other Vessel.

Thus, the title in the bunkers was to remain with the seller till the payment was done. The clause prohibited resale of the bunkers or its conversion in any form. However, it gave express permission to the buyer for consuming the bunkers for propulsion of the ship.

The PST Case: Rosneft Contract

It is common that the supply of bunkers happens through a chain of transactions. OWBM, thus, had entered into a contract with its parent company OWBAS to buy the bunker. OWBAS in turn had entered into a contract with a United Kingdom company, Rosneft Marine (UK) Ltd (Rosneft). Rosneft had entered into a contract with its Russian subsidiary, RN-Bunker Ltd. to buy the bunker. The Russian subsidiary came into the picture as the bunkers were to be supplied at the Russian port. It is the Russian subsidiary, RN-Bunker Ltd., which had physically delivered the bunkers to the ship.

The contract between OWBAS and Rosneft was on the standard contract terms of Rosneft. It was also titled as a sale contract governed by English law subject to arbitration in London. The contract gave a 30-day credit to the buyer and it too had a title retention clause. It declared: 'Title to the Marine Fuels shall pass to the Buyer upon payment for the value of the Marine Fuels delivered …'. The terms did not allow any use or conversion of the bunkers till the ownership transferred to the buyer. This was in contrast to the OWB terms which expressly allowed the use of the bunkers for propulsion of the ship. Rosneft knew that it might be selling to a trader for resale and thus, did not permit any conversion of the bunker or its use.

The PST Case: Insolvency of OWB

On 5 November 2014, OWBAS uncovered a major fraud committed by senior employees in a Singaporean subsidiary of the company. The group had also accumulated other losses. The total loss was estimated at about USD275 million. The company, on 6 November 2014, announced that it expected to be insolvent and was filing for an in-court restructuring procedure. The group had a financing agreement with ING Bank NV. Following the commencement of the insolvency proceedings, ING acquired the right of OWBM to recover the debt from the shipowner. The contract provided that the rights of OWBM to receive the money could be assigned to ING. The ship owners had agreed to it. ING communicated to the ship owners that the price should be paid to them.

In this while, RMUK too learnt of the insolvency. It realised that it might not receive payment from OWBAS. The contract between RMUK and OWBAS, as stated earlier, had a title retention clause with a 30-day credit period. By virtue of this, it continued to be the owner of the bunkers supplies to the ship owners. On 17 November 2014, RMUK asserted to the ship owners that it remained the owner of the bunkers and that the ship owners should pay them for it on the completion of the 30-day credit period. A part of the bunkers supplied got consumed by the 30th day and all of it by the 60th day. The ship owners were in a quandary, with payment demands from two parties. The ship owners had a contract with OWBM and not Rosneft. They could take only OWBM to arbitration and not Rosneft. In early December 2014, the ship owners began arbitration proceedings against OWBM and ING seeking a declaration that they were not bound to pay either of them for the bunkers as OWBM had not passed the ownership in the goods.

The PST Case: Contract of Sale of Goods

Section 2 of the Sale of Goods Act, 1979 defines a contract of sale of goods. The Act is a detailed code of the rights and obligations of the buyer and seller. It also vests numerous rights on the buyers and sellers. If the contract is not a sale of goods, not the act, but the general principles of contract law will apply. This makes a very significant difference. For this reason, since the beginning, whether a contract is a sale of goods or not, has been an important theme. In a sale contract, the seller has a right to claim the price if the ownership has transferred. As the property in the bunkers had not been passed to PST, it claimed that ING cannot raise a claim for the price.

ING claimed payment of USD 443,800 as the sum due from the owner. ING contended that the contract was not a contract of sale of goods and the Act did not apply to it. Within the contract terms, it was a simple obligation of the owner to pay the amount to ING. On the expiry of the 60-day credit period, the amount became due and the owners must pay ING.

The central question before the arbitrator, and later the courts, was whether the contract was a contract of sale of goods. The arbitrator, applying the definition of sale of goods, concluded that the contract was not a sale of goods. The ship owners challenged the award before the Commercial Court.

The PST Case: The Commercial Court

The ship owners argued that the contract was titled as a sale contract and described the parties as buyer and seller. It contained terms which use the language of sale of goods. Further, all the cases of bunkers trading had been recognised by the courts as a sale of goods. Thus, the contract was a contract of sale of goods. The court noted: [PST (HC): para 28].

> I accept that the ... contract is drafted as a contract of sale and contains numerous terms appropriate to such a contract. It is therefore a reasonable starting point that this is what the parties intended and is indeed the true nature of the contract which they have concluded. However, that is only a starting point. Ultimately the question must depend, not on the labels which the parties have used or on the form of contract which they have adopted (or adapted), but on an analysis of the obligations which they have undertaken.

The court proceeded to examine the substance of the contract. A contract for supply of bunkers without a retention clause is clearly a contract of sale of goods. The Sale of Goods Act, 1979 would apply to it. Within the Act, if a contract does not provide on the transfer of ownership, the ownership would transfer to the buyer when the bunker is delivered to the buyer. In this case, a permission to consume before payment is meaningless as the buyer has become the owner and he is free to do what he likes with the goods. The present problem arises 'only because of the combination of a retention of title clause and the imminent consumption or destruction of the goods' [PST (HC): para 35]. The court recognised that the bunkers business has chosen to 'operate with payment on credit terms, affording security to the supplier in the form of a retention of title clause' [PST (HC): para 36]. However, the title retention clause does not fit into the business context. The court noted: [PST (HC): para 36].

... Such a clause does not sit easily with a shipowner's need to be able to consume the bunkers once they are on board, which therefore has to be accommodated either expressly or by necessary implication by giving permission for such use, but which has the consequence that title in the bunkers will cease to exist. This is a materially different regime from that which would apply in the absence of a retention of title clause. It should not ultimately be surprising if that regime, essentially grafted on to what otherwise would certainly be a contract of sale, leads to a materially different legal analysis of the parties' contract.

The Commercial Court noted: 'A contract of sale of goods is a contract by which the seller transfers or agrees to transfer the property in goods to the buyer for a money consideration, called the price' [PST (HC): para 40]. The question was whether the contract was for transfer of ownership in bunker. The Commercial Court noted: [PST (HC): para 42].

> ... the whole object of a sale is to transfer property from one person to another. In the present case, however, the combination of features listed above means that it cannot have been the object of the contract to transfer property from OWBM to the Owners: both parties knew that this was unlikely ever to happen. Even if it did, because some bunkers remained unconsumed after 60 days, that was not fundamental to the transaction.

The Commercial Court concluded: [PST (HC): para 43].

> In those circumstances it is difficult to conclude, in my judgment, that OWBM undertook an obligation to transfer the property in the bunkers to the Owners. There is no good reason why it should undertake an obligation which both parties knew that it was unlikely to be able to perform. It is equally difficult to conclude that what the Owners were paying for was the transfer of title to them, when both parties knew that this was unlikely ever to happen. It stands to reason that what the Owners were paying for was not a title which they were never going to get but something else.

The dispute came in appeal before the Supreme Court.

The PST Case: The Supreme Court

The Supreme Court noted on the title retention clause with the permission to use the fuel for propulsion: [PST Energy 7 Shipping LLC and another v OW Bunker Malta Ltd, (2016) UKSC 23, hereafter PST(SC): para 27].

> The qualification clearly reflects a reality. Bunker suppliers know that bunkers are for use. If they grant relatively long credit periods combined with a reservation of title pending payment in full, it is unsurprising that they do so combined with an express qualification authorising use in propulsion, since standard terms prohibiting any use would be uncommercial or in practice, no doubt, simply ignored.

The Supreme Court, with reference to the contract, noted: [PST (SC): para 27].

> ... OWBM's (and RMUK's) contractual terms and the assumed facts ... together with an admissible modicum of commercial awareness on the court's part about how ships operate (and in particular how owners strive to keep them operating) and about the value of credit and the likelihood that full advantage of it will be taken—all point in one direction. They demonstrate that the liberty to use the bunkers for propulsion prior to payment is a vital and essential feature of the bunker supply business.

Thus, the contract was not a 'straightforward agreement to transfer the property' [PST (SC): para 28] in the bunkers to the owners for a price. The Supreme Court noted: [PST (SC): para 28].

> It was in substance an agreement with two aspects: first, to permit consumption prior to any payment and … without any property ever passing in the bunkers consumed; and, second, but only if and so far as bunkers remained unconsumed, to transfer the property in the bunkers so remaining to the owners in return for the owners paying the price. But in this latter connection it is to be noted that the price does not here refer to the price of the bunkers in respect of which property was passing, it refers to the price payable for all the bunkers, whether consumed before or remaining at the time of its payment.

The Supreme Court concluded that the contract was not a sale of goods contract and PST was required to pay to OWB. There was much discussion before the courts as to what should such a contract be called. The conclusion was what matters is the substance of the contract not what one calls it.

Transfer of ownership is a watershed moment in a sale of goods contract. Only when the ownership transfers to the buyer can the buyer resell the goods or use the goods. Once the ownership transfers to the buyer, the seller can only make a claim for the price and not have the ownership revest in him. To protect the seller, a title retention clause has come to be introduced in sale of goods contracts. The clause provides that the ownership would not pass to the buyer till the seller is fully paid. The negatively worded clause protects the interest of the seller. However, the clause has to be reconciled with business practices. In businesses where the seller gives a relatively long credit, the goods would have to sit idle with the buyer till the buyer pays up. This is no good either to the seller or to the buyer. To address this, the businesses have tweaked the title retention clause to allow the buyer to use the goods before paying for them. But this changes the very character of the contract—it ceases to be a sale of goods contract.

References

Aluminium Industrie Vaassen BV v Romalpa Aluminium Ltd., (1976) 1 WLR 676

FG Wilson (Engineering) Ltd v John Holt & Co (Liverpool) Ltd, (2014) 1 W.L.R. 2365

PST Energy 7 Shipping LLC and another v OW Bunker Malta Ltd, (2016) UKSC 23

PST Energy 7 Shipping LLC, Product Shipping and Trading S.A. v O.W. Bunker Malta Limited, (2015) EWHC 2022 (Comm)

Chapter 13
Carriage and Delivery: Incoterms

In a sale of goods contract, the goods have to be delivered to the buyer. As the delivery invariably happens through the intermediation of a carrier, price of the goods on its own is incomplete. The parties have to expressly address themselves as to who will bear the cost of carriage, insurance during transit, risk in goods and taxes and levies in moving the goods. Maritime trade developed its practices allocating cost and risk between the buyer and seller and gave cryptic names to these practices. As disputes developed between the parties over the terms, the courts gave judgments on the scope and meaning of the terms. The two significant terms were, cost insurance freight (cif) contracts and free on board (fob) contracts.

International Commercial Terms

As trade expanded, such terms became widely used in international trade. As would happen with any term, there also arose the problem of persons in different jurisdictions understanding and interpreting these terms differently. This led to disputes and uncertainties in international trade. To respond to this, the International Chamber of Commerce (ICC), a non-governmental body, based in Paris, took the initiative to standardise such terms. It picked up the terms in usage in international trade in relation to sale of goods, affixing responsibilities and liabilities between the buyer and seller. It called such terms 'International Commercial Terms' and abbreviated it as 'Incoterms'. It defined the terms for the first time in 1936. It has updated its definitions several times. The last edition of Incoterms is Incoterms 2020. The ICC is not a law-making body, and thus, the terms do not apply to contracts automatically. The contracting parties have to incorporate the incoterms in the contract.

The buyer and the seller may be based in different countries and the goods could be moving from one country to another. Also, the buyer and the seller may be based in the same country but the goods could still be moving from one country to another.

A. Pathak, *Contract Terms in International Business*,
https://doi.org/10.1007/978-981-96-8146-4_13

Incoterms can be applied in both the situations. It should also be borne in mind that this chapter is specifically with reference to contracts which have adopted English law as the law governing the contract. A large number of the countries, including the United States, Canada, China, Australia, Brazil and a large number of EU countries are signatory to the United Nations Convention on Contracts for the International Sale of Goods (CISG). CISG sets out detailed rules for international sale of goods, based on common law and civil law. However, the United Kingdom is not a signatory to the convention. As a result, the English rules on international sale of goods are the same as the domestic law. Thus, a sale of goods contract, where goods have to move from one country to another, with English law as the governing law, applies the domestic English law.

Shipping was the first mode of transportation. Subsequently, other modes of transportation, like the railways and airways, came into being. As a result, some commercial terms got developed specifically for maritime trade while other terms are used generally, for any mode of transportation. The Incoterms 2020 follows this as the basis for classification of the terms in the two categories. The classification and the terms are:

Sea and inland waterways transport only.

CFR—Cost and Freight.

CIF—Cost Insurance and Freight.

FAS—Free Alongside Ship.

FOB—Free on Board.

All modes of transport.

CIP—Carriage and Insurance Paid to.

CPT—Carriage Paid To.

DAP—Delivery at Place.

DPU—Delivered at Place Unloaded.

DDP—Delivery Duty Paid.

EXW—Ex Works.

FCA—Free Carrier.

The terms bear E, F, C and D as their first letters. This is another way of categorising the terms. The seller and buyer being at a distance, there can be two extreme arrangements. The parties can agree as a part of their sale contract that the buyer will take delivery of the goods at the seller's premises. From there, the buyer, at his own cost and risk, will take the goods to his destination. This is called an 'Ex' term contract, for example, an ex-warehouse contract. The second extreme arrangement could be one where the parties agree that the seller will bring the goods at his own cost and risk, all the way to the premises of the buyer and give delivery to the buyer. This is called a 'D' term contract. It covers different terms under which the seller brings the goods to the country of the buyer at his own risk and cost. In between are the 'F' term and 'C' term contracts. The 'F' term contracts begin with the word 'free'. Free signifies that the seller would bring the goods at his own cost and deliver them to a carrier, as instructed by the buyer. In the C group, the seller takes up the further costs of carriage of the goods as well. A brief description of all the Incoterms 2020 is as follows.

EXW—This term stands for 'EX Works' contract. The seller makes the goods available to the buyer at his premises. The buyer bears all the costs and the risk in taking the goods from the seller's premises to his own destination. Delivery of the goods happens when the seller places the goods at the disposal of the buyer at the named place and time. The risk in the goods passes to the buyer at delivery. The buyer has to arrange for the loading of the goods on the carrier. 'Works' stands for the premises of the seller. The other terms used for 'Works' are 'factory', 'plant' and 'warehouse'.

FCA—This term stands for 'Free Carriage'. The term is followed by a place where the buyer has to make available the goods. The term is available for all modes of transportation. The buyer organises for the carriage of the goods and informs the seller about the carrier and the time for delivering the goods at the named place. The delivery happens when the seller hands over the goods to the carrier. The risk passes when the goods are handed over to the carrier.

CPT—This term stands for 'Carriage Paid To'. The term is followed by a named place of destination. The term is available for all modes of transportation. The seller arranges for and pays the freight for the carriage of the goods to the named destination but does not insure the goods to the named destination. The seller hands over the documents to the buyer for the buyer to collect the goods at destination. The risk in goods passes to the buyer on delivery of the goods to the first carrier. Delivery of the goods happens when the seller hands over the goods to the carrier. Risk transfers from the seller to the buyer at the point where the goods are taken in charge by the carrier.

CIP—This term stands for 'Carriage and Insurance Paid To'. The term is followed by a named place of destination. The term is available for all modes of transportation. The seller arranges for and pays the freight for the carriage of the goods to the named destination and also insures the goods to the named destination. The seller hands over the documents to the buyer for the buyer to collect the goods at destination. Delivery of the goods happens when the seller hands over the goods to the carrier. Risk transfers from the seller to the buyer at the point where the goods are taken in charge by the carrier.

DPU—This term stands for 'Delivery at Place Unloaded'. The term is followed by the place where the goods are to be delivered in the country of the buyer. The term can be used for all modes of transportation. The seller pays for carriage to the named destination in the country of the buyer and also organises to unload the goods. However, the buyer organises for importing the goods and pays the import duty. The seller organises for the insurance of the goods and bears the risk of damage to the goods till the goods are delivered to the buyer. The delivery happens when the seller unloads the goods and handover to the buyer. Risk transfers to the buyer on delivery.

DAP—This term stands for 'Delivery at Place'. The term is followed by the place where the goods are to be finally delivered. This is the premises of the buyer or warehouse of the buyer. The term can be used for all modes of transportation. The seller pays for carriage to the named destination in the country of the buyer. The buyer has to organise for unloading of the goods at his place. However, the import duty is paid by the buyer. The seller organises for the insurance of the goods and bears the risk of damage to the goods till the goods are delivered to the buyer. The goods are delivered at the named place when the seller makes available the goods to the buyer. The risk passes to the buyer at the named destination, when the goods are made ready for unloading by the buyer.

DDP—This term stands for 'Delivery Duty Paid'. The term is followed by the place where the goods are to be finally delivered. This is the premises of the buyer or warehouse of the buyer. The term can be used for all modes of transportation. The seller pays for carriage to the named destination in the country of the buyer and also organises for import clearance and pays the customs duty. The buyer has to organise for unloading of the goods at his place. The seller organises for the insurance of the goods and bears the risk of damage to the goods till the goods are delivered to the buyer. The goods are delivered at the named place when the seller makes available the goods to the buyer. The risk passes to the buyer at the named destination, when the goods are made available to the buyer. The buyer organisation is to take the goods to his final destination.

The following are the four terms used exclusively in maritime trade or waterways.

FAS—This term stands for 'Free Alongside Ship'. The seller pays for the transportation of the goods to the port of shipment in his country. The buyer pays the loading costs, freight, insurance, unloading costs and transportation from the port of destination to his premises. The passing of risk occurs when the goods are delivered alongside the ship at the named port of shipment. The term is followed by the place from where the goods are to be shipped.

FOB—This term stands for 'Free On Board'. The term is followed by the name of the port in the country of the seller from where the goods would move to their destination. The seller pays for the transportation of the goods to the port of shipment and for their loading on the ship. The buyer pays the freight, insurance, unloading costs and transportation from the port of shipment to his destination. Delivery happens when the goods are loaded on the ship. Risk passes to the buyer when the goods are loaded on the ship. The buyer organises for the carriage and informs the seller about the time period when the ship would be at the port.

CFR—This term stands for 'Cost and Freight'. It is also written as C & F. The term is followed by the name of the destination port in the country of the buyer. The seller pays the costs and freight to bring the goods to the port of destination but not the cost of marine insurance. The delivery happens when the goods are loaded onto the vessel. The risk passes when the goods are loaded on the vessel.

CIF—This term stands for 'Cost, Freight and Insurance'. The term is followed by the name of the destination port in the country of the buyer. The seller pays for the transportation of the goods to the port of shipment, loading and freight as well as for marine insurance. The delivery happens the moment goods pass the ship's side at the port of loading. Risk also passes to the buyer when the goods pass the ship's side at the port of loading.

Can the Incoterms be used for domestic trade? The Incoterms have been developed specifically for international trade. However, the use of the terms is voluntary. There is no bar on a domestic sale contract using the Incoterms. In domestic trade, further, several variants of the Incoterms have been developed. Some examples of these are variants of FOB—'free on rail' and 'free on truck'. Such terms used in domestic trade are interpreted according to the meaning given to these terms by the common law. We can now explore some of the incoterms with the following review of cases. The first case is from the European Court of Justice on Ex Works.

Electrosteel Europe SA v Edil Centro SpA.

Edil Centro, an Italian company, entered into a sale of goods contract with a French buyer, Electrosteel. [Electrosteel Europe SA v Edil Centro SpA, Case C-87/10. Hereafter Case C-87/10.] The parties got into a dispute on the performance of the contract. The seller applied to an Italian court for an order directing the buyer to pay EUR 36 588.26 in payment for the goods purchased. The buyer objected that under the European Union Regulations, the Italian court lacked jurisdiction. The buyer contended that as it has its seat in France, it should be sued in a court in France, not Italy. The European Council Regulation No 44/2001 of 22 December 2000 provided on jurisdiction of courts in civil and commercial matters. The default position was to sue a person in a court where the person was domiciled. Article 5 of the Regulation provided that in the case of sale of goods the person was to be sued at 'the place in a Member State where, under the contract, the goods were delivered or should have been delivered'. The Italian court had made a reference to the European Court of Justice to settle the scope of the regulation.

The delivery terms were 'Resa: Franco ns. [nostra] sede', the English translation of which was 'Delivered free ex our business premises'. The seller claimed that the delivery terms in the contract corresponded to incoterm Ex Works. The court noted that the International Chamber of Commerce, in the version published in 2000 in English, had defined 'delivery' as: [Case C-87/10: para 12].

> The seller must place the goods at the disposal of the buyer at the named place of delivery, not loaded on any collecting vehicle, on the date or within the period agreed or, if no such time is agreed, at the usual time for delivery of such goods. If no specific point has been agreed within the named place, and if there are several points available, the seller may select the point at the place of delivery which best suits his purpose.

The court noted that rule required that the 'buyer must take delivery of the goods when they have been delivered in accordance' [Case C-87/10: para 12] with the delivery rule stated above. The court stated that the place where the goods sold were delivered or to be delivered under the contract was to be determined on the basis of the provisions of the contract. In this context, the court noted that trade terms developed by recognised professional organisation 'play an important role in the non-governmental regulation of international trade or commerce' [Case C-87/10: para 21]. The court noted: [Case C-87/10: para 21].

> They make it easier for traders to draft contracts because, through the use of short and simple terms, they can define many aspects of their business relations. The Incoterms drawn up by the International Chamber of Commerce, which define and codify the content of certain

terms and clauses commonly used in international trade or commerce, are particularly widely recognised and used.

The European Court of Justice, thus, directed that the referring courts towards determining the place of delivery in the contract take into account all the contract terms including 'the terms and clauses generally recognised and applied in international commercial usage, such as the Incoterms'. The courts should examine whether the terms stipulate only on the allocation of risks and the transportation cost or also identify the place of delivery of the goods. With reference to the Incoterm Ex Works, the court held that the clause provided for 'Delivery' and 'Taking delivery'. In conclusion, the court directed the national courts to take account of the terms and clauses of Incoterms in working out the place of delivery.

Cost, Insurance and Freight (Cif) Contracts

The letters of a cif contract stand for cost, insurance and freight. In a cif contract, the seller contracts with the carrier to ship the goods to the contracted destination. Following this, the seller ships the goods and gets the bill of lading in favour of the buyer. The seller also takes marine insurance cover. The seller submits the documents to the bank through which the letter of credit is arranged and gets the price. It is a very widely and frequently term used for sea transportation. A very large number of transactions of a staggeringly large value are carried out each year under cif contracts. It has been noted on the duties and rights of the seller: [Ross T Smyth & Co Ltd v. T D Bailey Son & Co, (1940) 3 All ER 60.]

> The seller has to ship ... On or after shipment, he has to obtain proper bills of lading and proper policies of insurance. He fulfils his contract by transferring the bills of lading and the policies to the buyer. As a general rule, he does so only against payment of the price, less the freight, which the buyer has to pay.

The following cases will bring out the nature, rights and obligations of the parties in a cif contract.

Manbre Saccharine Co, Ltd v. Corn Products Co, Ltd.

The parties had entered in a contract for the sale of American pearl starch and corn syrup. [Manbre Saccharine Co, Ltd v. Corn Products Co, Ltd, (1919) 1 K.B. 198. Hereafter Manbre (1919).] The sale was on cif terms. The vessel carrying the goods capsized and sank. The seller and buyer knew that the vessel was sunk. The seller tendered the document but the buyer refused to accept the documents and pay the money. The question before the court was: [Manbre (1919): page 201].

> Can a vendor, under an ordinary cif contract, effectively tender appropriate documents to the buyer in respect of goods shipped in a vessel which at the time of tender the vendor knows to have been totally lost?

The essential feature of a cif contract is that the seller performs the contract by 'delivery of documents and not by the actual physical delivery of goods by the vendor' [Manbre (1919): page 202]. The court noted: [Manbre (1919): page 202].

> All that the buyer can call for is delivery of the customary documents. This represents the measure of the buyer's right and the extent of the vendor's duty. The buyer cannot refuse the documents and ask for the actual goods, nor can the vendor withhold the documents and tender the goods.

The obligation of the seller is to deliver documents rather than the goods. The seller has 'to transfer symbols rather than the physical property represented thereby' [Manbre (1919): page 203]. This being the case, the court observed: [Manbre (1919): page 203].

> If the vendor fulfils his contract by shipping the appropriate goods in the appropriate manner under a proper contract of carriage, and if he also obtains the proper documents for tender to the purchaser, I am unable to see how the rights or duties of either party are affected by the loss of ship or goods, or by knowledge of such loss by the vendor prior to actual tender of the documents.

In a cif contract, by its very definition, the parties have already contemplated the potential loss of the goods and the remedy against it. And the remedy was, the court noted: [Manbre (1919): page 204].

> For the purchaser in case of loss will get the document he bargained for, and if the policy be that required by the contract and if the loss be covered thereby, he will secure the insurance moneys. The contingency of loss is within and not outside the contemplation of the parties to a cif contract.

The court concluded that the buyer was not entitled to reject the tender of the documents. We next review the following case.

Kwei Tek Chao v. British Traders and Shippers LD.

London exporters contracted under a c.i.f. contract to sell to a merchant in Hong Kong a quantity of chemical known as Rongalite C. [Kwei Tek Chao and Others (Trading As Zung Fu Co.) v. British Traders and Shippers LD., (1954) 2 Q.B. 459. Hereafter Kwei (1954).] The shipment was to be done not later than 31 October 1951 on cif terms. The seller was to receive payment against letter of credit on production of the shipping documents. The goods were not shipped until 3 November 1951. However, the sellers' forwarding agents at the port of loading forged the date of shipping. The seller had no knowledge of the forgery. The seller presented the documents to the bank on 10 November 1951. As the documents appeared to be in order, the bank paid the money to the seller.

The buyer had made sub-sale of the goods. Due to the delay in shipment of the goods, the buyer lost their contract for resale in Hong Kong. The goods arrived Hong Kong on December 17. They knew that the shipment was not done till October 31. Despite this, they took the goods from the ship and put them into a warehouse. Further, they gave the warehouse warrants to the bank as their security. The buyer subsequently discovered that the bills of lading had been forged. They were unable to sell the goods owing to a serious fall in the market price in Hong Kong. They moved to court claiming breach of contract and damages under the contract. The court noted on the forged bill of lading: [Kwei (1954): page 476].

If the bills of lading are a nullity, no doubt the property does not pass by their tender, but if a man, with knowledge of a bill of lading and the fact that it is a nullity, takes delivery of the goods, acts upon it and keeps them, it is not then open to him to avoid the transaction.

The court noted that the buyer had two rights, the right to reject the documents and the right to reject the goods, and the 'two things are quite distinct.' [Kwei (1954): page 480] The court explained: [Kwei (1954): page 480].

A c.i.f. contract puts a number of obligations upon the seller, some of which are in relation to the goods and some of which are in relation to the documents. So far as the goods are concerned, he must put on board at the port of shipment goods in conformity with the contract description, but he must also send forward documents, and those documents must comply with the contract.

If the seller delays in the shipment, he had breached a term of the sale of goods contract. At the same time, he has made it impossible to send a bill of lading bearing an appropriate date. Thus, the same act 'can cause two breaches of two independent obligations' [Kwei (1954): page 481]. Despite this, 'they are distinct obligations'. [Kwei (1954): page 481] The court noted: [Kwei (1954): page 481].

... the right to reject the documents arises when the documents are tendered, and the right to reject the goods arises when they are landed and when after examination they are found not to be in conformity with the contract. There are many cases, of course, where the documents are accepted but the goods are subsequently rejected.

In a cif contract, the ownership transfers to the buyer when the documents are given to the buyer. How can the buyer reject the goods when he has already become the owner of the goods? The judgment sorts out this puzzle. It distinguished between the delivery of goods and delivery of documents in a cif contract: [Kwei (1954): page 486].

In a c.i.f. contract the goods are delivered, so far as they are physically delivered, when they are put on board a ship at the port of shipment. The documents are delivered when they are tendered.

The buyer cannot and does not take physical delivery of the goods at destination, as he has already been given the delivery. The court noted: [Kwei (1954): page 486].

A buyer who takes delivery from the ship at the port of destination is not taking delivery of the goods under the contract of sale, but merely taking delivery out of his own warehouse, as it were, by the presentation of the document of title to the goods, the master of the ship having been his bailee ever since he became entitled to the bill of lading.

When the buyer gets the documents from the seller, he gets a title to the goods. The court noted: [Kwei (1954): page 487].

> ... the buyer obtains, when the title under the documents is given to him, is the property in the goods, subject to the condition that they revest if upon examination he finds them to be not in accordance with the contract. That means that he gets only conditional property in the goods, the condition being a condition subsequent.

As a result of this, the buyer has the right to examine the goods when the goods have been landed and reject them. In this case, the goods have to be physically returned to the seller and the ownership revests in the seller. The case thus resolved the puzzle as to how the buyer can reject the goods in a cif contract after having become the owner of the goods. The following is a judgment from the Singapore High Court.

Profindo Pte Ltd v Abani Trading Pte Ltd

Profindo Pte Ltd and Abani Trading Pte Ltd are trading companies based in Singapore. Profindo Pte Ltd (seller) entered into a contract with Abani Trading Pte Ltd. (buyer) for the sale of 2,750 metric tons of cement. [Profindo Pte Ltd v Abani Trading Pte Ltd (2013) SGHC 10. Hereafter Profindo (2013).] The cargo was to be loaded in China and delivered to a port in Madagascar. The contract was a CFR contract and provided for a discharge rate at which the cement would be unloaded. Within this, there was a total time of 2.75 days to discharge the load. The contract also provided the rate of demurrages.

The ship docked at the destination port and unloading started. However, the unloading got unexpectedly disrupted as the port authorities required the vessel to leave the berth and move to the anchorage to give priority to a tanker. By the time the vessel could dock back and unloading completed, demurrages had accumulated. The question was who would bear the demurrages, the buyer or the seller.

The Singapore High Court noted that a CFR contract was a variation of a "cost, insurance and freight" (CIF) sale contract, and the differences between the two types were not relevant to the present case. Thus, the rules of Incoterms on CIF could be applied. The court noted: [Profindo (2013): para 24].

> In this particular case it is helpful to consider the matter in light of the duties of a seller in a CIF/CFR sale contract. In Benjamin's at para 19-010, the learned author explained that the duties of a CIF seller are:
>
> ... first to ship (or procure a shipment of) goods in accordance with the contract and, where necessary, to appropriate such goods to the contract; secondly to procure or prepare the proper shipping documents, and thirdly to tender these documents to the buyer, or as the buyer directs. He is not under any duty to ensure the actual physical delivery of the goods at the c.i.f. destination, though he is under a duty not to take active steps to prevent such delivery.
>
> [emphasis added]

Thus, in a CIF/CFR contract, the seller is under no duty to ensure the physical delivery of the goods. Building on this, the court noted: [Profindo (2013): para 25].

> … it would be quite remarkable to hold that the risk of delay in unloading the goods at the port of discharge after laytime has commenced has to be borne by him. This is especially so when there is a demurrage clause in the contract since the raison d'être of the same must be to transfer the risk of delay in the discharge of goods to the buyer.

The court concluded: [Profindo (2013): para 25].

> It is more logical and more in line with commercial realities to hold that such risks, unless they have been expressly allocated to the seller by a specific term in the contract, are to be borne by the CIF/CFR buyer.

As the contract did not specify on whom the risk would fall if the unloading was disrupted, the costs were to be borne by the buyer.

The International Chamber of Commerce (ICC) is a non-governmental body, based in Paris. It publishes International Commercial Terms every ten years. The current edition is Incoterms 2020. The incoterms allocation the cost of carriage, insurance, passing of risk, time of delivery, loading and unloading costs and export and custom duties among the buyer and seller. It gives a menu of terms and the contracting parties can reference and employ and appropriate term. The terms are grouped into two categories, only sea and water transports and all modes of transportation. Only sea and water mode of transport Incoterms are CFR (Cost and Freight), CIF (Cost Insurance and Freight), FAS (Free Alongside Ship) and FOB (Free on Board). The terms which can be employed in any mode of transportation are CIP (Carriage and Insurance Paid to), CPT (Carriage Paid To), DAP (Delivery at Place), DPU (Delivered at Place Unloaded), DDP (Delivery Duty Paid), EXW (Ex Works) and FCA (Free Carrier). E term has the least obligations for the seller and D terms the most. In between, F and C terms are with reference to the point of shipment in the country of the seller.

References

Electrosteel Europe SA v Edil Centro SpA, Case C-87/10

Kwei Tek Chao and Others (Trading As Zung Fu Co.) v. British Traders and Shippers LD., (1954) 2 Q.B. 459

Manbre Saccharine Co, Ltd v. Corn Products Co, Ltd, (1919) 1 K.B. 198

Profindo Pte Ltd v Abani Trading Pte Ltd (2013) SGHC 10

Ross T Smyth & Co Ltd v. T D Bailey Son & Co, (1940) 3 All ER 60

Chapter 14
Description, Merchantability and Usefulness of Goods

A sale of goods is a contract where the seller agrees to transfer ownership in the goods to the buyer for a price in money. The kind, features and quality of the goods are important concerns for the buyer. A sale of goods contract would have clauses on the description, fitness, usefulness and characteristics of the goods. The clause may read:

1. All Goods shall be supplied strictly in accordance with the descriptions, specifications, drawings, data sheets, other attachments and conditions stated in the Contract.
2. All materials supplied by the SELLER are guaranteed to be of the best quality of their respective kinds and shall be free from faulty design, workmanship and materials, and to be of sufficient size and capacity and of proper materials so as to fulfil in all respects all operating conditions, if any, specified in the Contract.

A clause on the description, fitness and usefulness of the goods is in relation statutory protection given to the buyer. The protection comes from common law. Trade and commerce have been a part of the human society since quite a long time. Commercial laws have developed over the centuries. In the early stages, people and traders came from different areas, assembled in the marketplace, and bought and sold goods. There could be no account of it after the sale was done. Thus, the common law court formulated the maxim, *caveat emptor* (buyer beware). As trade and commerce developed, parties came to be at a distance. The seller alone could describe the goods he had and the buyer would get to see the goods only when it was delivered. Thus, the courts came to make an exception to the 'buyer beware' principle that the seller must deliver the described goods. If the seller failed, the buyer could terminate the contract.

As trade further developed, it became reasonable to insist that the seller must deliver goods which were fit for their basic ordinary purpose. The term developed for the goods being fit for their basic purpose was 'merchantable quality'. Thus, the second exception to 'buyer beware' became that the seller must supply goods

A. Pathak, *Contract Terms in International Business*,
https://doi.org/10.1007/978-981-96-8146-4_14

of merchantable quality. If the seller failed, the buyer could terminate the contract. With further development in trade and commerce, markets, shops and establishments emerged. The seller, by dealing in the goods, knew a lot more about them than a disparate buyer. The buyer came to rely on the skill and judgment of the seller to supply goods suitable for a particular purpose. Thus, entered the third exception to the maxim of *caveat emptor*, if a buyer described the purpose for which he wanted a thing, and relied on the skill and judgment of a seller, the goods should be fit for that purpose. If the goods did not serve the purpose, the buyer could terminate the contract.

Implied Conditions

To recall from the principles on termination of contracts, a core part of the contract is called a condition and a subsidiary part a warranty. A party can terminate the contract for a breach of a condition of the contract but not a warranty. Thus, the right came to be termed as a condition. Further, as the courts had developed the rights for the buyer and these were to apply to every sale contract, the rights came to be termed as conditions implied by law. The courts had developed several other rights for the buyers. Some of them were implied conditions and others, implied warranties. For example, in a sale of goods contract, if there are dues on goods, say taxes, it is only an implied warranty that there will be no encumbrances on the goods. If the seller has created encumbrances, the buyer can only claim damages but not terminate the contract. Similarly, the courts developed other implied conditions, for example, in a sale of goods contract, it is an implied condition that the seller will supply the exact quantity, not more or less.

The implied conditions developed by the common law courts were codified in England as the Sale of Goods Act, 1893. Let us become familiar with Sections 13 and 14 of the Sale of Goods Act, 1893. Section 13 provides that in a sale by description, there is an "implied condition that the goods shall correspond with the description". Section 14 (2) provides that in a sale by description, "there is an implied condition that the goods shall be of merchantable quality". Section 14 (1) is about the parties describing the use of the goods. A buyer may describe the goods and, in addition, state the purpose for which he wants them. Alternately, a buyer may only describe the purpose for which he wants the goods. If a buyer makes known the purpose for which he wants the goods, "there is an implied condition that the goods shall be reasonably fit for such purpose". Section 11 (b) provides that the buyer can terminate the contract for the breach of a condition, but for the breach of a warranty, he can only claim damages and not terminate the contract.

The Sale of Goods Act, 1893 has been re-enacted as the Sale of Goods Act, 1979. The act was further amended in 1994. The change, for our purposes, has been in changing the implied condition of merchantable quality to a higher requirement of satisfactory quality. Whether the supplied goods are of merchantable quality, satisfactory quality or useful for the stated purpose is fact specific. In commercial contracts, often, the subject matter specialists would be able to make a determination. As the term 'description', in the implied condition of description, is a general term of wide use, it has been subject of dispute and received judicial attention. We will explore the meaning and scope of the term.

Description and Examination

In a sale of goods contract, the buyer may like to examine the goods at the seller's premises itself before the goods are delivered. This minimises the inconvenience of the parties in rejecting the goods after these are delivered to the buyer. The contract terms introduce a right for the buyer to inspect and examine the goods. The clause may read:

Inspection, Testing & Expediting

1. The PURCHASER or its representative shall have the right to inspect and/or to test the GOODS to confirm their conformity to the CONTRACT specifications.
2. The inspections and tests may be conducted on the premises of the SELLER or his sub-contractor(s), at point of DELIVERY and/or at the GOODS' final destination.
3. Should any inspected or tested GOODS fail to conform to the specifications, the PURCHASER may reject them and the SELLER shall either replace the rejected GOODS or make all alterations necessary to meet Specifications' requirements, free of cost to the PURCHASER.

However, there is a risk in examining the goods. The common law principle on description being an implied condition has a disqualifier. If the buyer examines the goods, 'there shall be no implied condition as regards defects which such examination ought to have revealed.' [Section 14(2), Sale of Goods Act, 1893. There is a similar provision in the Sale of Goods Act, 1979.] The reason for the disqualifier is the founding principle was buyer beware and the implied condition of description was an exception to the rule. Thus, the balance of what an examination revealed was against the buyer. To reverse this, the inspection and examination clause ends with a clause like:

> Nothing in this clause shall in any way release the SELLER from the description of the goods in contract, requirement of merchantability of gods, usefulness of the goods any other obligations under this CONTRACT.

Thus, even if the buyer examines the goods and approves them, the contract terms on the goods stay unqualified.

Description: Identity of Goods

The Act provides on sale "by description" but does not define it. What is the meaning and scope of description has been a subject of judicial attention. In Ashington Piggeries v Christopher Hill Ltd, the House of Lords analysed the provisions: [Ashington Piggeries v Christopher Hill Ltd (1972) AC 441. Hereafter Ashington (1972): page 503].

> Not all statements about the characteristics of goods which are the subject-matter of a contract of sale form part of the "description" by which they are sold. Sections 13 and 14 draw a distinction between the description by which goods are sold, on the one hand, and their fitness for the particular purpose for which they are required and their quality, on the other.

Section 14 (4) provides that the parties can state express conditions and warranties in the contract. It can override the implied condition only if it is inconsistent with it. Referring to the provision, the House of Lords noted: [Ashington (1972): page 503].

> Section 14 (4) recognises that a contract for the sale of goods may contain an express statement about the fitness of the goods for a particular purpose or their quality which does not form part of the description by which they are sold but constitutes a separate stipulation in the contract which may be either a condition or a warranty, depending upon the construction of the contract.

Thus, a contract can a have stipulation on quality or fitness, and this need not be a part of the description of the goods. In a sale contract for ascertained goods, the property in the particular goods is passed to the buyer. In a sale of unascertained goods, the goods are physically identified and the property in them transfers to the buyer. The House of Lords, in Ashington Piggeries v Christopher Hill Ltd, delineated that the purpose of description was limited to identify the goods. The court noted: [Ashington (1972): page 504].

> The "description" by which unascertained goods are sold is, in my view, confined to those words in the contract which were intended by the parties to identify the kind of goods which were to be supplied. It is open to the parties to use a description as broad or narrow as they choose. But ultimately the test is whether the buyer could fairly and reasonably refuse to accept the physical goods proffered to him on the ground that their failure to correspond with that part of what was said about them in the contract makes them goods of a different kind from those he had agreed to buy. The key to section 13 is identification.

Thus, whether a term is a condition or a warranty has to be constructed from the contract. Does one weigh on the side of condition or warranty? Lord Justice Roskill, in the Hansa Case, sets the principle: [The Hansa Nord, Cehave NV v Bremer Handelsgesellschaft mbH, (1976) Q.B. 44: page 70].

> In my view, a court should not be over ready, unless required by statute or authority so to do, to construe a term in a contract as a 'condition' any breach of which gives rise to a right to reject … I deliberately avoid the use of the word 'warranty' at this juncture. In principle, contracts are made to be performed and not to be avoided according to the whims of market fluctuation and where there is a free choice between two possible constructions I think the court should tend to prefer that construction which will ensure performance, and not encourage avoidance of contractual obligations.

Description v Quality

The principles developed by the courts have found application in that a stipulation on quality of goods is not necessarily a description. In Tradax v Goldschmidt SA, [Tradax v Goldschmidt SA (1977) 2 Ll. Rep. 604.] the sale contract for barley provided that foreign matter should not be more than 4%. The court noted: [Tradax v Goldschmidt SA (1977) 2 Ll. Rep. 604.]

> It is accepted that the provision as to impurities was not part of the description of the goods so there was no implied condition under s. 13 of the Sale of Goods Act, 1893, entitling rejection on non-compliance.

In R G Grain Trade LLP (UK) v Feed Factors International Ltd, [R G Grain Trade LLP (UK) v Feed Factors International Ltd, (2011) EWHC 1889 (Comm). Hereafter Grain (2011).] the sale contract provided as follows: [Grain (2011): para 3].

> Commodity: UKRAINIAN ORIGIN SUNFLOWER EXPELLER
>
> In bulk, sound, loyal and merchantable quality.
>
> Specifications: Protein min 32%—Moisture max 7%—Fiber max 23%—Fat min 11%

The seller supplied goods whose fibre content was 26.57%, which was higher than the stipulated limit. The buyer contended that the fibre content was a description of the goods and thus an implied condition giving him the right to terminate the contract. The court did not agree and thus constructed the stipulation on fibre: [Grain (2011): para 41].

> … the term does not appear next to the description of the goods. On the contrary it appears under the heading "Specifications" and next to a specification characteristic which is clearly a matter of quality rather than description, namely protein. That too contained a specified limit ("min" rather than "max").

The following is a leading and the latest case on the theme description.

The Proton Energy Group Case: The Contract

Proton Energy Group SA is a company incorporated in Switzerland [Proton Energy Group SA v Orlen Lietuva, (2013) EWHC 2872 (Comm). Hereafter Proton (2013)]. It is engaged in international trading of oil and gasoline related products. Orlen is a petroleum refining company incorporated in Lithuania. By an email sent on 14 June 2012, Proton made a communication to Orlen stating a "firm offer" to sell CIF Butinge, Lithuania 25,000 metric tons ± 10% in the Seller's option of Crude Oil Mix CN27090090. The email had an attachment which provided the specifications for the same. The communication stated that the delivery would be made at the discharge port during 10–15 July 2012 along with its price. The parties continued the email communication, culminating in a one-word email from Orlen the same day stating, "Confirmed". Following this, Proton sent Orlen a draft of a detailed written contract for the sale. This provoked further email exchanges between the parties and finally Proton sent a revised draft to Orlen on 27 June 2012.

Orlen responded two days later by an email declaring that it was withdrawing from the negotiations. But Proton had already bought the cargo from a seller named, Trafigura, and sent it on a ship to Orlen. The shipment arrived at Butinge but Orlen did not take the delivery. On July 2, Proton communicated to Orlen that in not taking the delivery, it had made a repudiatory breach and for this, Proton was terminating the contract and would claim damages. Orlen asserted that the parties were still negotiating and there was no question of any concluded contract between them. Within the terms of its "firm offer", Proton claimed damages before the English court. The court first settled that a concluded contract was formed between the parties on June 14. It noted: [Proton (2013): para 39].

> This was a classic spot deal where the speed of the market requires that the parties agree the main terms and leave the details, some of which may be important, to be discussed and agreed later. … But overall the picture is clear. The language is that of commitment. One side, Proton, committed to Trafigura contractually as soon as this deal had been confirmed. This shows that it regarded itself as committed to Orlen … the fact that Orlen also saw itself as committed means that both sides did.

The reason for Orlen backing out "may well have been internal politics" [Proton (2013): para 57]. Proton claimed damages amounting to at least USD 1,363,255.59. Orlen claimed that Proton had misdescribed the goods for which Orlen would have the right to reject the goods and terminate the contract.

The Proton Energy Group Case: Contention of Orlen

Proton had attached the specifications of the product to all its offers and drafts. The specifications are relevant because refineries need to know the composition of the oil product and the prices also depend on them. Orlen had used the specification to work out its profit margin. The cargo despatched by Trafigura was tested by independent inspectors and following this, Proton had protested to Trafigura on 30 June 2012 that "there is a sharp deviation in several parameters which are guaranteed in our Contract". Orlen claimed that the goods Proton had shipped were materially different from the description. It further claimed that it would have been entitled to reject the cargo for misdescription. Proton contested that Orlen could not have rejected the goods.

Orlen submitted that the specifications of the product were a matter of description. In support, it quoted from a standard text, Benjamin on the Sale of Goods, [Bridge, Michael G., ed. (2010) Benjamin's Sale of Goods: 8th Edition. Common Law Library. Sweet & Maxwell, London, UK, 11–004.] that even a slight discrepancy from the description gives the right to the buyer to terminate the contract: [Bridge, Michael G., ed. (2010) Benjamin's Sale of Goods: 8th Edition. Common Law Library. Sweet & Maxwell, London, UK, 11–004.]

A buyer can refuse to receive something which is not what he promised to buy. The description of goods may be strictly interpreted with the result that a slight discrepancy may be treated as making the goods not what was stipulated for. Where goods are not what was stipulated for, they can be rejected.

Orlen referred to the following passage from the judgment of Lord Diplock in Ashington Piggeries v Christopher Hill Ltd. [Ashington (1972)] We have reviewed the passage earlier but it is reproduced for completeness. The House of Lords noted: [Ashington (1972): page 504].

The 'description' by which unascertained goods are sold is, in my view, confined to those words in the contract which were intended by the parties to identify the kind of goods which were to be supplied ... Ultimately the test is whether the buyer could fairly and reasonably refuse to accept the physical goods proffered to him on the ground that their failure to correspond with that part of what was said about them in the contract makes them goods of a different kind from those he had agreed to buy. The key to s.13 is identification.

Orlen, applying the principles, contended that as a matter of ordinary language and sense, the specification was a matter of description. It contended, in the words of the court: [Proton (2013): para 58].

As a non-standard product, it does not have a "name" like petrol or diesel. [Proton] had to give a "description" of the product in order to gauge the market interest. ... No refinery would purchase a cargo without knowing the specification. ... there are a wide variety of products which could be described as "Crude Oil Mix", which are all very different. ... describing the product as "oil blend": "doesn't tell the buyer very much" and that a buyer cannot work out how much it should pay for the product based on that information.

The court, however, noted that Proton had asked Orlen whether calling the product "Crude Oil Mix" was acceptable for it. This illustrated for the court that "the name applied to the product was a label of convenience, not something of fundamental importance".

The Proton Energy Group Case: Contention of Proton

Proton contended that the specification was neither an express nor an implied condition of the contract. The first argument that Proton made was to do with the nature of the business. It asserted, in the words of the court: [Proton (2013): para 59].

It would have been uncommercial for the parties to have agreed that since it is well known in the market that contractual specifications frequently vary from the final delivered specifications in a crude oil blend for mixing. ... Nor did the Contract contain an implied condition to that effect.

The second argument that Proton made was that the specification was to settle on the quality and not a description. It contended: [Proton (2013): para 59].

The condition implied by s. 13 of the Sale of Goods Act 1979 relates only to the "description" of the goods, not their quality. In contrast, the specification dealt only with the Product's quality, not its description. That specification was incorporated into the Contract's "Quality" clause, which as the name suggests dealt with quality. It was not incorporated into the "Product" clause. Accordingly, the delivery of a product matching that specification was not a condition of the Contract.

The Proton Energy Group Case: Decision

The court concluded: [Proton (2013): para 60].

> As I see it the specification was not part of a sale by description. As Benjamin points out, in principle description and quality are different notions. The key to description is identity. ... The cases show that the distinction between the concepts is sometimes blurred and that they may overlap where, for example, a word of description identifies the quality of the product.

In the instant case, the court did not see any blur or overlap. It noted: [Proton (2013): para 60].

> I see no such blur or overlap in this case. The contract document starts by confirming a sale of Oil Blend. Clause 3 headed "Product" describes it as "Oil Blend ... CN 2710". That is the description of the product. Clause 4 headed "Quality" sets out the details of the SGS Report of the analysis at the loadport. That is the quality of the product.

Having noted that the quality of the goods was distinctly and separately written, it turned to the business context. The judge noted: [Proton (2013): para 60].

> The document and my perception of it are consistent with the commercial reality that test results at the end of a voyage may differ from those at the outset. Further if the specification had been a sale by description Proton would have had to comply with it in every respect as a condition of the deal. Of course in another deal those considerations might have been addressed in the terms of the contract but they do point to the specification being the specified quality of the oil blend CN2710 and not part of its description. Further the fact that a buyer would not purchase without knowing the specification is as much an indication of concern about quality as it is about description. The parties are always free to make the quality a condition of the deal but, unlike description, it is not implied by statute.

The court, thus, concluded that the termination of the contract by Orlen was unjustified. Proton has the right to claim damages for the termination of the contract. However, the losses arising to Orlen from the lower quality of the product would be subtracted.

The law of sale of goods recognises that in a sale by description, it is an implied condition that the supplied goods would conform to the description. This gives the right to the buyer to terminate the contract if the goods are not as described in the contract. However, every aspect, characteristic or the quality of goods which are not mentioned in the contract does not fall under "description". The essence of description is to identify the goods to be delivered to the buyer. A contract has to be constructed to delineate the features which identify the goods and, thus, are implied condition as description. In constructing a contract, the courts are not eager to rule a term as a condition, so that the parties can be encouraged to perform the contract and not avoid them. Thus, it has to be constructed whether a stipulation on quality is essential for identifying the goods.

The law of sale of goods gives the protection to the buyer as implied conditions that the seller will supply goods which are in conformity with the description, the goods would be of merchantable quality and the goods would be suitable for the state use. However, these are only conditions implied by law. As contracts are voluntary, the parties are free to include express conditions in the contract on the goods. In fact, a sale of goods contract must provide on the features, characteristics, quality and usefulness of the goods.

References

Ashington Piggeries v Christopher Hill Ltd (1972) AC 441
Bridge MG (ed) (2010) Benjamin's Sale of Goods, 8th edn. Common Law Library. Sweet & Maxwell, London, pp 11–004
Proton Energy Group SA v Orlen Lietuva, (2013) EWHC 2872 (Comm)
R G Grain Trade LLP (UK) v Feed Factors International Ltd, (2011) EWHC 1889 (Comm)
The Hansa Nord, Cehave NV v Bremer Handelsgesellschaft mbH, (1976) Q.B. 44
Tradax v Goldschmidt SA (1977) 2 Ll. Rep. 604

Chapter 15
Exclusion of Implied Conditions: Sale of Goods

The common law courts developed certain protection for the buyer in a sale of goods contracts as implied conditions and warranties. The implied conditions included that the goods supplied by the seller will be in conformity with the description; the goods will be of merchantable quality; and the goods will be suitable for the use stated in the contract. It was a condition implied by law as the courts had recognised it and read it in every sale of goods contract. As contracts are voluntarily made, the contracting parties are free to set their own terms. The common law courts themselves recognised that they were only setting the default principles. Section 62 of the Sale of Goods Act, 1893 itself recognises that the rights can be 'negatived or varied by express agreement'. Thus, by express terms, a contract can vary or oust the implied terms. Contracts, where the seller has a better bargaining, have a clause to the following affect seeking to oust the rights of the buyer to terminate the contract:

> All warranties, conditions and other terms implied by law, including but not limited to those regarding quality, fitness for purpose, or merchantability relating to the goods are hereby specifically disclaimed and excluded from the Agreement.

For long, the contracting parting have attempted to oust the implied terms by such clauses. The disputes in these cases have been whether the implied conditions have been ousted or not. A chain of case law has developed over 100 years. We follow the development of the principles and their applications.

Implied Condition and Warranties

Sale contracts came to have exclusion clauses and disputes arose on the validity of the clauses in ousting the rights of the buyer. In Wallis, Son & Wells v. Pratt & Haynes, [Wallis, Son & Wells v. Pratt & Haynes, (1911) AC 394] the exclusion clause stated: "Sellers give no warranty express or implied as to … description or any other matters." The House of Lords stated that the parties 'must use apt language', [Wallis,

A. Pathak, *Contract Terms in International Business*,
https://doi.org/10.1007/978-981-96-8146-4_15

Son & Wells v. Pratt & Haynes, (1911) AC 394: p 395] as there was no mention of the implied conditions in the exclusion clause, these were not ousted. The court emphasised that the law provides for 'two things that are dealt with under different categories', 'one is 'warranty' and the other is 'condition' [Wallis, Son & Wells v. Pratt & Haynes, (1911) AC 394: p399]. In the next case, Baldry v. Marshall, the contract had the term: "Guarantee the same as received by us from the manufacturers' but "expressly excludes any other guarantee or warranty, statutory or otherwise". [Baldry v. Marshall, (1925) 1 KB 260.] The Court of Appeal ruled that the implied conditions were not ousted: [Baldry v. Marshall, (1925) 1 KB 260: p269].

> It said nothing about 'conditions,' and I do not think that the words 'any other guarantee' can be read as meaning 'any other condition,' merely because they are used in addition to the word 'warranty'.

The next case in the line of cases is Cammell Laird and Company, Limited v. The Manganese Bronze and Brass Company, Limited. [Cammell Laird and Company, Limited v. The Manganese Bronze and Brass Company, Limited, (1934) AC 402.] The sale contract had the clause: "To be guaranteed against defective material and workmanship for a period of six calendar months". The Court noted: [Cammell Laird and Company, Limited v. The Manganese Bronze and Brass Company, Limited, (1934) AC 402: Page 431].

> … the statutory conditions may be excluded or varied by the express agreement of the parties, yet such a clause as this, in which the word condition is not used, is ineffective to exclude the conditions implied under the Act. … The principle … is … once a condition always a condition: hence apt and precise words must be used to exclude it: the words guarantee or warranty are not sufficiently clear.

The court went as far as to say that if 'the word condition is not used', the implied condition would not get ousted. In a case to follow, Henry Kendall & Sons v. William Lillico & Sons, [Henry Kendall & Sons v. William Lillico & Sons, (1969) 2 AC 31.] the exclusion clause was worded as: "not warranted free from defect, rendering same unmerchantable … any statute or rule of law to the contrary notwithstanding". [Henry Kendall & Sons v. William Lillico & Sons, (1969) 2 AC 31: page 40] The court, building on the line of the cases noted: [Henry Kendall & Sons v. William Lillico & Sons, (1969) 2 AC 31: page 96].

> The words … are wholly inapt to exclude a condition of the contract. They do not refer to a condition. You do not exclude a condition by excluding or purporting to exclude a warranty.

The Mercini Lady Case [KG Bominflot Bunkergesellschaft für Mineraloele mbH & Co v. Petroplus Marketing AG (The Mercini Lady), (2010) EWCA Civ 1145. Hereafter The Mercini Lady (2010).], which we explore in detail, came in this line of cases.

The Mercini Lady Case: The Contract

The seller is KG Bominflot, a German company. The buyer is Petroplus Marketing AG, a company in Switzerland. The contract was governed by the English law and was for the sale of a quantity of gasoil [The Mercini Lady (2010)]. The cargo was to be delivered at a port in Spain. Clause 4 of the contract was headed "Quality" and it specified several properties of the gasoil. This included the "total sediment", which was to be a maximum of 10 mg/litre as tested by a specific method. Quality of the goods was to be determined by independent inspection at the loading port. Clause 18 was titled "Other Conditions" and it contained a number of terms including an exclusion clause. The exclusion clause read: [The Mercini Lady (2010): para 28].

> 18. OTHER CONDITIONS
>
> INCO Terms 2000 plus latest amendments...
>
> There are no guarantees, warranties or misrepresentations, express or implied, of merchantability, fitness or suitability of the oil for any particular purpose or otherwise which extend beyond the description of the oil set forth in this agreement.
>
> The buyers warrant that...
>
> Buyers further warrant that...
>
> The buyer warrants that...
>
> Buyer guarantees that...
>
> Buyers guarantee that...
>
> Buyers warrant, represent and undertake that...
>
> It is a condition of this agreement that buyer complies with its obligations under this clause. In the event that buyer is in breach of any of the provisions of this clause in whole or part, seller shall be entitled to terminate this agreement immediately.

The gasoil supplied by the seller failed the sediment test. The buyer rejected the goods, terminated the contract and claimed USD 3 million in damages. The question before the British courts was whether the exclusion clause had ousted the implied conditions. If the exclusion clause had ousted the implied conditions, the buyer would not be able to terminate the contract.

The buyer, relying on the chain of court judgments reviewed above, contended that the ousting of the implied conditions must happen cleanly and clearly. For this, there must be an express reference to the conditions which are being ousted. A reference to 'guarantees' is not the same as conditions. Referring to clause 18 of the contract, the buyer highlighted that the last paragraph had used the word 'condition' breach of which was to give the right to the buyer to terminate the contract. And yet, it was absent from the exclusion within the same clause, as a result, "the exclusion clause could sensibly speak in terms of warranties of quality and fitness without reaching as far as conditions" [The Mercini Lady (2010): para 56]. Thus, the implied conditions were not ousted.

The seller contended that the chain of the cases, reviewed above on the subject, is old. In the modern settings, the construction of exclusion clauses, particularly as between commercial parties, has become more realistic. The courts have come to insist on common-sense principles, reasonable understanding of persons, knowledge of the parties and the context of the contract. The courts have discarded "all the old intellectual baggage" [The Mercini Lady (2010): para 54]. The seller claimed the reference to "guarantees, warranties or representations" was a reference to all the express and implied conditions and warranties. Referring to clause 18, the seller constructed the clause uses 'condition' in two senses. The title of the clause itself is 'other conditions'. Here, the term is used for terms of the contract. The second sense is of a fundamental term for breach of which the buyer can terminate the contract. The reference in the exclusion clause to "merchantability, fitness or suitability of the oil for any particular purpose" is a clear ... old-fashioned, reference to the statutory Sale of Goods Act implied terms. Further, the term guarantee "is a strong and emphatic word" indicative of it "may amount to conditions themselves" [The Mercini Lady (2010): para 55]. In the view of the seller, "it is mere pedantry to demand that the general reference to "no guarantees, warranties or representations" must also include a reference to 'conditions' [The Mercini Lady (2010): para 55].

The Mercini Lady Case: Decision

The court recognised that it was 'not easy to choose between these submissions'[The Mercini Lady (2010): para 59]. It noted: [The Mercini Lady (2010): para 59].

> On the one hand a principle has been established, on the highest authority, that ... implied conditions cannot be excluded by reference to guarantees or warranties and require clearer language extending to 'conditions' themselves.

The court was of the view that clause 18, seen in a commercial context, was intended to exclude the rights of the buyer. The court noted: [The Mercini Lady (2010): para 60].

> On the other hand, it is extremely difficult to read our exclusion clause as not being intended to cover the exclusion of the statutory implications of ... merchantable quality and fitness for purpose.

The court conceded that if it had to construe the clause 'untrammelled by past authority,' [The Mercini Lady (2010): para 61] it would: [The Mercini Lady (2010): para 61].

> ... by considerations of the precise language and context of those particular clauses, I would feel it open, in the modern world, to give to clause 18 the construction which I believe that it realistically bears: that is to say, that 'guarantees' and 'warranties' are intended to cover all terms [including implied conditions].

The courts, however, are bound by precedence and 'not so free' [The Mercini Lady (2010): para 61]. The judge noted: [The Mercini Lady (2010): para 61].

> The jurisprudence extends beyond individual decisions and has become expressive of a principle, and what is more the principle also encompasses clauses very similar to clause 18.

> I must consider that the parties to this English law contract, foreign as both of them are and quite possibly ignorant of the consequences of their choice of language, intended to contract by reference to what English law had to say about the language which they have adopted.

Taking it forward, the judge quoted the following passage from Lord Diplock in Photo Production v. Securicor Transport Ltd. on interpretation of exclusion clauses: [Photo Production v. Securicor Transport Ltd (1980) AC 827: page 850].

> … exclusion clauses are to be construed strictly and the degree of strictness appropriate to be applied to their construction may properly depend upon the extent to which they involve departure from the implied obligations. Since the obligations implied by law in a commercial contract are those which, by judicial consensus over the years or by Parliament in passing a statute, have been regarded as obligations which a reasonable businessman would realise that he was accepting when he entered into a contract of a particular kind.

The court concluded the principle that as the rights to the buyer are given by law, a clause excluding the valuable right of the buyer has to be strictly constructed. Applying the principle, the court noted:[The Mercini Lady (2010): para 62].

> … the implied obligations which it is said on behalf of the seller have been excluded are not only fundamental obligations of English law, long enshrined in our Sale of Goods Acts, but there has also been a judicial consensus that such obligations can only be excluded by language which expressly (or perhaps one may add which must necessarily be taken to) refer to conditions: and that such language as has been used in our case falls within that consensus and principle.

The court emphasised that it is important for there to be certainty of commercial law. This is an abiding concern going beyond particular cases. The court concluded that it could not be said that the 'language is fairly susceptible of only one meaning,'[The Mercini Lady (2010): para 62] and concluded that the implied condition was not excluded. The following case arose soon after the Mercini Lady Case.

The Bombardier Case: The Contract

An Angolan company, Angoil SA entered into an Aircraft Purchase Agreement (the APA) with Bombardier Inc. in January 2007 to buy a Challenger 605 aircraft. [Air Transworld Ltd v Bombardier Inc. (2012) 1 C.L.C. 145. Hereafter Bombardier (2012).] On 26 April 2007, the APA was assigned to Air Transworld Ltd by an assignment agreement. Bombardier was also a party to the assignment agreement. Both the companies, Angoil and Transworld were controlled by a business person in Angola. The aircraft was to be used by the businessman. The aircraft was delivered to Transworld on 27 March 2009 and put into operation.

On 20 May 2010 the aircraft had to make an unscheduled landing at a military airfield in Algeria on one engine. There was a problem with one of the two engines. The aircraft was taken to the premises of Bombardier in Connecticut. The incident had happened due to the failure of the hydraulic system in the engine pump. The buyer got to know that other aircrafts of the Challenger 604/605 fleet had the same problem. The buyer, through a letter dated 5 July 2010 rejected the aircraft on the grounds that it did not correspond with description, was not of satisfactory quality and was unfit for purpose stated in the contract. Bombardier contended that the contract terms had excluded liabilities and replaced them with warranties. Thus, the buyer had no right to terminate the contract. Clause 4.1 of the APA was central to the contest between the parties. It read: [Bombardier (2012): para 8].

> 4. 1 The warranty, obligations and liabilities of seller and the rights and remedies of buyer set forth in the agreement are exclusive and are in lieu of and buyer hereby waives and releases all other warranties, obligations, representations or liabilities, express or implied, arising by law, in contract, civil liability or in tort, or otherwise, including but not limited to (a) any implied warranty of merchantability or of fitness for a particular purpose, and (b) any other obligation or liability on the part of seller to anyone of any nature whatsoever by reason of the design, manufacture, sale, repair, lease or use of the aircraft or related products and services delivered or rendered hereunder or otherwise.

The Bombardier Case: Review of the Principles

The buyer contended that the clause was ambiguous and did not exclude the implied conditions given to the buyer by the Sale of Goods Act 1979. The buyer claimed that Article 4 was in essence an exclusion clause, excluding the rights of the buyer. For this reason, the clause has to be construed strictly and any ambiguity in it will be determined in favour of the buyer. The buyer further claimed that following the decision of the Court of Appeal in The Mercini Lady Case [The Mercini Lady (2010)], the term 'implied condition' had to be used to exclude the right. As the article does not use the expression 'implied condition', the right of the buyer to terminate the contract is not ousted. The court reviewed the judgments given up to the Mercini Lady Case and summarised: [Bombardier (2012): para 16].

> The effect of these decisions is that liability cannot be excluded for a breach of a condition implied by the Sale of Goods Act by exclusions which refer merely to 'warranty' or 'guarantee', even if those words are cross-referenced to statutes or rules of law, which would otherwise give rise to an implication of such terms. These authorities require any term excluding a condition implied by the Sale of Goods Act to be in 'apt and precise words', if it is to be effective, for the clause 'expressly or by necessary inference' to negative such a condition and for sufficiently clear words to be used to achieve this result.

The court summarised the discussion in the Mercini Lady Case on interpretation of the clauses by the courts: [Bombardier (2012): para 26].

> In these cases the court refused to accept that there were two competing approaches to construction, struggling for supremacy, one of which required clear express words whilst the other favoured the natural meaning of the words used. ... it was important to remember that any clause in a contract had to be construed in the context in which it was found, meaning both the immediate context of the other terms and the wider context of the transaction as a whole.

The court tied up the discussion in the Mercini Lady Case with the approach of the courts in reading exclusion clauses. It noted: [Bombardier (2012): para 26].

> The court was unlikely to be satisfied that a party to a contract had abandoned valuable rights arising by operation of law, unless the terms of the contract made it sufficiently clear that this was intended. The more valuable the right the clearer the language would need to be. Similarly, the more significant the departure from obligations implied by the law or ordinarily assumed under contracts of the kind in question, the more difficult it would be to persuade the court that the parties intended that result.

The Bombardier Case: Decision

The court applied itself to the present case. On a detailed analysis of the clause, it found the clause to be comprehensive. The court noted: [Bombardier (2012): para 28].

> Article 4.1 ... refers to any implied warranty of merchantability or fitness for purpose as well as to any other obligation or liability of the seller 'of any nature whatsoever' by reason of the design, manufacture and sale of the aircraft. Whilst on the authorities, the use of the word 'warranty' here would not be sufficient to give rise to any exclusion of liability for breach of the implied conditions of satisfactory quality, merchantability or fitness for purpose, this part of Article 4.1 is only illustrative of the all embracing provision found in the first part of that Article.

The was emphatic that no person 'reading this Article could be in any doubt that every promise implied by law is excluded' [Bombardier (2012): para 29] and replaced by the contract terms, it noted: [Bombardier (2012): para 29].

It is right that there is no term which purports to exclude the buyer's right to reject the goods and recover the price, nor to the specific sections of the Sale of Goods Act, but the words 'all other ... obligations ... or liabilities express or implied arising by law', which the purchaser expressly waives, necessarily include the conditions implied by the Sale of Goods Act.

The court concluded:[Bombardier (2012): para 29].

> In my judgment these are apt and precise words which are sufficiently clear to exclude those implied conditions and the Article, by necessary inference does negative the application of those implied conditions. The parties' language is in my judgment fairly susceptible of only one meaning. There is no express reference to the word 'condition' but the language must necessarily be taken to refer to the implied conditions of the Sale of Goods Act, because they are obligations and liabilities 'implied, arising by law'.

The court found that there was 'no ambiguity in the clause' and it was capable of 'only one meaning which can fairly be given to it' [Bombardier (2012): para 31]. The court concluded that the implied conditions were ousted.

Dalmare SpA v Union Maritime Ltd.

A buyer bought a second-hand ship. [Dalmare SpA v Union Maritime Ltd, (2013) Bus. L.R. 810. Hereafter Dalmare (2013)]. The implied conditions and warranty apply to new and second-hand goods alike. Clause 11 of the contract provided: "The Vessel shall be delivered and taken over as she was at the time of inspection, fair wear and tear excepted. …". [Dalmare (2013): page 812] The vessel was inspected and delivered. About five weeks after delivery, the main engine broke down. The buyer contended it to be a breach of implied condition of merchantability and claimed to terminate the contract. The sellers argued that the implied conditions were ousted by the exclusion clause as the vessel was sold 'as she was' [Dalmare (2013): page 812]. The court noted: [Dalmare (2013): page 819].

> … it is instructive to consider the principle reiterated most recently … in The Mercini Lady and … in Air Transworld that clear language must be used in the contract, if the statutory implied terms which are conditions of the contract of sale, not mere warranties are to be excluded. It is clear from all the cases that that principle is strictly applied, …

The seller argued before the court that 'as is' means the same to be 'as is where is'. The court explored that it was not and even 'as is, where is' had no settled meaning. The court noted: [Dalmare (2013): page 832].

> In my judgment, the words 'as she was', in the context of the first sentence of clause 11, are incapable of bearing the same meaning as the free-standing words 'as is, where is' in a sale contract, assuming for the purposes of the argument that those words do exclude the statutory implied terms.

The court continued and concluded: [Dalmare (2013): page 835].

> .. if the sellers are right that the two short words 'as is' have the effect of excluding all the implied conditions, notwithstanding that the words do not have a customary meaning and are not a term of art, then I agree … that that conclusion rather drives a coach and horses through the authorities on the need for clear words to be used to exclude statutory implied conditions. If the implied terms can be excluded by the simple expedient of inserting a provision that the contract is to be on an 'as is' basis, then generations of commercial men have missed a trick in not adopting that two short word approach rather than devising detailed and supposedly all-encompassing exclusions in their contracts (some of which have successfully excluded the implied conditions as in Air Transworld, others of which have not as in The Mercini Lady). That suggests that the words 'as is' do not upon proper and detailed analysis have the meaning for which the sellers contend.

The exclusion clause can oust the rights of the buyer by using the term 'implied conditions' or without it. The term 'as is where is' is frequently used. However, even this expression does not have a settled meaning. Merely mentioning 'as she was' was far removed from ousting the implied conditions.

The Spicejet Lease Case

Spicejet Limited is an Indian commercial low-budget airliner. It leased three aircrafts on "dry" lease for a term of ten years. [Wilmington Trust SP Services (Dublin) Limited, Sabarmati Aviation Leasing Limited (formerly known as Sky Aircraft Cassia Two Limited), Falgu Aviation Leasing Limited (formerly known as Sky Aircraft Cassia One Limited) v Spicejet Limited, (2021) EWHC 1117 (Comm). Hereafter Spicejet (2021).] In a dry lease, the aircraft is handed over to the lessee who undertakes all risk and responsibility in the operation and maintenance of the aircraft. The obligation of the owner is limited to quiet enjoyment by the lessee. The aircrafts were one Boeing 737–800 and two Boeing 737-MAX 8 aircraft. The court captured the facts: [Spicejet (2021): para 3].

> ... the two MAX 8 aircraft have been grounded in India by the Indian Directorate General of Civil Aviation (the "DGCA") since early 2019 following the tragic fatal crashes of similar aircraft as a result of design defects. Similar bans were imposed by virtually all countries worldwide and although some countries have lifted their restrictions, the ban imposed by the Indian authorities remains in place for a period which is currently indefinite. It thus remains illegal for the Defendant to operate the aircraft at present, either internally or externally.

The lease was subject to the English law and thus, the Supply of Goods and Services Act, 1982 applied to it. Within the act, it is an implied condition that the goods leased would be of satisfactory quality. The lease agreement had an exclusion clause which read:[Spicejet (2021): para 6].

> 5(a) in reliance on lessee's representations, warranties and covenants contained in this lease, lessor has not and shall not be deemed to have made (whether by virtue of having leased the aircraft under this lease, or having acquired the aircraft, or having done or failed to do any act, or having acquired or failed to acquire any status under or in relation to this lease or otherwise) and lessor hereby specifically disclaims any representation or warranty, express or implied (except as herein below provided).

A question before the judge was whether the exclusion clause had ousted the implied condition of satisfactory quality. The judge noted that 'implied conditions can only be excluded by language which expressly or necessarily refers to such conditions' [Spicejet (2021): para 39]. The clause in question, the judge noted, 'refers only to representations or warranties' [Spicejet (2021): para 39]. The keyword condition 'are nowhere mentioned' [Spicejet (2021): para 39]. The judge referred to the Mercini Lady case and the Bombardier case and noted that unlike the Bombardier case: [Spicejet (2021): para 42].

> I cannot read the clause before me as necessarily excluding the statutory implied conditions. The critical distinction between this and the Bombardier case, as it seems to me, is the absence of any such general words as "obligation" or "liability". The clause refers specifically only to representations and warranties. A condition of satisfactory quality is not a representation and, as recognised by The Mercini Lady , wording excluding warranties is not effective to exclude conditions.

The judge concluded that the lease contract had not excluded the obligation of the aircraft being of a satisfactory quality.

The conditions implied by law can be ousted by express terms. Contracts where the seller has a better bargaining power tend to exclude the implied conditions by a stipulation in the contract. The term excluding the implied conditions is an exclusion clause. The courts have formulated that while the parties are free to oust the implied condition, as these are valuable rights given by law, apt and clear words must be used. The question has arisen whether the term 'implied condition' itself must be used to refer to it and oust it. In the Bombardier Case, the court has clarified that the requirement is not of use of any specific term, but of clear words. The requirement of clear words is proportion to the rights. An exclusion clause taking away a valuable right has to make it clear that there is only one meaning of the clause.

References

Air Transworld Ltd v Bombardier Inc. (2012) 1 C.L.C. 145
Baldry v. Marshall (1925) 1 KB 260
Cammell Laird and Company, Limited v. The Manganese Bronze and Brass Company, Limited (1934) AC 402
Dalmare SpA v Union Maritime Ltd (2013) Bus. L.R. 810
Henry Kendall & Sons v. William Lillico & Sons (1969) 2 AC 31
KG Bominflot Bunkergesellschaft für Mineraloele mbH & Co v. Petroplus Marketing AG (The Mercini Lady) (2010) EWCA Civ 1145
Photo Production v. Securicor Transport Ltd (1980) AC 827
Wallis, Son & Wells v. Pratt & Haynes (1911) AC 394
Wilmington Trust SP Services (Dublin) Limited, Sabarmati Aviation Leasing Limited (formerly known as Sky Aircraft Cassia Two Limited), Falgu Aviation Leasing Limited (formerly known as Sky Aircraft Cassia One Limited) v Spicejet Limited (2021) EWHC 1117 (Comm)

Chapter 16
Reasonable Care and Skill

The law of sale of goods was developed by the common law courts over the centuries. The comprehensive body of principles got codified as an act, the Sale of Goods Act, 1893. The act provided on the description, merchantability and usefulness of the goods. In contrast, service contracts are relatively newer phenomenon. Further, service contracts are diverse, ranging from carriage to banking. As a result, there was no comprehensive common law principles on the quality of service. The English common law courts developed a basic principle to imply in a service contract that the service provider will provide the service with reasonable care and skill. In Barton v Morris, the United Kingdom Supreme Court recognised: [Barton v Morris, (2023) UKSC 3: para 131].

> In the same way as the common law developed default rules, some in the form of standardised implied terms, that apply to contracts for the sale of goods, such rules were also developed in relation to the supply of services. One such rule imposes a duty on the supplier to exercise reasonable skill and care in doing the work.

In the United Kingdom, the protection has been codified in the Supply of Goods and Services Act, 1982. Section 13 of the act provides:

> Section 13: Implied term about care and skill: In a relevant contract for the supply of a service where the supplier is acting in the course of a business, there is an implied term that the supplier will carry out the service with reasonable care and skill.

As can be noted, unlike the sale of goods, the protection is not an implied condition, it is only an implied term. A breach of the term does not necessarily give the right to the service receiver to terminate the contract. Whether the party can terminate the contract would depend on the effect of the breach on the contract. Further, as contracts are voluntarily made, like the sale of goods, the Supply of Goods and Services Act, 1982 recognises the right of the parties to oust the implied term. Section 15 of the Act provides that the implied term can be 'negatived or varied by express agreement'. The ousting can take two forms.

A. Pathak, *Contract Terms in International Business*,
https://doi.org/10.1007/978-981-96-8146-4_16

The Quincecare Duty

In relation to the banking services, the implied term found elaboration in Barclays Bank Plc v Quincecare Ltd. [Barclays Bank plc v Quincecare Ltd (1992) 4 All ER 363. Hereafter Barclays (1992).] Barclays Bank entered into a contract with a company Quincecare Limited to lend it £400,000 to buy four chemist shops. The chairman of the company, Mr Harry Stiller, withdrew £340,000 and misapplied for his own dishonest purposes. Mr Stiller was prosecuted and convicted to a four-year prison term. However, almost the entire sum was lost. The bank sued the company for the repayment of the debt. The company maintained that the bank owed it a duty to have protected it from the withdrawals. The High Court held that the relationship between a banker and a customer in respect of the drawing and payment of cheques was a relationship of principal and agent. The bank had an elementary obligation to exercise reasonable care and skill in carrying out the instructions of their principal in executing the orders of the customers. The court, however, recognised that that duty to exercise reasonable skill and care "must generally speaking be subordinate to the bank's other conflicting contractual duties" [Barclays (1992): page 376–377]. The court sought that 'the law should guard against the facilitation of fraud, and exact a reasonable standard of care in order to combat fraud and to protect bank customers and innocent third parties. [Barclays (1992): page 376–377]'. However, this obligation was to be balanced by the duty of the bank in following the instructions of the customers.

The implied term has found expression in X v Kuoni Travel Ltd [X v Kuoni Travel Ltd, (2021) UKSC 34. Hereafter Kuoni (2021)], in relation to holidays and travels. The Supreme Court noted that following Sect. 13 of the Supply of Goods and Services Act 1982, tour operators were 'required to carry out the services promised under the contract with reasonable care and skill' [Kuoni (2021): para 7] The court noted: [Kuoni (2021): para 30].

> In the case of any contract for a package holiday the provider of the holiday necessarily undertakes to provide not merely transport, accommodation and meals but also to provide other services ancillary thereto. This is, in my view, inherent in the express obligations undertaken because it is only in this way that an enjoyable holiday of the reasonable standard contracted for can be provided.

Reasonable Skill and Care

The GCCs of service contracts have express terms requiring the service provider to carry out the service with reasonable care and skill. The GCCs may also have terms limiting or excluding liability arising from provision of service. For example, in the Triple Point Case, the contract for setting up a trading software platform had the express term: [Triple Point Technology, Inc v PTT Public Company Ltd, (2021) UKSC 29. Hereafter Triple Point (2021): para 12].

12.1 CONTRACTOR shall exercise all reasonable skill, care and diligence and efficiency in the performance of the Services under the Contract and carry out all his responsibilities in accordance with recognized international professional standards.

In Persimmon Homes Ltd v Ove Arup & Partners Ltd, which was on giving technical services on a project involving site clearance, reclamation and development of infrastructure, the obligation included: [Persimmon Homes Ltd v Ove Arup & Partners Ltd, (2017) EWCA Civ 373: para 24].

1.4. The Consultant warrants that it has exercised and shall continue to exercise in the performance of its duties under this Agreement all the reasonable skill and care as is to be expected of a properly qualified and competent member of its profession experienced in carrying out work such as its duties under this Agreement in relation to Projects of similar scope, size, nature, timescale and complexity and on a similar site or at a similar location to the Project.

1.5 A Notwithstanding any other term of this Agreement the Consultant's obligation in relation to the performance of the Services shall be to exercise the duty of care in clause 1.4 and the Consultant shall only liable if and to the extent that he has failed to exercise the duty of care and for the avoidance of doubt the Consultant shall not be under any fitness for purpose obligation under this Agreement.

The contract had put a limit on liability, which stated: [Persimmon Homes Ltd v Ove Arup & Partners Ltd, (2017) EWCA Civ 373: para 26].

4.3 The Consultant's aggregate liability under this Deed whether in contract, tort (including negligence), for breach of statutory duty or otherwise (other than for death or personal injury caused by the Consultant's negligence) shall be limited to £5,000,000.00 (five million pounds) with the liability for pollution and contamination limited to £5,000,000.00 (five million pounds) in the aggregate. Liability for any claim in relation to asbestos is excluded.'

The implied term requires the service provider to carry out the service with reasonable skill and care; the express terms of the contract on the standards of service and the deliverables; and the limitations clauses are applied together to work out the rights and liabilities of the parties. We would explore it with the following review of cases.

The Seadrill Case

Seadrill Management Services Ltd v OAO Gazprom, [Seadrill Management Services Ltd and another v OAO Gazprom (2010) EWCA Civ 691. Hereafter Seadrill (2010)] involved a contract for the hire of a drilling rig. Seadrill Management Services Ltd (Seadrill) was the owner and operator of a jack-up drilling rig. OAO Gazprom (Gazprom) entered into a contract with Seadrill to hire a drilling rig for doing explorations in the Bay of Bengal. The contract was entered on the terms of the International Daywork Drilling Contract-Offshore (IDDCO) form published by the International Association of Drilling Contractors.

The rig is effectively a floating barge with three legs. It can be lowered to the sea bed. Once in position, the entire weight of the rig is borne on the legs and the body of the rig is raised above sea level for the purposes of operations. To operate the drill, the legs of the drill are first stabilised. This is called pre-load. As the legs of the drill take the weight, these sink in the sea bed. Seawater ballast is used to put additional weight to drive the legs into the sea bed soil. This operation is carried out in several stages. Eventually, the legs and the drill will be stable for the drilling to be taken up.

Surveys were done to assess the nature of the sea bed soil. It was known that the legs would need to be penetrated to an unusual depth. The pre-loading work was carried out for a week. The legs penetrated unevenly and became jammed. These could not be moved up or down. The crew carried out numerous recovery operations which itself resulted in damage to the rig, the legs and the jacking system. The rig had to be towed away to a shipyard in Singapore for repairs. As a result, the drill was not available to Gazprom for its operations.

Gazprom considered that the damage to the rig was caused by the negligence of the master and the crew in carrying out the pre-load operations. It terminated the contract for breach by Seadrill. Seadrill contested that it was negligent in the pre-load operations. The judge, however, recorded: [Seadrill (2010): para 13].

> It seems that during the preloading operation, the Master paid no heed to the operations manual, but pursued the "Captain Alex" procedure as he had done before. However, at least by the time that the stage 4 loading recommenced … it should have been apparent to the Master that the rig was in trouble.

The court recognised: [Seadrill (2010): para 27].

> … unless the contract otherwise provides, it … assumes an obligation to carry out the work with reasonable skill and care, since that is an incident of any obligation of that kind, originally imposed by the common law and now by section 13 of the Supply of Goods and Services Act 1982.

Paragraph 501 of the contract provided on the responsibilities of the parties. It read: [Seadrill (2010): para 8].

> 501. Except for such obligations and liabilities specifically assumed by Contractor, Operator shall be solely responsible and assumes liability for all consequences of operations by both parties while on a daywork basis, including results and all other risks or liabilities incurred in or incident to such operations, notwithstanding any breach of representation or warranty, either expressed or implied, or the negligence or fault of Contractor, its employees, agents or servants, including sole, concurrent or gross negligence, either active or passive, latent defects or unseaworthiness of vessels (whether or not pre-existing) and any liability based on any theory of tort, breach of contract or strict liability, including defect or ruin of premises, either latent or patent.

Seadrill contended that even if its employees were negligent in operating the rig, under paragraph 501, it was liable only for the obligations which were 'specifically assumed'.

The court asserted that the express terms have to be read with the implied terms as the implied terms are inherent to the contract. It noted: [Seadrill (2010): para 28].

> It may, of course, be possible for the parties to agree otherwise, but unless they have done so, they can only be presumed to have accepted that the ordinary incidents apply. To proceed

> on any other basis would make commercial life impossible. To say, therefore, that under this form of contract the contractor specifically assumes an obligation to operate the rig but does not specifically assume an obligation to do so carefully is to approach the question from the wrong end. Prima facie it assumes the obligation as expressed and all that the law attaches to it, unless there is agreement to the contrary.

In assessing the rival claims of the implied terms and express terms attempting to oust them, the court relied on Modern Engineering (Bristol)Ltd v Gilbert-Ash (Northern) Ltd (1974) AC 689, where Lord Diplock had stated: [Modern Engineering (Bristol)Ltd v Gilbert-Ash (Northern) Ltd (1974) AC 689: page 717.]

> But in construing such a contract one starts with the presumption that neither party intends to abandon any remedies for its breach arising by operation of law, and clear express words must be used in order to rebut this presumption.

The contract had elaborate risk allocation provisions. Seadrill contended that the starting point should be the allocation of the risks. The court noted: [Seadrill (2010): para 29].

> … the principle encapsulated in Lord Diplock's dictum is, with respect, essentially one of common sense; parties do not normally give up valuable rights without making it clear that they intend to do so. The flaw in [Seadill's] argument is that it requires one to approach the question of construction making the contrary assumption, namely, that the parties did intend to give up their rights in favour of a set of comprehensive risk allocation provisions. However, … I do not think that one can properly start from that point when analysing the contract.

The court reasoned that 'paragraph 501 is not inconsistent with the existence of an obligation on the part of the contractor to operate the rig with reasonable skill and care' [Seadrill (2010): para 30].

The JP Morgan Chase Bank Case

The facts of the case are complex, covering a long period of time, from 1998 to 2013. In its skeletal form, in the late 1990s, the Nigerian government gave very valuable offshore oil and gas rights to a company, Malabu. [JP Morgan Chase Bank, N.A. v The Federal Republic of Nigeria, (2019) EWCA Civ 1641. Hereafter Morgan Chase Bank (2019).] The company was connected with a Minister in the government. Malabu entered into agreement with Shell group of companies to exploit the rights. There was a change of government, and the new government revoked the rights given to Malabu on the grounds of corruption. It gave the rights directly to the Shell group companies. Years later, Malabu got the legislature of Nigeria to uphold its rights and a settlement was reached reinstating the rights of Malabu.

Shell, deprived of the rights, sued the Federal Republic of Nigeria in the civil courts and in arbitration. In 2011, a series of multi-party settlement agreements were made. Within these, Malabu gave up its claims in favour of Shell in return for a payment by the Republic of $1 billion on certain conditions. JP Morgan Chase

Bank was the escrow agent for the transfer of the funds. Following the instructions from the authorised signatories to the depositories, the bank released the funds. Subsequently, the Republic asserted that the settlement arrangements themselves were corrupt and the Bank was grossly negligent in not realising this and in continuing to pay out the funds as instructed. The Federal Republic of Nigeria claimed that the bank did not meet the Quincecare duty and was liable for the losses. We have reviewed the Quincare duty earlier. The contract had the following entire agreement clause: [Morgan Chase Bank (2019): para 31].

> 5.1 The duties and obligations of the Depository in respect of the Depository Cash shall be determined solely by the express provisions of this Agreement. The Depository has no knowledge of the terms and provisions of any separate agreement or any agreement relating to the Depositor's Obligations, and shall have no responsibility for compliance by the Depositor with the terms of any other agreement, or for ensuring that the terms of any such agreement are reflected in this Agreement and shall have no duties to anyone other than the Depositor.

The bank claimed that the clause ousted the Quincare duty based on the obligation of the bank to provide the services with reasonable care and skill. In assessing the rival claims of the implied terms and express terms attempting to oust them, the court relied on Modern Engineering (Bristol)Ltd v Gilbert-Ash (Northern) Ltd (1974) AC 689, where Lord Diplock had stated that implied terms in sale of goods or provision of services can be ousted or limited: [Modern Engineering (Bristol) Ltd v Gilbert-Ash (Northern) Ltd (1974) AC 689: page 717].

> But in construing such a contract one starts with the presumption that neither party intends to abandon any remedies for its breach arising by operation of law, and clear express words must be used in order to rebut this presumption.

The court quoted the following passage from Stocznia Gdynia SA v Gearbulk Holdings Ltd, [Stocznia Gdynia SA v Gearbulk Holdings Ltd (2009) EWCA Civ 75.] where the Court of Appeal formulated: [Stocznia Gdynia SA v Gearbulk Holdings Ltd (2009) EWCA Civ 75: para 23].

> It is important to remember that any clause in a contract must be construed in the context in which one finds it, both the immediate context of the other terms and the wider context of the transaction as a whole. The court is unlikely to be satisfied that a party to a contract has abandoned valuable rights arising by operation of law unless the terms of the contract make it sufficiently clear that that was intended. The more valuable the right, the clearer the language will need to be.

The court relied on the Seadrill case, which we have reviewed above and noted: [Morgan Chase Bank (2019): para 40].

> … the Quincecare duty is one aspect of a bank's overall duty to exercise reasonable skill and care in the services it provides. It can therefore properly be described as one of the incidents which the law ordinarily attaches to the relationship between the bank and the client and it is a duty which is inherent in that relationship.

The court noted that the express terms require the bank to execute the instructions of the bank but the implied terms attach to them and require the bank to do it with reasonable skill and care. Clause 5.1 in no way has ousted it by merely stating that the rights and obligations of the bank are 'determined' by the express provisions. The court noted: [Morgan Chase Bank (2019): para 40].

> It is not, of course, impossible for a bank and its client to agree that the Quincecare duty would not arise and that the bank should be entitled to pay out on instruction of the authorised signatory even if it suspects the payment is in furtherance of a fraud which that signatory is seeking to perpetrate on its client. But the first sentence of clause 5.1 is nowhere near clear enough to indicate that the FRN and Morgan Chase intended that to be the case in relation to the depository cash.

The court concluded that Quincecare duty was not successfully ousted by the entire agreement clause.

The Triple Point Case

The Triple Point Case has been reviewed in an earlier chapter, where the Triple Point had a service contract to provide a software trading platform to PTT. The contract provided: [Triple Point (2021): para 12].

> 12.1 CONTRACTOR shall exercise all reasonable skill, care and diligence and efficiency in the performance of the Services under the Contract and carry out all his responsibilities in accordance with recognized international professional standards.

Clause 12.3 of the contract had a limitation of liability which had the following exception: [Triple Point (2021): para 12].

> This limitation of liability shall not apply to CONTRACTOR's liability resulting from fraud, negligence, gross negligence or wilful misconduct of CONTRACTOR or any of its officers, employees or agents."

PTT refused to pay Triple Point as it had not completed the work. On not being paid, Triple Point wrongfully abandoned the work. The Supreme Court noted: [Triple Point (2021): para 52].

> The first point to make is that the word "negligence" has an accepted meaning in English law, ... It covers both the separate tort of failing to use due care and also breach of a contractual provision to exercise skill and care. ... therefore ... the word "negligence" in the context of the final sentence of article 12.3 the effect of that clause is that liability for negligence does not exclude the breach of a contractual duty of care.

The contract made a distinction between services where Triple Point would be in breach of contract in providing the services to the stated specifications. This included a defect-free software and other deliverables. For the other services, Triple Point owed a duty of skill and care. The Supreme Court noted: [Triple Point (2021): para 100].

> The starting point must be that ... any breach of an obligation to exercise reasonable care and skill would, in common legal language, be called "negligence", whether the source of the obligation is a term of the contract or the law of tort. On a straightforward reading of article 12.3, therefore, liability resulting from breach of a contractual duty of care falls within the exception for "liability resulting from ... negligence" established by sentence 4. Hence such liability is not subject to the limitation on the liability of Triple Point to PTT.

The Supreme Court noted the principle for exclusion of the liability of reasonable skill and care. It noted: [Triple Point (2021): para 112].

> In Seadrill and in JP Morgan Chase Bank the obligation allegedly excluded by a clause in the contract was in each case an aspect of the obligation implied by law - originally at common law and now by section 13 of the Supply of Goods and Services Act 1982 - in a contract to supply services that the supplier will carry out the service with reasonable care and skill. In each case, applying the Gilbert-Ash principle, it was held that clear wording would be needed to exclude this obligation and that there was no such clear wording.

The court concluded that there was 'an obligation implied by law in the CTRM Contract' that Triple Point would carry out the services with reasonable care and skill. The parties have not attempted to exclude it, instead, 'they have positively reinforced it by article 12.1' [Triple Point (2021): para 113].

Philipp v Barclays Bank UK PLC

Dr Philipp is a retired doctor based in the United Kingdom. [Philipp v Barclays Bank UK PLC, (2023) UKSC 25. Hereafter Philipp (2023).] He held his savings with an investment firm Tilney. He was contacted in February 2018, by a person, who turned out to be a fraudster, claiming to be working for the Financial Conduct Authority. He represented that he was working in conjunction with the National Crime Agency and investigating a fraud within HSBC and the investment firm Tilney. The fraud operation played on Dr Philipp was very sophisticated. The telephone calls that were made to the mobile phone of Dr Philipp displayed to be coming from the telephone number of the National Crime Agency. The fraudster convinced Dr Philipp that his money was unsafe and needed to be moved to safe accounts.

Dr Philipp, convinced that his money was unsafe, transferred £ 950,000 from the investment account to his wife's current account with the Barclays bank. Mrs Philipp visited a branch of the bank on 10 March with her husband and instructed the bank to make an international transfer of £400,000 to a bank account in UAE in the name of Lambi Petroleum Ltd. The couple visited the bank again two days later and instructed the bank to transfer £300,000 to a bank account in UAE in the name of Bonito Systems Ltd. On both the occasions, they were following the instructions of the fraudster. For both the transfers, the Bank telephoned Mrs Philipp to seek her confirmation and she confirmed the instructions.

The police were on the trail of the fraud operations of the fraudster. They had credible information that Mrs Philipp's current account had been compromised by fraudsters in the UAE. The Police informed the bank of the fraud and the bank froze the account of Mrs Philipp. The couple attempted to make another international transfer but found that the account was frozen. Acting on the advice of the fraudster, Mrs Philipp called the fraud department of the bank and attempted to persuade the bank to lift the block on her account. But the bank refused to do it. They then realised that the officer on whose advice they were acting was a fraudster and they have been defrauded. The bank made efforts to get the money transferred back but did not succeed.

Mrs Philipp initiated proceeding with the High Court of Justice Business & Property that the bank was responsible for the loss. She contends that the Bank owed her a duty under its contract with her or at common law not to carry out her payment instructions, as the bank had reasonable grounds for believing that she was being defrauded. The dispute came in appeal before the Supreme Court. The Supreme Court stated the principles: [Philipp (2023): para 34].

> As with any contract for the supply of services in the course of a business, there is a term implied by law in the contract between a bank and its customer that the bank must carry out the services with reasonable care and skill. … A similar duty is owed in tort; but as the duty in tort arises out of the contractual relationship, it can be no more extensive than the contractual duty and adds nothing to the analysis for present purposes.

The Supreme Court next noted that the requirement of reasonable care and skill is only an implied term of a general nature. It would give way to specific stipulations in the contract on the manner of performance of the service or the outcomes of the service. The court noted: [Philipp (2023): para 35].

> The requirement to exercise reasonable care and skill only applies, and is only capable of applying, insofar as the contract gives the supplier any latitude in how the relevant services are carried out. Insofar as the contract prescribes what the supplier must do or achieve in carrying out the services, failure to do or achieve what is required will be a breach of the contract and it is irrelevant whether the supplier has acted with skill or care.

The recognised that when a customer orders a bank transfer in accordance with a mandate it 'leaves the bank with very little latitude in performing the obligation' [Philipp (2023): para 35]. Thus, it is only where the bank transfer order is not complete that the duty of the bank to perform that service with reasonable care and skill arises. An example is, a customer instructs the bank to transfer funds but does not specify the method of transfer. In this case, the bank must exercise reasonable skill and care in making its choice. Another example is the customer gives unclear instructions to the bank as to what the bank is instructed to do. The relationship of the bank and the customer is of agent and principal. The Supreme Court noted: [Philipp (2023): para 36].

> It is a general principle of the law of agency, applicable to a bank when acting in that capacity, that where the agent honestly and reasonably understands an instruction to bear a particular meaning and acts accordingly, the agent will not be in breach of contract by so acting.

When a customer orders a bank transfer which is 'clear and leaves no room for interpretation or choice', the bank is under a duty to 'simply to execute the order by making the requisite payment' and a 'duty of care does not' arise. [Philipp (2023): para 63] The Supreme Court engaged with and critiqued the foundations of Quincecare duty. The bank has to follow the transfer order of the customer. It is only when the transfer order is not clear that 'there is any scope for it' to apply itself. Only in this case, the bank is under a duty to use reasonable care and skill in executing the order of the customer. The court pointed out the flawed nature of the reasoning where the duty to execute an order of the customer itself could 'provide an independent basis for failing or refusing to execute a valid payment order' [Philipp (2023): para 64]. The court noted it was 'impossible to derive from a duty to observe reasonable skill and care in and about executing a customer's order a duty not to execute the customer's order' [Philipp (2023): para 64].

The relationship between a bank and the customer is governed by elaborate contract terms. The bank has to affect the express terms. Beyond the express terms, the court noted: [Philipp (2023): para 67].

... the aim of the courts is the more modest one of seeking to give effect to the presumed common intention of the contracting parties. A duty to combat fraud or to protect customers (let alone innocent third parties) against fraud is not an ordinary incident of the contractual relationship between a bank and its customer.

The court relocated that 'Quincecare duty' was 'simply an application of the general duty of care owed by a bank to interpret, ascertain and act in accordance with its customer's instructions' [Philipp (2023): para 97]. Its application arose in the context where an agent of the customer gave transfer instructions, as in the case of a company. In this case, if the bank had 'reasonable grounds for believing that a payment instruction given by an agent purportedly on behalf of the customer is an attempt to defraud the customer' [Philipp (2023): para 97], the bank should refrain from executing the instructions, make enquiries and verify with the customer. In this case, the court noted: [Philipp (2023): para 97].

If the bank executes the instruction without making such inquiries and the instruction proves to have been given without the customer's authority, the bank will be in breach of duty. It will also in making the payment be acting outside the scope of its own authority from the customer and will therefore not be entitled to debit the payment to the customer's account.

The court noted that the principle has no application, when the customer himself is giving instructions: [Philipp (2023): para 100].

> On the other hand, these principles have no application to a situation where, as in the present case, the customer is a victim of APP fraud. In this situation the validity of the instruction is not in doubt. Provided the instruction is clear and is given by the customer personally or by an agent acting with apparent authority, no inquiries are needed to clarify or verify what the bank must do. The bank's duty is to execute the instruction and any refusal or failure to do so will prima facie be a breach of duty by the bank.

A bank contracts with its customers on its standard contract terms. The bank had updated its customer terms for personal customers in January 2018. The terms provided the following warning to the customers: [Philipp (2023): para 112].

> If you authorise a payment and none of your details have been compromised, we have to assume it was a payment you wanted to make.
>
> If someone persuades you to pay them money and you feel you've been cheated or you should not have agreed to pay them, we are unlikely to be able to refund the money.

The terms make it clear that 'ordinarily a bank will not attract liability for APP fraud' [Philipp (2023): para 113]. The bank had further terms under the heading "When we do not have to follow your instructions". These listed the exceptions when the bank would not follow the express instructions of the customers. This included: [Philipp (2023): para 114].

> [the instruction] isn't complete or clear, or we don't think it came from you or someone authorised to give us the instruction on your behalf
>
> you don't have the money (including any available overdraft) to cover the payment
>
> by carrying out the instruction we might break a law, regulation, code or other duty that applies to us, or it might expose us to claims from third parties
>
> we reasonably think that a payment into or out of an account is connected to fraud or any other criminal activity, including where the funds are being obtained through deception

The last entry has a relationship to the case. The court interpreted that the term gave a right to the bank to decline a transaction. However, having 'a right … is obviously not the same as being under a duty'. It is following this right that the bank refused the third transfer order of Mrs Philipp. If the contract term were not there, Mrs Philipp could potentially have sued the bank for refusing to carry out her instructions.

The English common law courts developed the implied term in a service contract that the service supplier will exercise reasonable care and skill in providing the service. The protection has been codified in the Supply of Goods and Services Act, 1982. As contracts are voluntarily made, the common law courts and the Supply of Goods and Services Act, 1982 recognise that the implied term can be limited or ousted by express contract terms. The express terms can limit or oust the implied terms in different ways.

One, the contract provides the manner in which the service is to be provided. Two, the contract provides the deliverables as the outcome of the service. Three, the express term is in conflict with the duty of reasonable care and skill. Four, an express term clearly states to oust the implied term. The implied terms can be limited or ousted, however, as these are valuable rights, the courts insist that clear wording would be necessary to exclude the implied term of reasonable care and skill. GCCs have clauses making the implied term of reasonable care and skill express and also clauses limiting or even ousting it.

References

Barclays Bank plc v Quincecare Ltd (1992) 4 All ER 363
Barton v Morris, (2023) UKSC 3
JP Morgan Chase Bank, N.A. v The Federal Republic of Nigeria, (2019) EWCA Civ 1641
Modern Engineering (Bristol)Ltd v Gilbert-Ash (Northern) Ltd (1974) AC 689
Persimmon Homes Ltd v Ove Arup & Partners Ltd, (2017) EWCA Civ 373
Philipp v Barclays Bank UK PLC, (2023) UKSC 25
Seadrill Management Services Ltd and another v OAO Gazprom (2010) EWCA Civ 691
Stocznia Gdynia SA v Gearbulk Holdings Ltd (2009) EWCA Civ 75
Triple Point Technology, Inc v PTT Public Company Ltd, (2021) UKSC 29
X v Kuoni Travel Ltd, (2021) UKSC 34

Chapter 17
Indemnities

In business contracts, losses can arise from different sources. It is a concern for the party on whom the loss falls to cover the loss from the other party or a third party. A party may breach his contractual duties, leading to losses to the other. In this case, the suffering party would claim damages according to the terms in the contract for award of damages. A party may be negligent in performance of its contractual duties leading to a loss to the other. In this case, the suffering party may claim damages under negligence. Yet other times, a party may not be negligent, and a loss may simply arise in the course of performance of the contract or from the bargain itself. The loss would fall on one of the parties. The contracting parties allocate risk and losses among themselves by indemnity clauses.

The general meaning of the term indemnity is to cover a loss arising to another. It is a very versatile term in a contract. The parties do what the clause requires—cover the losses. The indemnifier, the person covering the losses, has the primary obligation for covering the losses. The indemnifier alone is liable to cover the losses. The indemnifier need not be the cause of the loss, he could be covering a loss caused by a third party. Unlike the award of damages, where several common law principles intermediate, there are no restraints on an indemnity. The only qualification on an indemnity is the claim arises when the loss has been incurred. For these reasons, while the losses in relation to the main transaction are covered by the damages clauses, all other losses which could arise in relation to the performance of the contract, are covered by indemnity clauses. A common form of indemnity is to seek protection against intellectual property law violations. It could read:

> Indemnities: The SELLER shall indemnify the PURCHASER against all third party claims of infringement of patent, trade mark, copyrights or industrial design rights arising from use of the GOODS or any part thereof in the PURCHASER's country.

Another common form of indemnity is to seek protection against the other party not complying with the laws. It could read:

A. Pathak, *Contract Terms in International Business*,
https://doi.org/10.1007/978-981-96-8146-4_17

> Indemnities: SELLER shall be responsible for compliance with all requirements under the laws and shall protect and indemnify completely the PURCHASER from any claims/ penalties arising out of any infringements.

In addition to such general clauses, contracts have specific indemnity clauses. As indemnity clauses are overarching, these have to be specifically worded to limit their ambit and scope. The disputes before the courts have been on interpreting the clause to ascertain whether the claims fall within them or not. Thus, the indemnity clauses have become about interpreting the contract terms. We will explore the theme with a review of the following cases.

Wood v Capita Insurance Services Ltd

Sureterm Direct Limited was a company which carried on business as a specialist insurance broker, primarily offering motor insurance for classic cars. [Wood v Capita Insurance Services Ltd, (2017) UKSC 24. Hereafter Capita (2017).] Mr Andrew Wood owned 94% share capital of the company, Mr Howard Collinge owned 5% and Mr Christopher Kightley owned 1%. Each was a director of the Company and Mr Wood was its managing director. The three entered into a contract with a company, Capita Insurance Services Ltd (Capita), dated 13 April 2010 to sell their shares. Following the sale, Capita came to own all the shares of the company. Mr Wood remained as managing director of the Company until the end of 2010. The Sale and Purchase Agreement (SPA) had an indemnity clause to indemnify Capita. It read: [Capita (2017): para 18].

> all actions, proceedings, losses, claims, damages, costs, charges, expenses and liabilities suffered or incurred, and all fines, compensation or remedial action or payments imposed on or required to be made by [Sureterm] following and arising out of claims or complaints registered with the FSA, the Financial Services Ombudsman or any other Authority against [Sureterm], the Sellers or any Relevant Person and which relate to the period prior to the Completion Date pertaining to any mis-selling or suspected mis-selling of any insurance or insurance related product of service.

The SPA also contained the following warranties: [Capita (2017): para 19].

> The Company conducts, and has conducted the Business in accordance with the requirements of all Competition laws and Applicable Financial Services Laws applicable to the business and has not been and is not being investigated for any alleged non-compliance or infringement of such Competition Laws and Applicable Financial Services Laws. ...
>
> The Company has no reason to believe that any action will be taken against it in relation to any of its current or past activities based on any alleged non-compliance or infringement of any Competition Laws and Applicable Financial Services Laws.

After completion of the acquisition, various employees of Sureterm raised concerns about Sureterm's sales processes. Sureterm had indulged in unfair dealings with customers and mis-selling. In response to these concerns, Sureterm carried out a review of its sales, and reported its findings to the FSA in accordance with its regulatory obligations. FSA conducted its investigations and concluded that customers had been treated unfairly. Following this, Sureterm was required to undertake a customer remediation exercise, which included paying approximately £1.35 million in compensation to the customers. Capita sought to claim this amount, together with costs relating to the remediation scheme and interest, from the Sellers under the indemnity.

The dispute between the parties was on the interpretation of the indemnity clause. The seller disputed the claim of indemnity. The seller contended that the clause applied only if there was a 'claims or complaint' against the company. In this case, there was no claim or complaint against the company, rather, Sureterm itself had reported the mis-selling. Capita read the indemnity clause differently. It claimed that 'claims or complaint' related to the second part of the indemnity clause and anything which got registered with FAS was covered.

The dispute came before the United Kingdom Supreme Court. The Supreme Court noted that the clause was not 'drafted with precision and its meaning is avoidably opaque' [Capita (2017): para 26]. Thus, the court moved to explore and detail the principles for interpreting contract terms in general and the indemnity clause.

Interpretation of Contracts

The Supreme Court observed that the role of the courts was in giving objective meaning to the language of the contract. This exercise was not to look at the words literally, pulling them out from the contract terms. Instead, the Supreme Court noted: [Capita (2017): para 10].

> ... the court must consider the contract as a whole and, depending on the nature, formality and quality of drafting of the contract, give more or less weight to elements of the wider context in reaching its view as to that objective meaning.

The exercise, however, may lead to rival contentions. In this case, the court can give weight to a view which is 'more consistent with business common sense' [Capita (2017): para 11]. The exercise has to be done in a reiterative process where the commercial consequences of each interpretation are taken up. The court noted: [Capita (2017): para 12].

> To my mind once one has read the language in dispute and the relevant parts of the contract that provide its context, it does not matter whether the more detailed analysis commences with the factual background and the implications of rival constructions or a close examination of the relevant language in the contract, so long as the court balances the indications given by each.

Thus, if rival interpretations of contract terms come up, the rival interpretations have to be weighed within the text of the contract and the business context of the provision. The court noted on reading the text in its context: [Capita (2017): para 13].

> Textualism and contextualism are not conflicting paradigms in a battle for exclusive occupation of the field of contractual interpretation. Rather, the lawyer and the judge, when interpreting any contract, can use them as tools to ascertain the objective meaning of the language which the parties have chosen to express their agreement.

In the light of its formulations on interpreting contract terms, the court, thus, examined the indemnity clause: [Capita (2017): para 26].

> Clause 7.11 has not been drafted with precision and its meaning is avoidably opaque. ... it is necessary to place the clause in the context of the contract as a whole, to examine the clause in more detail and to consider whether the wider relevant factual matrix gives guidance as to its meaning in order to consider the implications of the rival interpretations.

The contract had given wide-ranging warranties which could have covered the relevant losses. The losses, however, were to be claimed within two years. This was not an unreasonable time period to examine the sale practices and uncover regulatory breached. In contrast, the scope of the indemnity clause was unlimited in time. In this context, the court noted: [Capita (2017): para 28].

> All of the parties to the SPA were commercially sophisticated and had experience of the insurance broking industry. Capita was not involved in the management of the Company before the share purchase. The Sellers were the directors and the only shareholders of the Company. They were the people who knew or ought to have known how the Company had operated its business; Capita would in all probability not have that knowledge. The parties to the SPA would have known this.

This lack of knowledge explains why Capita required the disclosures and detailed warranties. However, the court noted, this did not 'assist the court to determine the scope of the indemnity clause' [Capita (2017): para 28]. Moving to the business context of the indemnity clause, the court noted: [Capita (2017): para 28].

> Business common sense suggests that Capita had an interest in obtaining as broad an indemnity against the adverse consequences of mis-selling as it could obtain. But the sellers had given warranties of compliance with regulatory requirements, which covered such mis-selling, subject to the agreed limits of quantum and time. The sellers were exposed to a potential liability under those warranties for the two years after the Completion Date, during which Capita could learn of the Company's sales practices.

From this, one can infer that the seller wanted to minimise its liability. The court commented that business common sense points to the purpose of a provision and its practical usefulness. The court, however, noted: [Capita (2017): para 28].

> But in the tug of war of commercial negotiation, business common sense can rarely assist the court in ascertaining on which side of the line the centre line marking on the tug of war rope lay, when the negotiations ended.

The court, therefore, turned to examine the clause in further detail before returning to the context. Following a detailed analysis, the court recognised that the general purpose of the clause was to indemnify Capital against losses caused by misspelling. Following this, it noted: [Capita (2017): para 40].

> Had clause 7.11 stood on its own, the requirement of a claim or complaint by a customer and the exclusion of loss caused by regulatory action which was otherwise prompted might have appeared anomalous. But clause 7.11 is in addition to the wide ranging warranties in part 14 of schedule 4 which probably covered the circumstances which eventuated.

In this arrangement, Capital had two years to examine the sale practices and make a claim. This was not an unreasonable time scale. In fact, Capita was able to send its findings to the FSA within 20 months of the Completion Date. Considering this, the court noted: [Capita (2017): para 40].

It is not contrary to business common sense for the parties to agree wide ranging warranties, which are subject to a time limit, and in addition to agree a further indemnity, which is not subject to any such limit but is triggered only in limited circumstances.

The court concluded that the 'SPA may have become a poor bargain' but it is 'not the function of the court to improve their bargain' [Capita (2017): para 41].

The Bahia Blanca Holiday Club Case

Timeshare is an arrangement to invest and in return, get access to holiday resorts for a limited period. [First National Trustco (UK) Limited v Bahia Blanca Holiday Club, (2020) EWCA Civ 107. Hereafter Bahia (2020).] A person makes a onetime payment and gets the right to enjoy a property for a certain period in a year in perpetuity but does not get the ownership of the property. Several entities and persons may be networked together to give effect to timeshare. The case involves timeshare resorts in Spain. In Spain, timeshare resorts are commonly held through a club trust structure. In this arrangement, the legal ownership of individual apartments is vested in an owning company, O. The owning company is in turn wholly owned by a trustee company T. The owning company O sells rights over the apartments to individuals. The individuals are constituted as members of a club. The trustee company holds and controls the owning company in trust for the benefit of the members of the club. The members, who have purchased occupation rights over the apartment in the form of individual weeks, become subject to the rights and obligations set out in the Constitution of the Club.

This dispute is on the Bahia Blanca Timeshare Resort (the Resort) in Gran Canaria, Spain. Bahia Blanca Club B Limited (BBCB) is the owning company. It holds title to apartments. First National Trustco (UK) Ltd (FNTC) is the trustee company controlling BBCB. The Bahia Blanca Holiday Club (the Club) comprises members who have bought timeshare interest in BBCB. Connecting the link, FNTC holds BBCB for the benefit of the persons who are the members of the club at any given point of time.

The resort was created in 1988 and the timeshare sold to the members of the public. TS International PLC (TSI) was the owner and developer of the property on which the apartments were built and was the Founder Member of the Club. The Club was established by a Constitution dated 1 January 1988. It was executed by

TSI as Founder Member and was subject to English law. TSI sold the ownership of the property to BBCB for memberships over the apartments sold. It then sold the memberships to the public. The membership of the Owning Company was limited to an independent custodian trustee who was to hold and control the Owning Company in trust for the benefit of the Members of the Club from time to time upon the terms of the Deed of Trust. The Deed of Trust made between the Founder Member and the Trustee sets out the rights and duties of the Trustee. The trustee company, when the dispute arose, was FNTC. At one point of time, TSI sold its rights to Bahia Blanca Leisure Limited (BBLL). Thus, BBLL came to stand in the shoes of the Founder Member.

Starting from 2000, the Spanish tax authorities, following tax audits, demanded tax arrears with penalties from BBCB. The demands were litigated by the club all the way up to the Supreme Court of Spain. The ruling was against BBCB. The tax authorities tried to auction the flats to recover the taxes. FNTL claimed indemnity from BBLL. The dispute was on the scope of the indemnity clause. The indemnity clause read: [Bahia (2020): para 15].

> 14. The Founder Member for itself and on behalf of the Club hereby undertakes to indemnify and hold harmless the Trustee from and against all costs, liabilities and expenses which may result from the performance by the Trustee of their duties hereunder and the Trustee shall be kept fully indemnified by the Club and the Founder Member against all losses, claims, demands, expenses and other liabilities made or incurred in connection with the Trust Property or in any other way in connection with the holding by the Trustee of the office of custodian trustee hereunder. The Trustee shall have the right if at any time it considers it desirable so to do to require that the Founder Member or the Club shall deposit with the Trustee as a reserve fund such sum as shall be reasonably necessary in support of the indemnity contained in this clause."

The court relied on the principles of interpretation of contracts developed in Wood v Capita Insurance Services Ltd, [Capita (2017).] of reading text and context iteratively to settle the rival contention. In addition, it relied on the following passage in LB Re Financing No 3 Ltd v Excalibur Funding No 1 Plc (2011) EWHC 2111 (Ch): [Bahia (2020): para 32].

> Commercial absurdity may require the court to depart even from the apparently unambiguous natural meaning of a provision in an instrument, because "the law does not require judges to attribute to the parties an intention they plainly could not have had"

The court, thus, formulated that the court should determine objectively the intentions of the parties when the contract was made. This will generally appear from what is stated in the contract. The court stated: [Bahia (2020): para 33].

> The court will not look for reasons to depart from the apparently clear meaning of the words they used, but elements of the wider documentary, factual and commercial context will be taken into account to the extent that they assist in the search for meaning. That wider survey may lead to a construction that departs from even the clearest wording if the wording does not reflect the objectively ascertained intention of the parties.

The court, looking at the wording of the indemnity clause, recognised that it gives two protections to the trust, (a) an indemnity against all liabilities resulting from the performance of its duties, and (b) an indemnity against all liabilities incurred in connection with the Trust Property or in any other connection with the office of Trustee. The trust was relying on the second limb. The court noted: [Bahia (2020): para 40].

> But in my view, the clause is clear both in its wording and, critically, in its intent. It is an indemnity given to the Trustee in respect of liabilities arising in connection with the Trust Property or the holding by the Trustee of the office. It is no more or less than a conventional indemnity clause for the protection of the Trustee. It has nothing to do with BBCB, or BBCB's liability for the Spanish Taxes, and it cannot sensibly be construed to extend to them.

The court then considered the commercial context of the contract. It noted: [Bahia (2020): para 42].

> For the scheme to be a commercial proposition, timeshare purchasers have to know their potential liabilities. Here, there is no indication that the parties to the Constitution or the Trust Deed intended the Members to be liable by way of an open-ended indemnity for general taxation in unspecified amounts.

If this were the intention, the court reasoned, the contract would have stated it. In fact, this would be necessary for the members to know of the liability and how it would get triggered. The court was of the view that there were 'matters of importance and the silence about them in documentation' [Bahia (2020): para 42] is instructive.

The trust contended that the members in the past had paid the taxes and they were being opportunistic. The court ruled that it was concerned with not that the actions 'might be regarded as opportunistic, but rather with their legal obligations under the agreement setting up the timeshare scheme' [Bahia (2020): para 39]. Assessing the commercial context, the court noted: [Bahia (2020): para 43].

> An arrangement by which the Members can pay what they want when they want by way of taxes and expenses may not be a tidy one, but the Resort has seemingly continued to operate.

The alternate proposed arrangement was 'far from obvious' [Bahia (2020): para 43] as it deprived the members of the choice of paying or not paying the taxes. The court noted the implications of not paying the taxes: [Bahia (2020): para 43].

> Of course, if they decide not to pay taxes, they may have to take any consequences. But that does not amount to commercial absurdity and there is nothing integral to the scheme as a whole that requires the Trustee to act as an enforcer for taxes levied on a third party that the Members do not wish to pay.

The court, thus, concluded that the indemnity clause does not extend to the claims made by the trustee company.

Gwynt y Mor OFTO Plc v Gwynt y Mor Offshore Wind Farm Ltd

A wind farm, consisting of 160 wind turbines, was developed by Gwynt y Mor Offshore Wind Farm Ltd and associated companies off the North Wales coast [Gwynt y Mor OFTO Plc v Gwynt y Mor Offshore Wind Farm Ltd, (2020) 4 WLUK 129. Hereafter Gwyny (2020)]. The farm was connected to the national power grid through sub-sea cables. Gwynt y Mor OFTO Plc (buyer) entered into a sale purchase agreement (SPA) with the developers and owners of the farm on 11 February 2015 to buy the 'business of owning, maintaining and operating the electrical transmission link between the farm and the national grid' [Gwyny (2020): para 1]. The transaction was completed on 17 February 2015 and the title passed to the buyer.

On 2 March 2015, one of the cables failed. A second cable failed on 25 September 2015. On both the occasions, the buyer undertook urgent repairs. This cost the buyer about 15 million in repair. The cables had suffered severe corrosion for months and years. Seawater had penetrated the polyethylene sheath surrounding the cables. The most likely cause of it was damage during the manufacturing process. The claimant could assess the fault only after completing the repairs. The SPA had an indemnity clause under which the buyer claimed the amount. The indemnity clause 8.2 read: [Gwyny (2020): para 18].

> 8.2 If any of the Assets are destroyed or damaged prior to Completion (Pre-Completion Damage), then, following Completion, the [seller] shall indemnify the [claimant] against the full cost of reinstatement of any Assets affected by Pre-Completion Damage. Without prejudice to any claim made by the [claimant] under this Clause 8.2, to the extent that the [seller] receive any payments from insurers or third parties in connection with any Pre-Completion Damage, such amounts shall, for the purposes of calculating the total liability of the Vendors [under limitations on liability provisions] only, be deducted from the amount of the Claim.

The seller contended that the indemnity was available only for damages to the assets 'prior to completion', that is, during the parties entering into the contract and completing the transaction. This period was 11–17 February 2015. The seller contended that the indemnity did not apply to damages caused in the earlier periods. The court noted the text of the clause: [Gwyny (2020): para 37].

> The SPA must be interpreted as at the date it comes into force, so the natural and ordinary meaning of the phrase "If any of the Assets are destroyed or damaged prior to Completion..." is that it applies to destruction or damage which occurs thereafter, that is, after execution. Such wording, on its face, does not include damage which had already occurred at the date of the SPA.

Clause 8.1 dealt with the signing of the contract and clause 9 with the completion of the contract. In this sequencing of the provisions, the court noted that 8.2 was inserted in between. The court put the contract in its context: [Gwyny (2020): para 38].

> The insertion, between those provisions, of an indemnity against Pre-Completion Damage, is readily understood as intended to relate to damage occurring between execution and Completion.

The need for the indemnity in this context was obvious. The court stated: [Gwyny (2020): para 38].

> … as at the date of execution the claimant is obliged to purchase the Assets, but does not have title to them or risk in them and so does not have an insurable interest. An indemnity to cover the risk to which the claimant was exposed between signing and Completion was an obvious solution.

The seller had given specific warranties as to the absence of damage to the assets as at the date of the SPA. The warranty had been limited to what had been discovered and had been reasonably likely to cause material disruption to the offshore transmission system. The court noted on the warranties: [Gwyny (2020): para 39].

> Such carefully structured and limited provisions would be rendered pointless [by] … a broad indemnity against any and all damage suffered prior to execution of the SPA. Such indemnity would apply to any damage, even if not discovered, not reasonably likely to disrupt the transmission system.

Thus, the specific wording of clause 8.2, the structure of the clauses, and the commercial sense supported the construction that the indemnity related only to damage occurring between the execution of the SPA and completion of the contract. The vendors had given the warranty in relation to the period up to the SPA, the indemnity for the period between execution of the SPA and completion and a further indemnity in respect of ongoing works. The court concluded: [Gwyny (2020): para 44].

> In my judgment, therefore, both the specific wording of clause 8.2 and the broader structure, provisions and commercial sense of the SPA support … that the Indemnity relates only to damage occurring between the execution of the SPA and Completion.

The court also explored whether corrosion of the cables was covered under the words “are destroyed or damaged”. The court observed that there was no basis to confine the term to ‘entirely new damage, or to damage caused by an external event’ [Gwyny (2020): para 57]. The court illustrated that if one of the cables failed during the period of the indemnity it would ‘plainly be described as having been destroyed or damaged.’ [Gwyny (2020): para 57] The court, however, noted: [Gwyny (2020): para 58].

> … the phrase requires damage to be patent, in the sense of being readily observable or discoverable … for the following reasons: … the word "damaged" is coupled with and follows "destroyed", indicating that either destruction or damage short of destruction is contemplated: the phrase is inapposite to encompass the slow process of continuing corrosion …

The court concluded that ‘on a textual reading of the SPA, corrosion of cables as occurred in the present case does not fall within clause 8.2’ [Gwyny (2020): para 59]. The court concluded: [Gwyny (2020): para 75].

> I conclude that the Indemnity, on a true interpretation, was limited to damage occurring in the period between signing of the SPA and Completion and to damage which was patent. ... As changes to the cables during the period of the Indemnity were limited to unobservable corrosion, no damage was suffered during that period.

Thus, the interpretation of the indemnity clause, based on a textual analysis and the business context, was limited to the narrow period between signing of the contract and transfer of title to the buyer.

The Indemnity clauses tend to cover losses other than contractual damages for the breach of the contract and other specific warranties given by the party. For this reason, their scope is often wide. Several disputes have come before the courts in the past years. In interpreting the indemnity clauses, the courts have given effect to the intentions of the parties, as stated in the contract. If the textual meaning of the clause is clear, the courts give effect to it. However, if the meaning of the text is not clear and there are rival interpretations, the courts put the clause in its context and give weight to a view which is more consistent with the business common sense. The texts and the context of the contract, are not in conflict. The courts go iteratively from one to the other to find an objective meaning the parties have given to their agreement in the contract.

References

First National Trustco (UK) Limited v Bahia Blanca Holiday Club, (2020) EWCA Civ 107
Gwynt y Mor OFTO Plc v Gwynt y Mor Offshore Wind Farm Ltd, (2020) 4 WLUK 129
Wood v Capita Insurance Services Ltd, (2017) UKSC 24

Chapter 18
Guarantees

Contracts have clauses creating payment mechanisms. In this context, the terms surety and guarantee feature prominently. A contract of surety or guarantee involves three parties and two contracts. The two contracts are the main contract and the payment contract, associated with the main contract. In the main contract, one party comes to owe obligation or a sum of money to the other, for example, a buyer will come to owe the price to the seller. The party to whom the money or the obligation is owed is called the creditor and the other party, principal. The surety or guarantor, as a part of the main contract, steps in to make a contract with the creditor to stand for the default of the principal. Thus, if the principal defaults, the creditor can require the surety to meet the obligations. In a contract of guarantee, the liability is of the principal, not the surety. For this reason, the liability of the surety does not arise till the principal defaults. Further, the surety, having paid up to the creditor, has the right to recover the amount from the principal. A guarantee, however, has come to take several forms, depending on how the instrument is structured. At times, a surety may undertake to pay a sum on a simple demand of the creditor. This is a demand bond, expressed in the terminology of a guarantee. The financial instruments, employing the terminology of a guarantee, have very different rights and obligations but have come to be on a spectrum. Disputes continue to come before the courts requiring the courts to characterise a guarantee instrument. We will first review the principles and applications of guarantee.

Principles and Forms of Guarantees

In Vossloh Aktiengesellschaft v. Alpha Trains (UK) Limited, [Vossloh Aktiengesellschaft v. Alpha Trains (UK) Limited, (2010) EWHC 2443 (Ch). Hereafter Alpha (2010)], the court has formulated, what has come to be known as the modern statement of the principles and use of contract of guarantee. The court noted that a contract

A. Pathak, *Contract Terms in International Business*,
https://doi.org/10.1007/978-981-96-8146-4_18

of surety is 'an area of law bedevilled by imprecise terminology' [Alpha (2010): para 20], and effect has to be given to the substance of obligations created in them. The court explored a contract of guarantee: [Alpha (2010): para 23].

> A contract of guarantee, in the true sense, is a contract whereby the surety (the guarantor) promises the creditor to be responsible for the due performance by the principal of his existing or future obligations to the creditor if the principal fails to perform them or any of them. Depending on its true construction, the obligation undertaken by the surety may be no more than to discharge a liability, for example a particular debt, if the principal does not discharge.

In this case, the surety is liable only so long as the principle is liable. If the principle is discharged from liability or pays the creditor, no liability can arise for the surety. In contrast are the 'see to it' guarantees where the surety 'undertakes that the principal will carry out his contract and will answer for his default' [Alpha (2010): para 23]. In this case, the court noted: [Alpha (2010): para 23].

> ... if for any reason the principal fails to act as required by his contract he not only breaks his own contract, but he also puts the surety in breach of his contract with the creditor, thereby entitling the creditor to sue the surety, not for the unpaid debt, but for damages. The damages are for the loss suffered by the creditor due to the principal having failed to do what the surety undertook that he would do.

A contract of indemnity is in contrast to a contract of guarantee. The court noted that in 'one sense all contacts of guarantee (strictly so-called) are contracts of indemnity' [Alpha (2010): para 25] because an indemnity is about covering losses of another. The court noted on indemnity: [Alpha (2010): para 25].

> In the narrower sense ... a contract of indemnity denotes a contract where the person who gives the indemnity undertakes his indemnity obligation by way of security for the performance of an obligation by another.

The essential distinction between the two is the liability of the giver of the indemnity is primary and that of the surety is secondary. The surety having discharged the liability has the right to be paid by the principal as the obligation of the principal was primary. An indemnifier meets only his own obligations in covering the losses. The court explored yet another form of payment mechanism: [Alpha (2010): para 28].

> This brings me to the so-called "performance bond", sometimes known as a "performance guarantee", often as a "demand bond" or "demand guarantee" or even as a "first demand guarantee".... In essence, it is a particularly stringent contract of indemnity. It is a contractual undertaking by a person, usually a bank, to pay a specified amount of money to a third party on the occurrence of a stated event, usually the non-fulfilment of a contractual obligation by the principal to that third party.

The court concluded: [Alpha (2010): para 34].

> ... there is in this field of law a spectrum of contractual possibilities ranging from the classic contract of guarantee, properly so called, at the one end ... to the performance or demand bond (or demand guarantee) at the other end, where liability in the giver of the bond may be triggered by mere demand and without proof of default ...There may be little to distinguish (and it may not matter) whether the obligation undertaken is in the nature of a guarantee (strictly so called) or an indemnity.

Several disputes have come before the courts requiring the court to characterise an instrument and settle the rights and obligations of the parties. We will explore the theme with the following review.

GPP Big Field LLP v Solar EPC Solutions SL

Solar EPC Solutions SL was a Spanish company which was the parent company of a group specialising in the construction of solar power plants [GPP Big Field LLP v Solar EPC Solutions SL, (2018) EWHC 2866 (Comm). Hereafter GPP (2018)]. From about 2009, Solar group had collaborated with the funds managed by Mr Gaarn-Larsen on solar projects in Spain and elsewhere in Europe. In about 2011, seeing an opportunity created by the favourable renewable energy tariffs in the United Kingdom, Solar and Mr Gaarn-Larsen decided to work together on a number of projects in the United Kingdom. For the operations in the UK, a special purpose limited liability partnership was incorporated in England. The partnership comprised of GPP Big Field LLP, GPP Langstone LLP.

GPP Big Field LLP entered into an Engineering, Procurement and Construction contract with Prosolia UK Ltd. Thus, GPP was the employer and Prosolia, the contractor. The contract turned out to be unprofitable and Prosolia turned insolvent. Solar was the parent company of Proslia and had given guarantees/indemnities in favour of GPP. There were several disputes between the parties. We will explore one on the guarantees/indemnities. Clause 6 of the contract provided: [GPP(2018): para 118].

> 6.1 [Solar] guarantees the due and punctual performance by the Contractor of the Contractor's duties and obligations to [GPP] under this Agreement.
>
> 6.2 If the Contractor fails to observe and perform any of its duties or obligations to [GPP], [Solar] (as a separate and independent obligation and liability from its obligations and liabilities under this Agreement) shall indemnify [GPP] against all loss, debt, damage, interest, cost and expense incurred by [GPP] by reason of such failure or breach and shall pay to the [GPP], without any deduction or set-off, the amount of that loss, debt, damage, interest, cost and expense.

GPP claimed liquidated damages and damages from Solar under the above indemnity clause for late and/or non-completion of the works required by the EEC. Solar asserts that within the clause, it was only a guarantor and it was discharged from obligations and the parties had changed the main contract. GPP contests and claims that 'Solar's liability under clause 6.2 is that of an indemnifier, and that the doctrines of guarantee law relied on by Solar as discharging it from liability do not apply to contracts of indemnity' [GPP(2018): para 120].

The court turned to examine whether clause 6.2 was a guarantee or indemnity. The court noted the difference between a contract of guarantee and indemnity: [GPP(2018): para 122].

> Whether any particular contractual promise is to be classified as a guarantee so as to attract the full range of the doctrines evolved in equity for the protection of guarantors depends upon the nature of the obligations thereby created. That, in turn, depends upon the correct interpretation of the particular words in which the parties have expressed the promise.

The court delineated a contract of guarantee: [GPP(2018): para 123].

> One touchstone which distinguishes contracts of guarantee, properly so called, from other contracts serving the same economic function is that, under a guarantee, the guarantor's liability is secondary and ancillary to that of the principal debtor. ... By contrast, an indemnity is a form of independent and primary obligation and so is not secondary to, nor dependent upon, the liability of any other obligor.

The court noted that a contract of guarantee could take at least two forms, including: [GPP(2018): para 124].

> One is a contract that creates a 'conditional obligation', ie a promise by the guarantor to pay or perform if the principal debtor fails to do so. The other is a contract which creates a 'see to it' obligation, i.e. an undertaking by the guarantor that the principal debtor will perform its contract with the creditor.

The court applied to clause 6 before it and noted that it contained pointers in both the directions and commented that words were not determinative: [GPP(2018): para 125].

> Just as it is clear that the use of the word "guarantee" is not in itself conclusive, the use of the word "indemnity" is similarly no more than a pointer. In one sense all contracts of guarantee (strictly so called) are contracts of indemnity (as indeed are many contracts of insurance): and it would be possible to read clause 6.2 as merely describing the consequences of the "see to it" guarantee promise given in clause 6.1. Clause 6.2 does not expressly state that Solar's liability is to be as primary obligor and not merely as guarantor.

The court on balance characterised the instrument as an indemnity. The court gave effect to the words used in the clause: [GPP(2018): para 126].

> The promise given in clause 6.2 is described as "a separate and independent obligation and liability". It is expressed as a promise to "indemnify"; and it is written in the language characteristic of indemnities, focusing on the "loss, debt, damage, interest, cost and expense incurred" by the first claimant, and promising to pay that amount without set-off or deduction.

Thus, clause 6.2 was constructed to be an indemnity and admitted of no exception, requiring Solar to indemnify GPP.

The Wuhan Shipbuilding Case

Wuhan Guoyu Logistics Group Co Ltd and Yangzhou Guoyu Shipbuilding Co. Ltd operated a shipyard in Yangzhou in the People's Republic of China. [Wuhan Guoyu Logistics Group Co Ltd v Emporiki Bank of Greece SA., (2012) EWCA Civ 1629. Hereafter Wuhan (2012).] They entered into a contract for the construction and sale of two ships to Swissmarine Inc of Liberia. Under article 3(b) of the shipbuilding contract, the second instalment of US$10,312,500 was payable within five New York banking days of receipt by the buyer of a refund guarantee issued by the seller's bank together with a certificate of the cutting of the first steel plate of the vessel in the seller's workshop. The article provided that the seller: [Wuhan (2012): para 4].

> shall notify with a telefax notice to the Buyer stating that the 1st 300 mt of steel plate has been cut in its workshop approved by the Buyer's representative and demand for payment of this instalment.'

Under clause 7 of the shipbuilding contract, payments were to be refunded in the event that the contract was rescinded or cancelled in accordance with the terms of the contract.

Emporiki Bank of Greece SA is a Greek bank, which provided finance to the buyer for its purchase of the vessel. By a deed of assignment, the buyer assigned to the Bank all moneys and claims including 'the refund guarantee and any other guarantee given to the buyer as security for money due to it under the shipbuilding contract' [Wuhan (2012): para 9]. Notice of the assignment was given to the seller and the seller accepted the assignment.

The first instalment was paid. The bank issued 'the payment guarantee' in respect of the second instalment of the price of the vessel under the shipbuilding contract. The instrument provided as follows: [Wuhan (2012): para 12].

> Dear Sirs,
>
> (1) In consideration of your entering into a Shipbuilding Contract dated 29th November 2006 ("the Shipbuilding Contract") … we, EMPORIKI BANK OF GREECE SA, hereby IRREVOCABLY, ABSOLUTELY and UNCONDITIONALLY guarantee, as the primary obligor and not merely as the surety, the due and punctual payment by the BUYER of the 2nd instalment of the Contract Price …
>
> (2) ….
>
> (3) We also IRREVOCABLY, ABSOLUTELY and UNCONDITIONALLY guarantee, as primary obligor and not merely as surety, the due and punctual payment by the BUYER of interest on the second Instalment guaranteed … from and including the first day after the date of instalment in default until the date of full payment by us of such amount guaranteed hereunder.
>
> (4) In the event that the BUYER fails to punctually pay the second Instalment guaranteed hereunder or the BUYER fails to pay any interest thereon, and any such default continues for a period of twenty (20) days, then, upon receipt by us of your first written demand stating that the Buyer has been in default of the payment obligation for twenty (20) days, we shall immediately pay to you or your assignee the unpaid 2nd Instalment, together with the Interest as specified in paragraph (3) hereof, without requesting you to take any or further action, procedure or step against the BUYER or with respect to any other security which you may hold.
>
> (5) We hereby agree that at your option this Guarantee and the undertaking …
>
> (6) …
>
> (7) Our obligations under this Guarantee shall not be affected or prejudiced by any disputes between you as the SELLER and the BUYER under the Shipbuilding Contract or by the SELLER's delay in the construction and/or delivery of the VESSEL due to whatever causes or by any variation or extension of their terms thereof or by any security or other indemnity now or hereafter held by you in respect thereof, or by any time or indulgence granted by

> you or any other person in connection therewith, or by any invalidity or unenforceability of the terms thereof, or by any act, omission, fact or circumstances whatsoever, which could or might, but for the foregoing, diminish in any way our obligations under this Guarantee.

The first cutting of steel for the vessel is said by the seller to have taken place on 18 April 2009. No representative of the buyer was present and there has been a dispute as to whether the steel cutting took place at all. The seller provided a refund guarantee which the buyer contended was not in the appropriate form. Thus, the parties got in dispute over the performance of the contract. The buyer contended in respect of the second instalment: [Wuhan (2012): para 18].

> (a) that there is no proof that the first 300 mt of steel for the vessel has, in fact, been cut; (b) that the condition of approval by the buyer of such cutting has not been met; and (c) that the seller has not provided in respect of the second instalment the refund guarantee required by the shipbuilding contract, namely a guarantee in the form finally approved by the banks of the buyer and the seller.

Both the seller and the buyer claim that the other party was in repudiatory breach and that they have terminated the contract. The seller claimed the encashment of the payment guarantee issued by the bank. The seller claimed that the payment guarantee was in the nature of a demand or performance bond. Payment was due upon a written demand, whether or not the payment which the bond 'guarantees' is actually due by the buyer to the seller. The Bank contends that the instrument is a guarantee properly so-called. If the second instalment is not due, there can be no liability for the bank to pay under the guarantee. The question before the court was whether the instrument issued by the bank was a demand bond or a proper guarantee.

The Court of Appeal noted that the judge of the High court 'did not find this case particularly easy and neither do I'. The difficulty in the case was that there were pointers in different directions. The court listed the following points in favour of the document being a traditional guarantee.

1. The document was called a 'payment guarantee' not an 'on-demand bond'.
2. Clause 1 states that the guaranteed 'the due and punctual payment by the Buyer of the 2nd instalment'.
3. Clause 3 guarantees the due and punctual payment of interest.
4. Clause 4 requires the bank to pay 'in the event that the Buyer fails punctually to pay the second instalment'.
5. Clause 7 is typical of guarantee contracts, insisting on non-release of the guarantor even if the main contract is changed.

The court listed the following points in favour of the document being an 'on-demand' bond.

1. Clause 4 states that the bank has to pay immediately on the first written demand of the seller.
2. Clause 7 provides that the obligations of the bank are not affected or prejudiced by any dispute between the seller and the buyer.
3. Clause 10 provides a limit to the guarantee and does not envisage any further delays or accumulations.

The Court of Appeal noted on the pointers in both the directions: [Wuhan (2012): para 25].

> In deciding whether the document is a traditional 'see to it' guarantee or an 'on-demand' guarantee, it would be obviously absurd to say that there are six pointers in favour of the former and only four pointers in favour of the latter and it must therefore be the former. But if the law does not permit boxes to be ticked in this way, commercial men will need some assistance from the courts in determining their obligations.

The court stated the way forward in making a resolution: [Wuhan (2012): para 25].

> The only assistance which the courts can give in practice is to say that, while everything must in the end depend on the words actually used by the parties, there is nevertheless a presumption that, if certain elements are present in the document, the document will be construed in one way or the other.

The court found 'exactly this kind of assistance' in *Paget's Law of Banking, edition 11,* under the heading 'Contract of suretyship v. demand guarantee' and quoted as below: [Wuhan (2012): para 26].

> Where an instrument (i) relates to an underlying transaction between the parties in different jurisdictions, (ii) is issued by a bank, (iii) contains an undertaking to pay "on demand" (with or without the words "first" and/or "written") and (iv) does not contain clauses excluding or limiting the defences available to a guarantor, it will almost always be construed as a demand guarantee. …
>
> In construing guarantees it must be remembered that a demand guarantee can hardly avoid making reference to the obligation for whose performance the guarantee is security. A bare promise to pay on demand without any reference to the principal's obligation would leave the principal even more exposed in the event of a fraudulent demand because there would be room for argument as to which obligations were being secured.

The court noted that every document has to be construed in accordance with its terms and concluded that 'the document sued on is an on-demand guarantee' [Wuhan (2012): para 33].

Shanghai Shipyard Co. Ltd. v Reignwood International Investment (Group) Company Limited

Shanghai Shipyard Co. Ltd is a company incorporated in the People's Republic of China. [Shanghai Shipyard Co. Ltd. v Reignwood International Investment (Group) Company Limited, (2021) EWCA Civ 1147. Hereafter Shanghai (2021).] As the name suggests, the company is operating a shipyard in Shanghai and provides ship-building and ship repairing services. Reignwood International Investment (Group) Company is a Hong Kong company. It is a part of an international multi-industrial conglomerate first established in Thailand in 1984. Reignwood offers investment services and invests in airport construction, metal processing, food manufacturing and technology sectors.

Shanghai Shipyard Co. Ltd (builder) entered into a contract with Reignwood International Investment (Group) Company (Reignwood) on 21 September 2011 to build an offshore drillship hull, Tiger 1, for a total price of US$ 200 million. Reignwood was only an investor, working with other individuals who would be operating the vessel. The parties formed a single-purpose vehicle, Opus Tiger 1 Pte. Ltd., in Singapore. Through novation, Opus Tiger 1 Pte. Ltd., became the buyer of the vessel. The buyer was to pay the price in three instalments. The final instalment of US$170 million became due upon delivery. Within the contract, Reignwood gave an 'Irrevocable Payment Guarantee' to support the buyer's obligation to pay the final instalment to the builder.

The builder gave a notice of completion of the vessel to the buyer on 12 December 2016. Within the contract, the builder made a demand on 11 January 2017 on the buyer to pay the final instalment. The buyer failed to pay the final instalment. Following this, on 23 May 2017, the builder made a demand on Reignwood to pay the amount under the guarantee. Alongside, the buyer had claimed that the vessel had short comings and was not in a deliverable stage. As Reignwood failed to pay, the builder initiated proceedings to claim the amount before the British court, which had jurisdiction within the contract. After the demand was made by the builder, arbitration Reignwood started arbitration proceedings against the builder and Opus Tiger 1 Pte. Ltd. The dispute was whether the guarantee was payable on the demand of the buyer or a 'see to it' guarantee that the buyer performed its duties. The dispute came before the Court of Appeal.

The Court of Appeal summarised the law and principles of guarantees: [Shanghai (2021): para 22].

> Suretyship ... in the modern era has come to be known more commonly as a guarantee. A traditional guarantee by way of suretyship is an undertaking by the guarantor to be answerable for the debt or obligation of another if that other defaults. Traditional guarantees by way of suretyship are sometimes called "see to it" guarantees.

Guarantee use varied terminologies. The surety is alternately called guarantor. The principal is also called debtor or obligor. Correspondingly, the beneficiary is also called creditor or obligee. The essential feature of such guarantees is the liability of the guarantor is secondary to the liability of obligor/debtor. In some cases, however, the guarantor can take further obligations of the debtor onto himself independently. In this case, the court noted: [Shanghai (2021): para 22].

> ... the default of the obligor gives rise to an independent and primary liability of the guarantor, who is liable and in breach of his obligation by the very fact of default by the obligor without more; hence the "see to it" characterisation of the guarantor's obligation. I shall refer to such an instrument as a surety guarantee.

The court introduced a third kind of a guarantee where there is an undertaking to pay a sum on demand irrespective of the liability of the obligor/debtor. The court noted on these documents: [Shanghai (2021): para 23].

> Such undertakings are also commonly termed guarantees, but their defining characteristic for present purposes is that they are payable on or by reference to an event, namely the demand,

> and without reference to the obligor's liability. The demand may have to be in prescribed form, and/or may have to be accompanied by prescribed documents, but it is the demand which triggers the liability to pay. I shall refer to such undertakings as demand guarantees.

A surety guarantee may also require a demand to be made for the payment, in addition to the requirement of the liability of the debtor. In this case, 'a requirement for a demand is not itself determinative' [Shanghai (2021): para 23]. It is only a variation of the standard suretyship arrangement. In contrast, the court noted: [Shanghai (2021): para 23].

> ... a demand is of the very essence of a demand guarantee. The defining characteristic of a demand guarantee, for present purposes, is that the guarantor's obligation to pay arises by reason of the demand, without the beneficiary having to establish a liability of the obligor.

The court further noted that the liability of the obligor is not irrelevant to a demand guarantee as a demand can be made only in good faith. For this reason, the court noted: [Shanghai (2021): para 24].

The demand must say in what respect the obligor is in breach of its obligations under the underlying relationship. ... Demand guarantees therefore necessarily have to make reference to the obligations for which they provide security.

There are further reasons for the demand making reference to the underlying obligations of the obligor. After the demand is paid, if it turns out that the debt or the obligation was not owned by the obligor, the excess amount would have to be restored to the obligor. In this context, the court noted: [Shanghai (2021): para 25].

> A demand guarantee provides that where there is a dispute, the guarantor must "pay now and argue later". It would be surprising if it gave the beneficiary a "pay now and never have to argue" entitlement. If that be right, the underlying liability for which the demand guarantee is security remains relevant to the ultimate accounting between the parties.

A demand guarantee can also have conditions attached to it, for example, happening of an even, for example, an arbitration award. The court analysed it: [Shanghai (2021): para 25].

> Guarantees ... in which case they may be described as a conditional bond. Analytically demand guarantees form a subset of conditional bonds in this sense, the demand being merely one type of event upon which liability may be conditional.

The purpose of a surety guarantee is to provide the creditor with security against the risk of failure of the contract arising from 'the financial or commercial probity of the obligor' [Shanghai (2021): para 27]. The beneficiary is concerned that the guarantor is reliable and has 'sufficient financial and commercial probity' and 'the obligation can readily be enforced in an accessible jurisdiction' [Shanghai (2021): para 27]. The court considered this as 'usually an important consideration' [Shanghai (2021): para 27] in shipbuilding contracts and illustrated it: [Shanghai (2021): para 27].

> Ownership of ships is often vested in companies with no other business or assets, which are incorporated in jurisdictions which offer not only tax advantages but secrecy as to beneficial ownership of so called "one ship companies". Shipbuilding contracts are often made with

such special purpose vehicles, who during construction are "no ship companies", with no assets other than the shipbuilding contract itself, the benefit of which may be mortgaged to the person financing the purchase, and beneficial ownership of which may change hands without the knowledge of the shipbuilder.

For these reasons, a shipbuilding contract is therefore 'a paradigm example of cases in which one party, the shipbuilder, needs protection from counterparty risk' [Shanghai (2021): para 27]. A demand guarantee also meets the ends of reducing counterparty risk. It, however, serves additional purpose of cashflow. The court noted: [Shanghai (2021): para 28].

In the shipbuilding context, as in other areas of commerce, cashflow is important, and is sometimes described as the lifeblood of the business. It is as important for a buyer, who will often have financing obligations, as it is for a builder, whose ability to fund the building of the vessel in question or other vessels depends upon timeous receipt of the instalments.

The court stated that the principles for interpreting the document to be 'the well-established rules of construction' [Shanghai (2021): para 32], where effect has to be given 'the words used by the parties and the commercial context in which they are used' [Shanghai (2021): para 35]. The court applied to the payment guarantee. An edited version of the document is below.

"IRREVOCABLE PAYMENT GUARANTEE

To: Shanghai Shipyard Co., Ltd...

1. In consideration of your entering into the Shipbuilding Contract with [Reignwood] as the buyer ("the Owner") for the construction of one (1) self propelled drill ship with Shipyard's Hull No. S6030 ("the Drillship"), we, [Reignwood] hereby IRREVOCABLY, ABSOLUTELY and UNCONDITIONALLY guarantee in accordance with the terms hereof, as the primary obligor and not merely as the surety, the due and punctual payment by the OWNER of the Final Instalment of the Contract Price amounting to a total sum of United States Dollar US$170,000,000 as specified in (2) below... .

2. The instalments guaranteed hereunder, pursuant to the terms of the Contract, comprise the Final Instalment in the amount of U.S. Dollars One Hundred and Seventy Million (US$ 170,000,000) payable by the Owner.

3. We also IRREVOCABLY, ABSOLUTELY and UNCONDITIONALLY guarantee, as primary obligor and not merely as surety, the due and punctual payment by the Owner of interest on the Final Instalment guaranteed hereunder ....

4. In the event that the Owner fails to punctually pay the Final instalment guaranteed hereunder in accordance with the Contract or the Owner fails to pay any interest thereon, and any such default continues for a period of fifteen (15) days, then, upon receipt by us of your first written demand, we shall immediately pay to you or your assignee all unpaid Final instalment, together with the interest as specified in paragraph. (3) hereof, without requesting you to take any or further action, procedure or step against the Owner or with respect to any other security which you may hold.

The court observed that the guarantee put in its commercial context, 'points in neither direction'. The court turned to the language of the document. The court found the following critical strongly bringing out that the document was a demand guarantee.

1. In clause 1 and 3 words the words "ABSOLUTELY and UNCONDITIONALLY" were capitalised. The court noted that 'this language would convey to a businessman is that the obligations were not conditional on the liability of the Buyer' [Shanghai (2021): para 37].
2. Clause 1 has words 'as the primary obligor and not merely as the surety'. The court noted that this 'is a clear indication that the document is not a surety guarantee'. It is 'at the heart of the obligation which is identified by clause 1 of the document' [Shanghai (2021): para 37].
3. Clause 4 has the words "upon receipt by us of your first written demand". The court noted this to be Payment 'the hallmark of a demand guarantee' [Shanghai (2021): para 37].
4. Clause 4 has the words "[upon receipt by us of your first written demand] we shall immediately pay to you…" The court noted: [Shanghai (2021): para 37]

> Immediate payment would not be appropriate in the case of a surety guarantee, in which some period would be needed for the guarantor to investigate and form a view on whether there was an underlying liability to make the final instalment payment under the Shipbuilding Contract.

The court, thus, concluded that the document was a demand guarantee.

There was a second issue to be resolved in the case. The guarantee had made the following proviso:

> In the event that there exists dispute between the Owner and Builder as to whether:
>
> (i) the Owner is liable to pay to the Builder the Final Instalment; and
>
> (ii) the Builder is entitled to claim the Final Instalment from the Owner,
>
> and such dispute is submitted either by the Owner or by you for arbitration in accordance with Clause 17 of the Contract, we shall be entitled to withhold and defer payment until the arbitration award is published. We shall not be obligated to make any payment to you unless the arbitration award orders the Owner to pay the Final Instalment. If the Owner fails to honour the award, then we shall pay you to the extent the arbitration award orders.

Reignwood claimed that as disputes have been taken to the arbitrator, it was freed from paying the builder till the arbitration award was finalised. The court noted on the proviso: [Shanghai (2021): para 54].

> It defines the circumstances in which the demand guarantee ceases to be payable on demand and becomes payable against an award. It provides, unsurprisingly, that the commencement of an arbitration is necessary to convert the obligation to become one to pay against an award. That is the natural meaning of the words: it requires not only that there is a dispute but also that the dispute "is submitted" to arbitration. Both are expressed as the condition on which the Guarantor is "entitled to withhold or defer payment."

The court, however, noted that the demand was made by the builder before disputes were submitted to the arbitrator. The proviso does not suggest that a right which is already accrued, suspended or remains pending till the award. The court ruled in favour of the builder on this issue also.

A contract of surety is a classical form of contract. In a contract of surety, a surety stands for the debt or default of a principal to the creditor. This classical form has taken varied forms in the modern era. The parties have come to be called surety and guarantor; principal, debtor and obligator; and creditor and oblige; and the contract, guarantee. In its traditional form, a guarantor stands for the debt or default of another. In this, the liability of the guarantor is secondary. In a variant, the guarantor takes additional and independent and primary liability. These are called 'see to it' guarantees. In this case, a breach by the debtor leads to primary obligations for the guarantor. A third form is a guarantee where there is an undertaking to pay a sum on demand irrespective of the liability of the obligor. While this is payable on demand, it needs to make reference to the obligations for which it provides security. A demand guarantee may have conditions attached to it. The different forms of guarantee form a spectrum but have very different rights and obligations. The courts use the well-established principles of interpretation of contracts and give effect to the text used in document by putting it in its commercial context.

References

GPP Big Field LLP v Solar EPC Solutions SL, (2018) EWHC 2866 (Comm)

Shanghai Shipyard Co. Ltd. v Reignwood International Investment (Group) Company Limited, (2021) EWCA Civ 1147

Vossloh Aktiengesellschaft v. Alpha Trains (UK) Limited, (2010) EWHC 2443 (Ch)

Wuhan Guoyu Logistics Group Co Ltd v Emporiki Bank of Greece SA., (2012) EWCA Civ 1629

Chapter 19
Interpreting Contract Terms

The contract is of the contracting parties, not the courts. When disputes come before the courts, the courts objectively assess the contract terms and give effect to them. If the meaning of a contract term is clear and it is capable of only one meaning, there can be no rival contentions. The problem arises if alternate constructions can be given to a contract term. The courts, over the decades, have developed principles for giving an objective meaning to the contract. The principles fall in three categories. One, the principles for interpreting the text of a contract by putting it in the context of the contract. Two, a contract may not have provided on an aspect or be silent on it. In this case, terms are implied in the contract to make the contract work. The courts have developed the principles for implying terms into contracts. Three, an exclusion clause limits or ousts the rights of a party. If there is an ambiguity in an exclusion clause, it should be resolved with the sensitivities to the right. The courts have developed principles for interpretation of exclusion clauses.

Interpretation of Contracts

In reading and understanding any text, one reads the texts as a whole, trying to integrate different parts of it. If there are doubts, as every text is in a context, one locates the text in its context to give meaning to it. The courts too have done this in interpreting contract terms. If the meaning of a contract term is clear, no dispute arises. However, if it is capable of rival meanings, the term could be read with the other terms in the contact to settle a meaning. A contract is about a transaction. The context of the contract is the exchange or the business. If there are rival constructions of a term, the term can be put in its business context to settle its meaning. The courts have recognised to read the text of the contract in its context.

In Wood v Capita [Wood v Capita Insurance Services Limited, (2017) UKSC 24. Hereafter Capita (2017).], the Supreme Court observed that the role of the courts

A. Pathak, *Contract Terms in International Business*,
https://doi.org/10.1007/978-981-96-8146-4_19

was in giving objective meaning to the language of the contract. This exercise was not to look at the words literally, pulling them out from the contract terms. Instead, the Supreme Court noted: [Capita (2017): para 10].

> … the court must consider the contract as a whole and, depending on the nature, formality and quality of drafting of the contract, give more or less weight to elements of the wider context in reaching its view as to that objective meaning.

The exercise, however, may lead to rival contentions. In this case, the court can give weight to a view which is 'more consistent with business common sense' [Capita (2017): para 11]. The exercise has to be done in a reiterative process where the commercial consequences of each interpretation are taken up. The court noted: [Capita (2017): para 12].

> To my mind once one has read the language in dispute and the relevant parts of the contract that provide its context, it does not matter whether the more detailed analysis commences with the factual background and the implications of rival constructions or a close examination of the relevant language in the contract, so long as the court balances the indications given by each.

Thus, if rival interpretations of contract terms come up, the rival interpretations have to be weighed within the text of the contract and the business context of the provision. The court noted on reading the text in its context:[Capita (2017): para 13].

> Textualism and contextualism are not conflicting paradigms in a battle for exclusive occupation of the field of contractual interpretation. Rather, the lawyer and the judge, when interpreting any contract, can use them as tools to ascertain the objective meaning of the language which the parties have chosen to express their agreement.

Thus, if there is rival construction on a contract term, it can be resolved by reading the contract term with the rest of the text of the contract; and the term and the contract in its business context.

Implying Terms into a Contract

A contract may not have contemplated and provided on an aspect of a contract. This is different from interpreting a contract. A textual and contextual interpretation of the contract will not fill the gap. The courts have developed the principles for implying terms from the context to make the contract complete. The United Kingdom Supreme Court formulated the principles for it in Marks and Spencer plc v BNP Paribas Services Trust Company (Jersey) Limited [Marks and Spencer plc v BNP Paribas Services Trust Company (Jersey) Limited (2015) UKSC 72].

Marks & Spencer, a United Kingdom retail chain store, in 2006, leased premises from BNP Paribas. Under the Lease, the rent was payable 'yearly and proportionately for any part of a year by equal quarterly instalments in advance on the usual quarter days'. The agreement had an exit clause. Marks & Spencer could terminate the lease by giving a six-month notice. Marks & Spencer gave a termination notice in July

2011 to bring the lease to an end on 24 January 2012. Alongside, within the terms of the contract, in December 2011, it had to pay for the quarter ending 24 March 2012.

It claimed a refund of rent for the period 24 January 2012 to 24 March 2012. It argued that as it did not occupy the premises, BNP should refund the amount. BNP refused and claimed that the parties had only followed the terms of the contract. The contract did not provide for a refund. Marks & Spencer conceded that the contract did not provide for a refund but contended that a refund should be implied into the lease. The United Kingdom Supreme Court thus summarised the principles it formulated in its judgment: [https://www.supremecourt.uk/cases/docs/uksc-2014-0158-press-summary.pdf].

> The judicial approach to the implication of contractual terms represents a clear, consistent and principled approach. A term will only be implied if it satisfies the test of business necessity or it is so obvious that it goes without saying; it will be a rare case where only one of those two requirements are met.

The court applied the principle to the case before it. It noted that it was a well-established common law principle that rent 'whether payable in arrear or advance, is not apportionable in time'. The court noted: [https://www.supremecourt.uk/cases/docs/uksc-2014-0158-press-summary.pdf].

> Given the clear, general understanding that neither the common law nor statute apportion rent payable in advance on a time basis, it would be wrong, save in a very clear case, to attribute to a landlord and a tenant, particularly where they have entered into a full and professionally drafted lease, an intention that the tenant should receive back an apportioned part of rent payable and paid in advance.

M&S argued that when the quarter rent, £919,800 plus VAT, was paid in December, it was known to both the parties that the lease would come to an end in January itself. It reasoned that 'commercial common sense therefore mandated that it should be in the same position whether it paid ... before or after 25 December 2011' [https://www.supremecourt.uk/cases/docs/uksc-2014-0158-press-summary.pdf]. The Supreme Court rejected the argument, noting: 'Any anomaly in the working of the lease does not establish that the contract is unworkable or that the result is commercially or otherwise absurd' [https://www.supremecourt.uk/cases/docs/uksc-2014-0158-press-summary.pdf]. Thus, working out the rent on a pro rata basis was neither so obvious that it went without saying nor did it make the renting itself completely unworkable.

The Court of Appeal in J N Hipwell & Son v Szurek [J N Hipwell & Son v Szurek (2018) EWCA Civ 674. Hereafter Hipwell (2018)] has summarised the principles of implying into a contract, developed by the Supreme Court. The court has stated:

1. First, the contract terms have to be interpreted to determine whether the contract expressly provides for it. Only after this exercise, can one move to exploring implying a term into the contract.
2. It could be that the parties deliberately had decided not to provide the term which is being sought to be implied. The court must take this possibility into account.
3. The reference frame for implying a term is to be 'judged at the date when the contract is made' [Hipwell (2018): para 30].

4. The test for implying a term is 'necessity, not reasonableness'. [Hipwell (2018): para 30] However, absolute necessity may be a steep requirement. It may be 'more helpful to ask the question whether without the term the contract would lack commercial or practical coherence' [Hipwell (2018): para 30].
5. Both, interpreting a contract term and implying term are for determining the meaning and scope of a contract. But the two are different exercises. Implying a term 'calls for strict restraint' [Hipwell (2018): para 30].

In Triple Point, the contract had provided for payment by the employer on a milestone basis [Triple Point Technology, Inc. v PTT Public Company Ltd, (2019) EWCA Civ 230. Hereafter Triple Point (2019)]. Triple Point contended to make the contract 'commercially workable, a term must be implied that Triple Point could suspend work in the event of non-payment' [Triple Point (2019): para 64]. Triple Point submitted that 'without the suggested implied term the contract would lack practical coherence' [Triple Point (2019): para 64]. The Court of Appeal disagreed. It noted: [Triple Point (2019): para 65].

> If PTT failed to make payments on the due dates, Triple Point would have all the usual remedies for non-payment. These would include suing for the money due, applying for summary judgment, treating non-payment as a repudiation and so forth. There was no need for the contract to incorporate a provision that Triple Point could suspend work for non-payment, even though from one party's point of view such a term would have been nice to have.

Triple Point contended that without the implied term, the contract would be 'wholly one-sided' [Triple Point (2019): para 65]. The court quipped, 'even if the contract were to favour one party strongly, that is no reason for the court to redress the balance by implying terms' [Triple Point (2019): para 65].

A clause which ousts or limits a right of a person is described as an exclusion clause. The approach of the courts in interpreting such terms has developed over the decades. The modern approach is to interpret the term like any other term of the contract. The requirement is that clear words must be used to oust or limit the rights. Nobahar-Cookson v Hut Group Ltd. [Nobahar-Cookson v Hut Group Ltd., (2016) EWCA Civ 128. Hereafter Nobahar (2016)] is a significant judgment which has consolidated the principle. We would explore the interpretation of exclusion clauses with the case.

Nobahar-Cookson v Hut Group Ltd.: the Contract

Mr Oliver Nobahar-Cookson was based in north England and started a company named Cend, trading as MyProtein. The company started trading in 2004. Its annual online sales of whey-based sports nutrition products grew to £27 m by September 2011. For tax purposes, Mr Cookson formed a trust in 2009. Mr Cookson held half the shares in Cend and the other half, with non-voting rights, came to be owned by the trust. Mr. Cookson got keen to sell the company and the business. He was represented by auditors and financial advisors to find a buyer.

The Hut Group Ltd (THG) was a company based in Northwich with an online retail business. It was set up in 2003 by Mr Moulding and had grown organically and significantly by way of acquisitions. Its revenue in 2013 was around £185 m. From about 2009, Mr Moulding was preparing for a future listing by way of Initial Public Offering (IPO) on the main market of the London Stock Exchange. A team of auditors and consultants were preparing numerous documents for the company. THG emerged as a potential buyer of the shares in Cend.

THG made an offer based on an enterprise value for Cend of £58 m. This is made up of £30 m in cash and the balance as shares in THG. A share purchase agreement (SPA) was entered between Mr Cookson and the trust as the seller, and THG as the buyer in May 2011. In performance of the contract, the seller transferred their shares in Cend Ltd to THG, and THG transferred shares in THG and paid the cash.

After the completion of the sale, THG claimed £8,567,085 as damages for breach of warranty regarding Cend's Management Accounts for the period 30 September 2010 to 30 March 2011. The seller counterclaimed £12.5 m as damages for breach of warranty regarding THG's Accounts and Management Accounts. The SPA had warranties for the buyer and seller. The seller warranted:

> "[Cend's] Management Accounts have been prepared on a basis consistent with that used in the preparation of [Cend's] Accounts and the past practice of the Business in the 12 months prior to the date of Completion [31 May 2011] and fairly present the assets and liabilities and profits and losses of [Cend] for the period from the Accounts Date [30 September 2010] to the Management Accounts Date [30 March 2011]"

The buyer, THG, warranted:

> The Buyer's Management Accounts have been prepared on a basis consistent with that used in the preparation of the Buyer's Accounts and the past practice of the business of the Buyer (Buyer's Business) in the 12 months prior to the date of Completion and fairly present the assets and liabilities of the Buyer as at the Buyer's Management Accounts Date and profits and losses of for the period from the Buyer's Accounts Date to the Buyer's Management Accounts Date."

The parties led proceedings in the Commercial Court claiming the warranties. The SPA had the following Clause 5.1 in Schedule 5 for the buyer to serve notice to claim warranties: [Nobahar (2016): para 5].

> 'The Sellers will not be liable for any Claim unless the Buyer serves notice of the Claim on the Sellers (specifying in reasonable detail the nature of the Claim and, so far is practicable, the amount claimed in respect it) as soon as reasonably practicable and in any event within 20 Business Days after becoming aware of the matter.'

The Buyer had served notice on 6 February 2012 of its warranty claim that Cend's Management Accounts did not give a true and fair view of Cend's financial position. The seller contended before the commercial court that the Buyer had become 'aware of the matter' by 9 January 2012 and was time-barred from making claims under clause 5.1. The dispute came before the Court of Appeal.

Nobahar-Cookson v Hut Group Ltd.: the Court of Appeal

The Buyer had served notice of its warranty claim under clause 5.1 on 6 February 2012. The parties were agreed that if the Sellers could show that the Buyer had become 'aware of the matter' within the meaning of clause 5.1 by 9 January 2012, the warranty claim of the buyer would be time-barred. The seller presented three alternative constructions of the phrase 'aware of the matter': [Nobahar (2016): para 9].

> (a) aware of the facts giving rise to the Claim (even if unaware that those facts did give rise to a claim);
>
> (b) aware that there might be a claim under the warranties; and,
>
> (c) aware of the Claim, in the sense of an awareness that there was a proper basis for the Claim.

The court noted on the three options: [Nobahar (2016): para 9].

> If the court was to prefer (a) or (b) over (c) then it is common ground that this appeal should be allowed. It is plain that interpretation (a) gives the broadest, and (c) the narrowest, effect to clause 5.1, and it is well-settled that contractual limitation periods for the notification or bringing of claims are forms of exclusion clause.

As a clause limiting the time period within which a claim should be made limits the rights of a person, it is taken to be an exclusion clause. The court noted the established principles on the interpretation of exclusion clauses: [Nobahar (2016): para 16].

> ... recent decisions about exclusion clauses have continued to affirm the utility of the principle that, if necessary to resolve ambiguity, they should be narrowly construed, including in relation to commercial contracts.

The court elaborated that an exclusion clause has to be narrowly constructed as: [Nobahar (2016): para 18].

> Ambiguity in an exclusion clause may have to be resolved by a narrow construction because an exclusion clause cuts down or detracts from the ambit of some important obligation in a contract, or a remedy conferred by the general law such as (in the present case) an obligation to give effect to a contractual warranty by paying compensation for breach of it.

The justification for narrowly constructing the terms is: [Nobahar (2016): para 18].

> The parties are not lightly to be taken to have intended to cut down the remedies which the law provides for breach of important contractual obligations without using clear words having that effect.

The court continued: [Nobahar (2016): para 19].

> Commercial parties are entitled to allocate between them the risks of something going wrong in their contractual relationship in any way they choose. Nor is it simply to be mechanistically applied wherever an ambiguity is identified in an exclusion clause.

Thus, the court set it up that it must use 'all its tools of linguistic, contextual, purposive and common-sense analysis' [Nobahar (2016): para 19] to determine the meaning of the clause. In doing this, it must keep the principle before it that 'parties do not normally give up valuable rights without making it clear that they intend to do so' [Nobahar (2016): para 19]. The court proceeded to construct clause 5.1 on the principle: [Nobahar (2016): para 21].

> … an ambiguity in its meaning may have to be resolved by a preference for the narrower construction, if linguistic, contextual and purposive analysis do not disclose an answer to the question with sufficient clarity.

The court first looked at the language of the clause.

Nobahar-Cookson v Hut Group Ltd.: Language

The court turned to the language employed to express the warranties and the limitations. It noted that the word 'claim' was used three times in clause 5.1. The contract defines it as 'any warranty claim'. This in turn has been defined in the contract as 'a claim by the Buyer for breach of a Warranty'. The seller contended that clause 5.1 uses the term 'aware of the matter' rather than 'aware of the claim'. Following this, the seller claims the contract intended to identify something other than the claim. The buyer countered that 'aware of the matter' must take the reader back to clause 5.1 to find out what it was. The only answer was the claim which was repeated three times in the clause. The court, using 'the natural meaning of language as the best guide to interpretation' [Nobahar (2016): para 29] did not find a clear answer. It recorded that the word 'matter' within clause 5.1 'does not clearly mean Claim and perhaps could not strictly do so' [Nobahar (2016): para 29]. The court concluded that a linguistic analysis has not given it the basis to choose among the three alternatives. The court proceeded: [Nobahar (2016): para 29].

> The natural meaning of the language is by no means so clear as to preclude serious consideration of the commerciality or otherwise of rival interpretations or, for that matter, to preclude recourse to the principle that ambiguous exclusion clauses should be construed narrowly.

Nobahar-Cookson v Hut Group Ltd.: Commerciality

The court next turned to put the contract and the clause in its commercial context. Appraising the contentions of the two sides, the court observed that option (b) 'requiring notification of a Claim when it was merely suspected, as so uncommercial that it ought to be rejected' [Nobahar (2016): para 34]. The same could not be said of the other two options (a) and (c). The court did not find either of the options commercially untenable. Becoming aware of a fact and investigating it to work out the claim and notify it to the other party does not 'seem to be so draconian that the parties cannot have intended it' [Nobahar (2016): para 35]. The court noted the purpose behind clause 5.1 was to push the buyer to expeditiously analyse and obtain advice once he got to know of a fact than 'keep it up its sleeve' [Nobahar (2016): para 32]. With this being the objective, it is 'better served by an interpretation which focuses upon awareness of the Claim than upon awareness of the underlying facts' [Nobahar (2016): para 37]. In conclusion, the court noted:

> Clause 5.1, interpreted as contended for by the Sellers, would make such a large inroad into the Buyer's entitlement to compensation for breach of warranty, for no sensible purpose, that it would have taken clearer words than the parties have chosen to use to achieve that result.

Thus, the court found both options (a) and (c) were commercially possible. It interpreted the clause narrowly to rule in favour of the buyer.

Persimmon Homes Ltd v Ove Arup & Partners Ltd

Barry is a seaside town in Welsh, close to Cardiff in the United Kingdom [Persimmon Homes Ltd v Ove Arup & Partners Ltd, (2017) EWCA Civ 373. Hereafter Persimmon (2017)]. It was once a thriving port through which much coal was exported. As coal mining came to a close in the UK, the docks got abandoned. In the early 1990s, Associated British Ports (ABP) and the Welsh Development Agency (WDA) decided to develop 170 acres of land adjacent to Barry Number 1 Dock. The project involved site clearance, reclamation and development of infrastructure.

ABP engaged Ove & Arup to advice on the project and supervise the work. ABP also engaged many other consultants and contractors. One of them was Berridges to investigate and report on the presence of contaminants, in particular asbestos. Investigating for contaminants was not surprising. Barry was a major industrial centre in the past, and most likely, asbestos was used for different purposes. Arup started their work in May 1992. There was a time lag of some four years before the parties got round to drawing up and executing a formal contract.

In February 1996, ABP and Arup entered into an appointment contract to provide engineering and environmental services. The scope of the contract included a wide range of advisory, design and supervisory services. The subject matter included testing for site contamination, traffic issues, archaeology, ecology, drainage, statutory services, road links, integration with rail links and compliance with local authority requirements.

After completing the regeneration project, ABP invited tenders for the purchase of the site. A consortium comprising Persimmon Homes Limited (Persimmon), Taylor Wimpey UK Limited (Taylor Wimpey) and BDW Trading Limited (BDW) was interested. The Consortium approached Arup for it to act as a consultant to help them develop a bid for the project. Arup and Consortium had several email exchanges and through this, the two entered into a contract for Arup to help develop a bid for the project. The Consortium put in a successful bid and purchased the site for £53 million in September 2007. The Consortium intended to develop the site for commercial and residential use.

In the course of the purchase negotiations, the Consortium discussed with Arup the possibility of Arup providing further professional services for developing the site. Arup put up a proposal listing several services it could provide and the parties entered into a contract in 2009. Arup were not the only engineers involved in the project. The Consortium also engaged the services of other consultants and specialist contractors. The Consortium had engaged Cuddy for groundworks. While doing excavation, Cuddy encountered asbestos. The Consortium was of the view that the quantity of asbestos was substantially more than they expected. This led them to claim that Arup had been negligent in failing to identify and report upon that asbestos at an early stage.

The Consortium and the constituent companies, Persimmon, Taylor Wimpey and BDW claimed damages against Arup for breach of contract and negligence. The claims were of two types. First, if Arup had properly advised, the Consortium would have bought the site for £51 million, rather than £53 million. Second, the late discovery of the asbestos caused the Consortium to incur additional costs which they could have avoided, if properly advised at an early stage. Arup denied liability. It contended that its liability, if any, in respect of the asbestos was excluded by clause 6.3 of the 2009 agreement and clause 4.3 of the warranties given to each of the Consortium companies. The dispute came before the Court of Appeal. The question was on the interpretation of clause 6.3 of the 2009 agreement and clause 4.3 of the warranties as 'the exemption clauses'. Clause 6.3 read: [Persimmon (2017): para 24].

> 6.3 The Consultant's aggregate liability under this Agreement whether in contract, tort (including negligence), for breach of statutory duty or otherwise (other than for death or personal injury caused by the Consultant's negligence) shall be limited to £12,000,000 (twelve million pounds) with the liability for pollution and contamination limited to £5,000,000 (five million pounds) in the aggregate. Liability for any claim in relation to asbestos is excluded.

Clause 4.3 of the contract read: [Persimmon (2017): para 26].

> 4.3 The Consultant's aggregate liability under this Deed whether in contract, tort (including negligence), for breach of statutory duty or otherwise (other than for death or personal injury caused by the Consultant's negligence) shall be limited to £5,000,000.00 (five million pounds) with the liability for pollution and contamination limited to £5,000,000.00 (five million pounds) in the aggregate. Liability for any claim in relation to asbestos is excluded.'

The court noted that both the exemption clauses have three separate limbs. The first is an overall limit of liability; the second is a limit on liability for pollution and contamination; and the third is an exclusion in relation to asbestos. There is no dispute between the parties on the first limb. It imposes a limit on the liabilities of Arup. The consortium interpreted limb 2 to mean that Arup had caused pollution and contamination by failing to advice on it. Arup countered that the interpretation made no sense. It was only engaged to investigate and advice about contamination. There was no 'possibility of Arup causing contamination to move from one place to another because of clumsy investigation procedures cannot possibly be the target of limb 2' [Persimmon (2017): para 45]. The parties advanced the same arguments on limb 3. The consortium contended that 'limb 3 applies to any claim for causing the spread of asbestos' [Persimmon (2017): para 46]. Arup contended that limb 3 related to any claim concerning asbestos.

The court noted that Arup's 'interpretation accords with the natural meaning of the words used' [Persimmon (2017): para 48]. From a commercial point also, 'it would be nonsensical for the parties to agree that Arup are not liable if asbestos is moved from one part of the site to another, but are liable if it is left in place' [Persimmon (2017): para 48] The court concluded: [Persimmon (2017): para 49].

> Both the language used by the parties and any application of business common sense lead to the same conclusion. Limb 2 of the exemption clauses limits Arup's liability for claims in relation to pollution and contamination to £5 million. Limb 3 of the exemption clauses excludes Arup's liability for claims in relation to asbestos.

The court then turned to the principles for interpretation of exemption clauses. It stated that in the past, the courts used to interpret the exemption clauses very stringently but in the recent years they have 'softened their approach to both indemnity clauses and exemption clauses' [Persimmon (2017): para 56]. The court noted: [Persimmon (2017): para 57].

> In major construction contracts the parties commonly agree how they will allocate the risks between themselves and who will insure against what. Exemption clauses are part of the contractual apparatus for distributing risk. There is no need to approach such clauses with horror or with a mindset determined to cut them down.

If a party takes a larger risk, it will charge for it and take appropriate insurance. A contractor or consultant takes lesser risk, it will 'presumably reflect that in the fees which they agree' [Persimmon (2017): para 57]. The court noted that clause 6 and clause 4 were integrated. It provided what risk Arup would accept and insure against and what risk it would not accept and insure against. All these were factored in the fee charged by Arup, even if it was not separately identified.

The contracting parties may dispute the meaning and application of a contract term. The courts have developed the principles for interpreting terms of a contract. The disputed term is read with the other terms in the contract to elucidate its meaning. Alongside, or in addition to it, the contract term is put in its business context. The term can also be put reiteratively within the text of the contract and the context. The court settle the meaning of a disputed term by this play of text and context. A contract may be silent on a question, that is, the contract may not have provided for it. In this case, the courts only imply a term which is so obvious that it goes without saying, or secures business efficacy to the contract. A contract term limiting or excluding a contractual right is called an exclusion clause. The courts in the past used to interpret exclusion clauses very stringently. Now, the exclusion clauses are interpreted like any other clause. The qualification which is put is clear words that must be used for limiting or excluding rights. The reason for this is the parties are not lightly to be taken to cut down their rights without using clear words.

References

https://www.supremecourt.uk/cases/docs/uksc-2014-0158-press-summary.pdf
J N Hipwell & Son v Szurek (2018) EWCA Civ 674
Marks and Spencer plc v BNP Paribas Services Trust Company (Jersey) Limited (2015) UKSC 72
Nobahar-Cookson v Hut Group Ltd., (2016) EWCA Civ 128
Persimmon Homes Ltd v Ove Arup & Partners Ltd, (2017) EWCA Civ 373
Triple Point Technology, Inc. v PTT Public Company Ltd, (2019) EWCA Civ 230
Wood v Capita Insurance Services Limited, (2017) UKSC 24

Chapter 20
Assignment

A person can ordinarily transfer his property to another person. Rights arising from a contract are also a form of property. Thus, ordinarily, a contracting party would be able to transfer his rights in the contract to a third party. The transfer of a right to another person is called assignment. A party to a contract, however, would not like to be exposed to deal with a third party. In several kinds of contracts, the party has a commercial interest in dealing with only the person he has contracted with. In other cases, the uncertainties of coming to owe obligations to a stranger are an undesirable prospect. At the same time, it is advantageous for the parties to have the freedom to deal with their rights as they wish. Thus, contracts attend to the question of assignment. A clause on assignment may read:

> Neither party may without the prior written consent of the other party assign a benefit or obligation imposed in this Agreement.

A distinction should be made between the assignment of a right and an obligation. It is common sense that one cannot freely transfer a liability. If this were allowed, a person could freely transfer the liability to an insolvent party or a financially weak party, nullifying the rights of the other party. Thus, assignment can only be of a right not an obligation. There is nothing called 'assignment of contract'. The term is imprecise and inaccurate. The House of Lords noted on the term in Linden Gardens Trust Ltd v Lenesta Sludge Disposals Ltd: [Linden Gardens Trust Ltd v Lenesta Sludge Disposals Ltd., (1994) 1 A.C. 85. Hereafter Linden (1994): page 103].

> It is trite law that it is, in any event, impossible to assign "the contract" as a whole, i.e. including both burden and benefit. The burden of a contract can never be assigned without the consent of the other party to the contract in which event such consent will give rise to a novation. Therefore one has to discover what the parties meant by this inelegant phrase.

A transfer of obligation can happen only with the consent of all the parties and this is called novation. In a novation, the existing contract is transformed into a new contract where the party owing responsibility steps out leaving the third party as the contracting party. The House of Lords commented: [Linden (1994): page 103].

A. Pathak, *Contract Terms in International Business*,
https://doi.org/10.1007/978-981-96-8146-4_20

> Although it is true that the phrase "assign this contract" is not strictly accurate, lawyers frequently use those words inaccurately to describe an assignment of the benefit of a contract since every lawyer knows that the burden of a contract cannot be assigned

If the phrase is used, the court has to 'discover what the parties meant by this inelegant phrase' [Linden (1994): page 103]. The principles of assignment have been given statutory force. Section 136 of the Law of Property Act 1925 provides:

> (1) Any absolute assignment by writing under the hand of the assignor (not purporting to be by way of charge only) of any debt or other legal thing in action, of which express notice in writing has been given to the debtor, trustee or other person from whom the assignor would have been entitled to claim such debt or thing in action, is effectual in law (subject to equities having priority over the right of the assignee) to pass and transfer from the date of such notice –
>
> (a) the legal right to such debt or thing in action;
>
> (b) all legal and other remedies for the same; and
>
> (c) the power to give a good discharge for the same without the concurrence of the assignor ...

A novation is an agreement among three parties A, B and C. A and B have a contract and rights and obligation to one another. C comes in and contracts with A and B and assumes all the rights and obligations of A. A new contract is formed between B and C and the original contract between A and B extinguished. All the parties must agree to the novation. The followings are the main differences between an assignment and novation: [The Argo Fund Ltd v Essar Steel Ltd (2005) EWHC 600: para 61].

> First, a novation requires the consent of all three parties involved ... But (in the absence of restrictions) an assignor can assign without the consent of either assignee or the debtor. Secondly, a novation involves the termination of one contract and the creation of a new one in its place. In the case of an assignment the assignor's existing contractual rights are transferred to the assignee, but the contract remains the same and the assignor remains a party to it so far as obligations are concerned. Thirdly a novation involves the transfer of both rights and obligations to the new party, whereas an assignment concerns only the transfer of rights.

We can explore assignment and novation with the following review of cases.

Linden Gardens Trust Ltd v Lenesta Sludge Disposals Ltd

Stock Conversion and Investment Trust Plc. (Stock Conversion) was the owner of a leasehold interest in third to sixth floor of a building in London [Linden (1994)]. In June 1979, it entered into a contract with McLaughlin and Harvey Plc. (MH) to remove blue asbestos from the property. Clause 17 of the contract provided:

> (1) The employer shall not without the written consent of the contractor assign this contract.
>
> (2) The contractor shall not without the written consent of the employer assign this contract...

MH appointed Lenesta Sludge Disposals Ltd as a subcontractor to do the work. MH completed the work on 25 March 1980 and was paid for it. Later, Stock Conversion found more asbestos on the property, which MW should have removed. In February 1985, Stock Conversion entered into a contract with Ashwell Construction for removal of this asbestos. On 3 July 1985, Stock Conversion initiated court proceedings against Lenesta Sludge Disposals Ltd and MH to claim damages for the deficient work. The second contract was completed in August 1985 and Stock Conversion paid the contractor.

Alongside, on 1 April 1985, Stock Conversion assigned to Linden Gardens Trust Ltd. (Linden Gardens) its leasehold interest in the third, fifth and sixth floors. In December 1986, Stock Conversion assigned its leasehold interest in the fourth floor to Linden Gardens. As Stock Conversion had no interest left in the property, it executed a deed of assignment in favour of Linden Gardens to pursue the court action to claim the damages. The deed read: [Linden (1994): page 100].

> In pursuance of the said agreement and in consideration of the sum of One pound (the receipt of which sum the assignors hereby acknowledge) the assignors hereby assign to the assignees, (a) all their rights of action as pleaded in the said proceedings or otherwise ... (b) all other rights of action currently vested in the assignors which are or were incidental to their leasehold in the said premises."

Clause 17(1) of the contract required Stock Conversion to secure a written consent of MH to the assignment. MH refused to give the written consent. In 1987 and 1988, Linden Gardens found yet more asbestos in the premises. Linden Gardens took up further work to have the asbestos removed and bore the cost of it. Linden Gardens initiated court proceedings against all the past contractors for damages for not having removed the asbestos. The dispute was whether Stock Conversion had assigned the rights to it to proceed with legal action and claim damages.

The House of Lords, in this landmark case, highlighted that the phrase 'assign this contract' was inaccurate and imprecise wording. It pointed out that only rights can be assigned and not obligations. A contract has both rights and obligations. For this reason, a contract cannot be assigned, it can only be novated with the consent of all the parties. However, lawyers use the term and it is not fatal. The court has to 'discover what the parties meant by this inelegant phrase' [Linden (1994): page 103]. The court readily concluded that 'clause 17(1) of the contract prohibited the assignment by the employer of the benefit of the contract' [Linden (1994): page 103].

An assignment of the rights in a contract gives two rights to the assignee. One, the assignee gets all the rights which have already accrued under the contract. Two, the assignee gets all the rights to require the future performance of the contract. The distinction was highlighted and contended before the court that clause 17 only prohibited the assignments of the right to future performance of the contract and not the rights which had already accrued. The House of Lords noted: [Linden (1994): page 105].

> In the context of a complicated building contract, I find it impossible to construe clause 17 as prohibiting only the assignment of rights to future performance, leaving each party free to assign the fruits of the contract. The reason for including the contractual prohibition

> viewed from the contractor's point of view must be that the contractor wishes to ensure that he deals, and deals only, with the particular employer with whom he has chosen to enter into a contract.

In a building contract, the parties have numerous claims and counter claims. Much confusion would arise if a third party were brought in and the rights forked in the two categories. The court concluded: [Linden (1994): page 106].

> … parties who have specifically contracted to prohibit the assignment of the contract cannot have intended to draw a distinction between the right to performance of the contract and the right to the fruits of the contract. In my view they cannot have contemplated a position in which the right to future performance and the right to benefits accrued under the contract should become vested in two separate people.

The House of Lords recognised that the parties are, of course, free to distinguish the two rights and treat them differently. However, it could be done only with 'careful and intricate drafting' [Linden (1994): page 106]. The court noted: [Linden (1994): page 106].

> But in the absence of such a clearly expressed intention, it would be wrong to attribute such a perverse intention to the parties. In my judgment, clause 17 clearly prohibits the assignment of any benefit of or under the contract.

The court concluded that 'the purported assignment to Linden Gardens without the consent of the contractors constituted a breach of clause 17' [Linden (1994): page 106].

The Energy Works Case: The Contract

Energy Works (Hull) Ltd (EWHL) entered into a contract with MW High Tech Projects UK Ltd (MW) as its main contractor for the design, procurement, construction, commissioning and testing of a waste-to-energy plant in the north of England. [Energy Works (Hull) Limited v MW High Tech Projects UK Limited, (2020) EWHC 2537 (TCC). Hereafter MW (2020).] The contract was based on the IChemE Red Book, with bespoke amendments (the Main Contract). The Main Contract provided for the appointment of subcontractors. MW appointed Outotec (USA) Inc (Outotec) as the subcontractor to supply elements for the plant. The subcontract was also based on the IChemE Yellow Book. Both the contracts had elaborate provisions.

The project ran into difficulty including significant delays and defects which could not be rectified. EWHL terminated the main contract within the terms of the contract. Clause 44.3(d) of the contract provided, that on termination of the contract '(d) the Contractor shall, if so required by the Purchaser and to the extent permitted by the subcontract, assign any subcontract to the Purchaser' [MW (2020): para 23]. Exercising the right, EWHL served a notice on MW requiring it to assign the sub-Contract. The sub-Contract had several warranties from Outotec. Clause 4.1 of the warranty read: [MW (2020): para 38].

> 4.1 If the employment of the Main Contractor under the Main Contract is terminated, the Beneficiary may within 28 days after the date of termination give notice requiring the Sub-Contractor to enter into a new contract (New Contract) with the Beneficiary or its appointee on the same terms as the Sub-Contract, executed as a deed, but with such revisions as the Beneficiary may reasonably require to reflect altered circumstances, for the continuation and completion of the Sub-Contract Works; and the Sub-Contractor shall comply with such notice.

Alongside, using the warranty, EWHL gave notice to Outotec requiring 'as the Sub-Contractor, to enter into a New Contract with us, the Beneficiary, subject to agreement on terms' [MW (2020): para 49].

Clause 9.1 of the sub-Contract made a corresponding provision that 'if so required by the Purchaser under the Main Contract the Contractor may assign the Subcontract to the Purchaser' [MW (2020): para 27]. Following the provisions, MW assigned the subcontract to EWHL. EWHL and Outotec were still negotiating the terms of their agreement.

The net effect of the arrangement was as MW was in breach, it was liable to EWHL for damages. However, it had no rights against Outotec who was in breach of the subcontract as MW had assigned the rights to EWHL. In a letter to EWHL, MW stated: [MW (2020): para 54].

> However, it appears that M+W no longer has the benefit of these rights under these subcontracts, including the right to enforce performance of the subcontract and bringing claims.
>
> Having exercised its right to assign all subcontracts, EWH has deprived M+W of its ability to enforce performance of the subcontracts and to bring claims.

There was no dispute between the parties that there was a valid assignment of the Subcontract by MW to EWHL. The dispute was on the effect of the assignment. The questions were, one, did the assignment transfer all benefits, including accrued benefits, or only future rights under the Sub-Contract? Two, if the assignment has transferred all benefits, then, have all the obligations also have been transferred, amounting to a novation?

The Energy Works Case: Assignment

The court summarised the principles of assignment after a review of the Linden Gardens Case: [MW (2020): para 62].

> (i) Subject to any express contractual restrictions, a party to a contract can assign the benefit of a contract, but not the burden, without the consent of the other party to the contract.
>
> (ii) In the absence of any clear contrary intention, reference to assignment of the contract by the parties is understood to mean assignment of the benefit, that is, accrued and future rights.
>
> (iii) It is possible to assign future rights under a contract without the accrued rights but clear words are needed to give effect to such intention.

The starting point has to be 'the words used by the parties in the relevant contracts and notices'[MW (2020): para 67]. The contract terms and the correspondence among the parties had used the term assign the subcontract. The court noted: [MW (2020): para 67].

A natural and ordinary reading of the words used in the Main Contract and Sub-Contract leads to the conclusion that the agreement to *"assign the Sub-Contract"* was an agreement to assign all MW's benefits under the Sub-Contract to EWHL, both future rights and accrued rights. ... this is what parties usually mean when they refer to assigning a contract.

The contract terms and the correspondence between the parties did not bring out that 'the parties intended to separate future and accrued rights for the purpose of the assignment' [MW (2020): para 68]. The parties are free to limit the rights that are being assigned but only by clear drafting. But there 'is no careful drafting in the Main Contract or Sub-Contract or in a bespoke assignment notice or deed, setting out the parties' intention to divide the accrued and future rights under the Sub-Contract as between MW and EWHL' [MW (2020): para 69]. The court noted that the 'parties could have used clear words to indicate that the permitted assignment was limited to future rights but there are no such words' [MW (2020): para 72].

The court recognised that MW has taken a commercial risk by the arrangement to assigning its rights against the subcontractor to the employer. The court, however, noted: [MW (2020): para 77].

> It is not for the Court to re-write the contractual arrangements entered into by the parties or to impose what it considers would be an equitable and fair commercial bargain by reference to the events that have unfolded. Effect must be given to the clear provisions for assignment.

Thus, MW had assigned all the accrued and future right of the subcontract to EWHL. The next question was, were all its obligations also transferred making it a novation.

The Energy Works Case: Novation

The court explored and summarised the principles of novation as the following points. One, in a novation, the original contract between A and B is extinguished and replaced by a new contract between A and C. It requires 'the consent of all parties to the original and new contract' [MW (2020): para 95]. The consent can be given in the original contract itself. However, 'clear words are needed to express such intention and the terms of the new contract must be sufficiently certain to be enforceable' [MW (2020): para 95]. Whether a novation has been created or not will depend on the intentions of the parties as expressed in the contract. The court must not confine the interpretation exercise to 'the descriptions or labels used by the parties' but apply 'the established rules of construction'[MW (2020): para 95]. Interpreting the terms of the contracts, the court noted: [MW (2020): para 98].

The use of the words *"assign the Sub-Contract"* in the Main Contract and in the Sub-Contract are very strong indications that the parties intended assignment and not novation. … there are no words in any of the relevant documents that indicate an intention to extinguish the Sub-Contract and replace it with a new sub-contract.

The court noted: [MW (2020): para 100].

Novation and assignment are very different legal concepts and it must be assumed that the parties meant what they said in referring to assignment rather than novation.

In the cases where advance consent to novation is given, the terms of the new contract would be 'identical in all material respects to the existing contract'. However, in this case, the court noted: [MW (2020): para 104].

… the proposed terms of any new contract between EWHL and Outotec would not be identical to the terms of the Sub-Contract; the terms of any new contract were not identified, let alone agreed, at the date of the original contracts.

The court took the point further and noted: [MW (2020): para 106].

Therefore, even if the reference to assignment could be construed as consent to novation of the Sub-Contract, the parties did not reach agreement on the terms of the intended novation. It follows that there was no novation of the Sub-Contract.

The court, thus, concluded that MW had assigned all its accrued and future rights in the subcontract with Outotec to EWHL and the assignment was not a novation. In the next case, we see the effects when a written consent to assignment is not give.

Sumitomo Mitsui Banking Corporation Europe Limited v Euler Hermes Europe SA (NV)

Derbyshire City Council was the public body intending to create a facility for waste treatment. [Sumitomo Mitsui Banking Corporation Europe Limited v Euler Hermes Europe SA (NV), (2019) EWHC 2250 (Comm). Hereafter Sumitomo (2019)] At the other end, in the Public Private Partnership, there were several companies involved in creating the project company and securing investments. The Council entered into a contract, termed the Project Agreement, with Resource Recovery Solutions Derbyshire Ltd (RRS), as the project company. RRS was responsible for designing, constructing, commissioning and operating the facility. RRS procured funding from the lenders and contracted with Interserve Construction Ltd (ICL) for the design, construction, commissioning and completion of the Facility. Under the Construction Contract, ICL was responsible for discharging substantially all RRS's obligations under its contract with the Council.

Under the terms of the Construction Contract, ICL provided RRS a performance bond against ICL turning insolvent and defaulting on the construction project. The performance bond was issued by Euler Hermes Europe SA (NV) (EH) and was in favour of RRS. RRS assigned its rights of being a beneficiary of the bond to the lender for the project as security. A dispute would arise whether the assignment was successful. The relevant terms in the performance bond were: [Sumitomo (2019): para 15].

Assignment

> Subject to the assignee confirming to the Bondsman in writing its acceptance of the Employer's repayment obligation pursuant to clause 8, the Employer may assign the benefit of this Bond to any party (or trustee or agent thereof) acquiring an interest in the Works and/or providing finance in respect of the Works or taking an assignment of the Contract under and in accordance with the terms of the Contract or the Senior Lenders' Direct Agreement (as such term is defined in the Contract) but, otherwise, this bond, or its benefit, may not be assigned without the prior written agreement of the Bondsman.

Non-Waiver

> 12.1 No failure or delay by either party in exercising any right or remedy under this Bond shall operate as a waiver; nor shall any single or partial exercise or waiver of any right or remedy preclude the exercise of any other right or remedy, unless a waiver is given in writing by that party.
>
> 12.2 No waiver under clause 12.1 shall be a waiver of a past or future default or breach, nor shall it amend, delete or add to the terms, conditions or provisions of this Bond unless (and then only to the extent) expressly stated in that waiver.

Sumitomo Mitsui Banking Corporation Europe Limited (SMBCE) was a lender for the project. The lending was happening through debentures of RRS and the lending contract was called Borrower Debenture. Under the terms of lending, RRS assigned its rights in the bond to SMBCE. Following the assignment, RRS sent a standard form titled 'Notice of Assignment and Acknowledgement of Receipt' to EH. The form notified that RRS had assigned all its rights to SMBCE and any money payable under the performance bond should be paid to SMBCE. RRS had sent two copies of the signed notice to EH. The form had the following at the bottom addressed to SMBCE: [Sumitomo (2019): para 19].

> "We acknowledge receipt of the notice of assignment of which this is a copy and confirm each of the matters referred to in the notice of assignment."

This was to be signed by EH as acknowledgement. EH duly signed it and returned the duplicate form to RRS.

Subsequently, the council terminated the contract with RRS for breach. Within the terms of the contract, which were networked, the construction contract got terminated. Following this, SMBCE made an application to EH for encashment of the performance bond. The basis for it was the ICL had turned insolvent and defaulted. It claimed to be the sole beneficiary, as the rights under the bonds were assigned to it. EH refused to pay SMBCE. EH contended that there was no effective assignment of the performance bond, because there had not: [Sumitomo (2019): para 34].

> … prior to the assignment of the Performance Bond … been either a confirmation given to EH by SMBCE that it accepted the obligation of RRS under clause 8 of the Performance Bond, or a written agreement (by EH) that there could be an assignment to SMBCE without its having given such a confirmation.

SMBCE asserted that there was no dispute that the assignment was valid between RRS and SMBCE. The only question was: [Sumitomo (2019): para 35].

> … whether, because of non-compliance with clause 9 of the Performance Bond, and in the absence of waiver or agreement to the contrary, there was no transfer of the chose in action on the Performance Bond.

The court observed that signing of the form by EH was only an acknowledgement of having received the notice; it was not written consent to it. The court concluded the signing of the notice form by EH 'did not meet the requirements of clause 12.2 and that as a result was not an effective waiver'. The court concluded: [Sumitomo (2019): para 57].

> In those circumstances, I consider that the alleged waiver was not effective. The effect of that conclusion is that there was not an effective assignment for the purposes of transferring the chose in action under the Performance Bond and SMBCE did not become a "permitted assignee" thereunder.

The assignment of the bond, thus, was not effective against EH. The next case is on assignment caused by the operation of law.

Dassault Aviation Sa v Mitsui Sumitomo Insurance Co Ltd

Dassault Aviation Sa (Dassault), the aircraft manufacturer of France, entered into a contract with Mitsui Bussan Aerospace Co. Ltd. (MBA) in Japan to sell two Falcon maritime surveillance aircraft and spares. [Dassault Aviation Sa v Mitsui Sumitomo Insurance Co Ltd, (2024) EWCA Civ 5. Hereafter Dassault (2024).] The sale contract was governed by English law. The aircrafts were for the Japanese Coast Guard. MBA had entered into a sub-sale contract the same day, with the Japanese Coast Guard. The sub-sale contract was governed by Japanese law. The aircrafts were delivered late to MBA and it got delayed in its delivery to the Japanese Coast Guard. MBA was held liable for it. However, it had taken an insurance with Mitsui Sumitomo Insurance Co Ltd (MIS) covering the risk of late delivery of the aircrafts. MBA claimed the insurance amount. Section 25 of the Japanese Insurance Act provided: [Dassault (2024): para 5].

> An insurer, when the insurer has made an insurance proceeds payment, shall, by operation of law, be subrogated with regard to any claim acquired by the insured due to the occurrence of any damages arising from an insured event …, up to the smaller of the amounts listed below …

Following this, MBA's claims against Dassault were transferred to MSI by operation of law. The main contract, however, had the following article 15 on assignment: [Dassault (2024): para 2].

> this Contract shall not be assigned or transferred in whole or in part by any Party to any third party, for any reason whatsoever, without the prior written consent of the other Party and any such assignment, transfer or attempt to assign or transfer any interest or right hereunder shall be null and void without the prior written consent of the other Party.

The contention of Dassault was MIS could not have a claim against it as the assignment clause has not been followed. The Court of Appeal noted: [Dassault (2024): para 11].

> The essential point is that I do not think that the words of article 15 are ambiguous or unclear. They prevent any transfer that is effected by a party to the sale contract, but not a transfer that is effected by operation of law.

The Court of Appeal explored the assignment clause: [Dassault (2024): para 28].

> The words of article 15 are clear. They provide that the sale contract "shall not be assigned or transferred in whole or in part by any Party to any third party, for any reason whatsoever". As it seems to me, the key words for our purposes are "by any Party". The central question is whether the transfer of MBA's claims against Dassault ... was a transfer by MBA.

It was claimed that MBA by voluntarily taking out the insurance and claiming it has voluntarily caused the transfer. The court of Appeal differed on it. It noted: [Dassault (2024): para 29].

> The correct question was whether the transfer was made by MBA, not whether the transfer was caused as a consequence of certain actions taken by MBA. The transfer was ... not made by MBA. The transfer was made by operation of law.

The court, thus, concluded that the assignment was made by the operation of law and the assignment clause did not prohibit it.

Assignment is a transfer of a right in a contract to another party. It transfers the rights which have already accrued to the party in the contract and all the rights to require the future performance of the contract. The parties are free to make a distinction and limit the rights that are being assigned. However, this can be done only by employing clear words. Obligations of a contract cannot be assigned. For transferring both, the rights and obligations of a contract, a novation has to be done. For the contracting parties A and B, novation happens when C comes in and contracts with A and B and assumes all the rights and obligations of B. A new contract is formed between A and C and the original contract between A and B is extinguished. The consent for a novation can be given in advance but it must be expressed in clear words. Whether an arrangement is an assignment or novation is not to be determined by labels and descriptions but interpreting the terms of the contract to objectively assess the intention of the parties.

References

Dassault Aviation Sa v Mitsui Sumitomo Insurance Co Ltd, (2024) EWCA Civ 5
Energy Works (Hull) Limited v MW High Tech Projects UK Limited, (2020) EWHC 2537 (TCC)
Linden Gardens Trust Ltd v Lenesta Sludge Disposals Ltd., (1994) 1 A.C. 85
Sumitomo Mitsui Banking Corporation Europe Limited v Euler Hermes Europe SA (NV), (2019) EWHC 2250 (Comm)
The Argo Fund Ltd v Essar Steel Ltd (2005) EWHC 600

Chapter 21
Non-disclosure and Restraint of Trade

When a person works with another or contracts another person, he would get access to information from the other person. The information can range from being confidential or a trade secret to ordinary business information. Disclosure of the information to a third party can be prejudicial to the other party. A non-disclosure agreement (NDA), also called a confidentiality agreement or secrecy agreement, protects against this. The non-disclosure clause, like any other clause in a contract, is binding on the parties, unless a law has prohibited it, or it is opposed to public policy or suffers from a similar vice. In Dorchester Project Management Limited v BNP Paribas Real Estate Advisory & Property Management UK Limited, [Dorchester Project Management Limited v BNP Paribas Real Estate Advisory & Property Management UK Limited, (2013) EWCA Civ 176] the Court of Appeal, recognising the validity of such clauses noted that these clauses have to be construed and given effect to by applying the principles of interpretation of contracts: [Dorchester Project Management Limited v BNP Paribas Real Estate Advisory & Property Management UK Limited, (2013) EWCA Civ 176: para 28].

> The primary aim of the court in contractual interpretation is to ascertain the meaning of an agreement which the document would convey to a reasonable person having all the background knowledge which would reasonably have been available to the parties in the situation in which they were at the time of the contract.

Applying the principles the court protected against the risks of both unauthorised disclosure and circumvention. A non-disclosure agreement has come to be tied up with putting restrictions on employment or business activities of the recipient of the information. This restriction is called restraint of trade. There are two reasons for the joining of the two. One, a breach of a non-disclosure agreement is difficult to establish, while it is easier to prevent the deployment of the information for a business gain. Second, in the information age, most businesses have come to be about access, sharing and use of information. Information is at the centre of restraint of trade. The validity of a restraint of trade clause in a contract, however, is subject to it being reasonable. An unreasonable restraint on trade is void.

A. Pathak, *Contract Terms in International Business*,
https://doi.org/10.1007/978-981-96-8146-4_21

The restraint of trade started out with the question of employment. The UK Supreme Court has noted in Tillman v Egon Zehnder Ltd: [Tillman v Egon Zehnder Ltd, (2019) UKSC 32. Hereafter Tillman (2019): para 22].

> The doctrine is one of the earliest products of the common law. It epitomises … central importance to the freedom of all of us to work—in the interests both of the self-sufficiency of ourselves and our families and of our common prosperity.

In the beginning, any restraint on employment or vendor of a business was void. However, by the seventeenth century, the absolute nature of the right of an ex-employee or a vendor of a business began to be tempered. In Nordenfelt v The Maxim Nordenfelt Guns and Ammunition Co Ltd, the court explained:[Nordenfelt v The Maxim Nordenfelt Guns and Ammunition Co Ltd (1894) AC 535: page 564].

> … it was found that a rule so rigid and far-reaching must seriously interfere with transactions of every-day occurrence. Traders could hardly venture to let their shops out of their own hands; the purchaser of a business was at the mercy of the seller; every apprentice was a possible rival. So the rule was relaxed.

The law came to recognise that 'the employer or the purchaser of a business had legitimate interests which might justify his placing limited restrictions on his employee or vendor' [Tillman (2019): para 24]. Since the scope of the doctrine also expanded to take more business relations in its folds, its scope also has also been kept in bounds by case law. Restraint of trade has come to include employees, seller of business, exclusive dealings, franchisees and exclusive service agreements. In Harcus Sinclair LLP v Your Lawyers Ltd, the United Kingdom Supreme Court stated the principle of the restraint being reasonable for it not to be help void: [Harcus Sinclair LLP v Your Lawyers Ltd, (2021) UKSC 32. Hereafter Sinclair (2021)].

> … two principles must be applied … The first principle is that it is for the promisee … to establish that the non-compete undertaking is reasonable as between the parties. To satisfy this burden, the promisee must show, first, that the non-compete undertaking protects legitimate interests of the promisee and, secondly, that the non-compete undertaking goes no further than is reasonably necessary to protect those interests.

A further third requirement is for the promisee to establish that 'the restriction is commensurate with the benefits secured to the promisor under the contract' [Sinclair (2021): para 48]. If the promisee succeeds in establishing the three requirements, an opportunity still remains for the promisor. The promisor can take the burden and establish 'that the undertaking is unreasonable as being contrary to the public interest' [Sinclair (2021): para 49]. We will explore the working of a non-disclosure agreement and restraint on trade with a review of the following two cases from the United Kingdom Supreme Court.

The Your Lawyers Case: The Contract

Volkswagen is a major manufacturer of automobiles. [Sinclair (2021)] In September 2015, the United States Environmental Protection Agency alleged that the manufacturer had fitted its cars with 'defeat device' to manipulate the tests of compliance with emission standards. Mr Aman Johal, a solicitor, was of the view that there could be a group claim against the manufacturer by the buyers of the car in the United Kingdom. He was the director of a limited company carrying on the business of solicitors, Your Lawyers Limited (Your Lawyers).

Your Lawyers made preparations and on 26 October 2015, sent a letter to Volkswagen United Kingdom Limited (VWUK), the company in the United Kingdom, a cause of group action for fraudulent misrepresentation, unjust enrichment and violations of consumer regulations. Following this, Your Lawyers engaged in correspondence with the solicitors of VWUK. On 26 January 2016, Your Lawyers made a claim in a court on behalf of five buyers of the car, as representatives for a group litigation. By April 2016, Your Lawyers had obtained consent from about 4000 potential claimants for the proposed group claim.

For a group action, funding has to be secured for the legal costs from a third party and also insurance against the risk of the judgment going against the group and the court imposing the legal costs on the group. Your Lawyers was new and did not have experience of group action. Mr Johal was suggested to collaborate with a larger law firm, which had experience of group action, and could secure funding. Mr Johal identified a law firm Harcus Sinclair for collaboration.

Mr Johal got in touch with Mr Parker at the law firm Harcus Sinclair. On 10 April 2016, Your Lawyers sent a draft non-disclosure agreement (NDA) to Mr Parker. Mr Parker asked Ms Morrissey, a senior solicitor at Harcus Sinclair to review it. She suggested some amendments. Mr Parker signed the amended document expressly for and on behalf of Harcus Sinclair on 11 April 2016 without reading it himself. The agreement was headed as a non-disclosure agreement and identified Your Lawyers as 'the Discloser' and Harcus Sinclair as 'the Recipient'. The relevant provisions were as follows: [Sinclair (2021): para 13].

> 1. The Discloser intends to disclose information (the Confidential Information) to the Recipient for the purpose of obtaining legal advice on behalf of Claimants in a large Group Action (the Purpose).
>
> 2. The Recipient undertakes not to use the Confidential Information for any purpose except the Purpose, without first obtaining the written agreement of the Discloser. The Recipient further undertakes not to accept instructions for or to act on behalf of any other group of Claimants in the contemplated Group Action without the express permission of the Discloser.
>
> 3. The Recipient undertakes to keep the Confidential Information secure and not to disclose it to any third party except those who know they owe a duty of confidence to the Discloser and who are bound by obligations equivalent to those in clause 2 above and this clause 3.
>
> 7. The undertakings in clauses 2 and 3 will continue in force for six years from the date of this Agreement.

After the NDA had been signed, Your Lawyers provided Harcus Sinclair with its 'Litigation Pack' later the same day. It contained all the information Your Lawyers had on the group action. On 12 April 2016, Mr Parker sent Mr Johal a draft collaboration agreement, where the two firms will work together and each would have its own clients. There was a meeting between the parties but no formal agreement to collaborate was reached. The parties proceeded to informally collaborate on the basis that they would agree to a written agreement. Further drafts were exchanged and from the clauses it was clear that each party would have its own clients.

Mr Parker had not read the NDA and assumed that he could pursue a group action on his own or in collaboration with another firm. Without the knowledge of Your Lawyers, he formed his own claimant group, collaborated with another group and proceeded to initiate legal action. In the coming months, the collaborations between Your Lawyers and Harcus Sinclair did not work out. Your Lawyers could not secure funding for the group action. Mr Parker, in collaboration with other law firms, proceeded towards group action against Volkswagen.

Your Lawyers initiated court proceedings restraining Harcus Sinclair from violating the NDA. The action was on the second line in clause 2 which stated that the Recipient of the confidential information, that is, Harcus Sinclair 'undertakes not to accept instructions for or to act on behalf of any other group of Claimants in the contemplated Group Action without the express permission of the Discloser [Your Lawyers]' [Sinclair (2021): para 13].

In the case, Harcus Sinclair was the promisor and the promise was being put up to Your Lawyer, the promisee. The Supreme Court stated the principle that the burden was on Your Lawyer to establish that the non-compete undertaking was to protect legitimate interests of Your Lawyers and further, the non-compete undertaking 'goes no further than is reasonably necessary to protect those interests' [Sinclair (2021): para 48]. If Your Lawyers is successful in this, the burden would shift to Harcus Sinclair to establish that the undertaking is unreasonable as contrary to public interest.

The Your Lawyers Case: Unilateral Contract

The first question was on the nature of the NDA contract. In the contract, neither party had undertaken to do anything. The NDA only stated that if Your Lawyers gave confidential information, Harcus Sinclair would be bound not to disclose it and to the undertaking of non-compete. Your Lawyers was under no obligation to give any confidential information. Such contracts are called unilateral contracts, in contrast with bilateral contracts, where both the parties bind themselves to do something. In this contract, Your Lawyers provided confidential information the day the NDA was signed and the obligations of Harcus Sinclair of non-disclosure and non-compete started from that day itself, that is, 11 April 2016.

This raised a critical question for law. The question was should the court confine itself only to the express and implied provisions of the contract, that is, the NDA? If the answer were to be yes, there would be no legitimate interests as there were no binding obligations on the parties. Or, should the court in addition 'assessed at the time the NDA was made—the parties' non-contractual intentions or what they contemplated would occur as a consequence of entering into the contract' [Sinclair (2021): para 62]. The Supreme Court was clear that 'there is no need for the legitimate interests to be spelt out, or referred to, in the contract' [Sinclair (2021): para 63]. For example, the trade secrets have not to be mentioned in a contract prohibiting an employee from disclosing trade secrets. Similarly, a legitimate interest of a party may flow from several contracts taken together. The court, thus, formulated: [Sinclair (2021): para 63].

> Therefore, the question we are asking is not whether a legitimate interest has to be mentioned in the contract or must flow from the contract taken in isolation from other contracts. Rather the question is whether, in determining the promisee's legitimate interests, one can take into account not only the contractual obligations of the parties but also (assessed objectively at the time the contract was made) their non-contractual intentions, or what they contemplated, as a consequence of entering into the contract.

The Supreme Court answered: [Sinclair (2021): para 70].

> In determining the legitimate interests of the promisee one can take into account what the parties (objectively) intended or contemplated, consequent on the contract, at the time the contract was made as well as the contract terms.

The first reason for the affirmative answer was if the parties contract to give protection to their interests and contemplations, there is no reason for the court to deny it. There was no 'good reason of principle or policy' as to why 'a party should be prevented from seeking to protect its interests by a clause which anticipates what both parties intended, or contemplated' [Sinclair (2021): para 70]. The second reason was the phrase which has been adopted is "legitimate interests" rather than "legally protected interests". This brings out that 'one is not just concerned with what flows from the parties' legal rights' [Sinclair (2021): para 70]. The third reason was in other areas of contract law, the term 'legitimate interest' 'can extend beyond the contractual rights of the parties. Following this, the Supreme Court concluded that 'Your Lawyers did indeed have legitimate interests, flowing from the intended informal collaboration, which it was protecting by the non-compete undertaking' [Sinclair (2021): para 71].

Thus, it got established that Your Lawyers had a legitimate interest to protect. The next Your Lawyers has to establish is 'the undertaking does not go further than is reasonably necessary to protect those interests' [Sinclair (2021): para 72]. The challenge here was the length of time for the NDA, which was six years. Harcus Sinclair argued that it was too long to protect any legitimate interest of Your Lawyers. A shorter period, 'say, a six-month non-compete undertaking which would have served to protect Your Lawyers' head-start in the emissions litigation' [Sinclair (2021): para 73]. A claimant could make a claim against Volkswagen for six years. After that, a claim would be time-barred by law. The six-year period was 'rational and necessary in order to keep Harcus Sinclair out of the emissions litigation' [Sinclair (2021): para 74], other than with Your Lawyers consent. The Supreme Court concluded: [Sinclair (2021): para 75].

> ... it was logical and necessary for the non-compete undertaking to last for a six-year period that would roughly equate to the limitation period for claims in the emissions litigation. And

of course the restriction was solely concerned with the emissions litigation. Harcus Sinclair was not being restricted in any way from carrying on all the rest of its normal business as solicitors.

The additional burden on Your Lawyers was to establish that the restriction was commensurate with the benefits to the other party, that is, Harcus Sinclair.

The Your Lawyers Case: Benefits to Harcus Sinclair

The question arose here too, whether the benefits to Harcus Sinclair from the NDA should be confined to the provisions of the contract or should extend to include 'non-contractual intentions of the parties, or what they contemplated, at the time the contract was made' [Sinclair (2021): para 78]. The court answered it would be illogical to take the non-contractual intentions of Your Lawyers but confine to the contractual benefits when determining the benefits of Harcus Sinclair. The court concluded, 'for essentially the same reasons that we have set out above in relation to the promisee's legitimate interests, the benefits to the promisor can extend beyond the contractual consideration' [Sinclair (2021): para 79]. Thus, the court was to explore in addition to the confidential information provided by Your Lawyers, 'the benefits intended or contemplated as flowing from the informal collaboration' [Sinclair (2021): para 79] for Harcus Sinclair. The court, linking to the legitimate interests of Your Lawyers, noted on the intentions and benefits of Harcus Sinclair: [Sinclair (2021): para 80].

> … the informal collaboration would give Harcus Sinclair access to the work already done, and information already acquired, by Your Lawyers as well as knowledge of any deficiencies in the approach of Your Lawyers which could be exploited. … In short, there was a potentially lucrative business opportunity arising from the intended informal collaboration.

A third requirement for establishing reasonableness of the restriction is to put it in the context of the relative bargaining position of the parties. As the parties were of equal bargaining position, it was not an important point. The Supreme Court noted: [Sinclair (2021): para 84].

> … we do regard it as being of general relevance in considering reasonableness between the parties that the parties here were two law firms of equal bargaining power. If anything … Harcus Sinclair may be regarded as being the "stronger" party, because it was more experienced in these matters, than Your Lawyers.

Once it was established that Your Lawyers has legitimate interests and the restraint was reasonable, the burden shifted to Harcus Sinclair to establish that the restraint was contrary to public policy. The court concluded against Harcus Sinclair for the following reasons. One, there was no public policy against a solicitor undertaking not to act for a client. In general, solicitors are entitled to refuse to act for a particular person. Two, there is a public interest in law firms knowing that the courts will enforce a NDA and non-compete undertaking as 'non-enforcement would undermine firms seeking external advice and assistance in respect of a proposed group claim' [Sinclair (2021): para 87]. Three, the restraint was very narrow, limiting Harcus Sinclair from taking up group action on emission standards against Volkswagen and 'such a limited restriction was not damaging any public interest' [Sinclair (2021): para 87]. Four, there were a large number of firms willing and able to take up the group action. It was 'not contrary to the public interest for Harcus Sinclair to be removed from the pool (other than if acting with Your Lawyers)' [Sinclair (2021): para 87]. As a result of these, 'the choice of solicitor, and hence access to justice, was not being significantly affected' [Sinclair (2021): para 87]. In conclusion, the Supreme Court held the NDA to be valid and enforced it. We next review the following Supreme Court case on restraint on an employee.

Tillman v Egon Zehnder Ltd: The Contract

Egon Zehnder Ltd (Egon) is a UK subsidiary of a Swiss company [Tillman (2019)]. Egon group companies are in the business of searching and identifying specialist executives and make recruitments. The group has nine practice areas. Its customers were companies, availing its services for their needs of executives. A customer was put in one practice area, depending on its business activities. Financial service was one of the practice areas of Egon.

Ms Tillman was employed by J P Morgan as European Managing Director. Egon considered her valuable for their financial services practice area. She was prospected and employed as a consultant in January 2004 at an annual salary of £120,000 for the first year and a bonus of £100,000. The company considered her "a bit special" and she was expected to be promoted soon. She was promoted to be a principal in 2006 and a partner in 2009. As a condition of being elevated to being a partner, she began to hold shares in the Swiss parent company. In 2012, she became joint global head of the financial services practice area for the company.

Ms Tillman's employment with the company came to an end on 30 January 2017. Shortly thereafter, she informed the company that she intended to start work for a company which was in competition Egon. At the time of joining the company in 2004, she had signed an employment contract. The contract had stipulated restraints after she left the employment of the company. The restrictions were contained in Clause 13 of the contract. The clause was titled 'Covenants' and it provided for five restraints, all limited to a period of six months.

Clause 13.1 provided that she would not 'endeavour to entice away from the company any of its employees in specified senior positions' [Tillman (2019): para 6].

Clause 13.2 had the following introductory lines: [Tillman (2019): para 7].

> You [Ms Tillman] shall not without the prior written consent of the company directly or indirectly, either alone or jointly with or on behalf of any third party and whether as principal, manager, employee, contractor, consultant, agent or otherwise howsoever …

The introductory line was followed by four stipulations. By the first stipulation, clause 13.2.1, Ms Tillman covenanted 'not to solicit the custom of, nor to deal with, specified suppliers of services to the company' [Tillman (2019): para 7]. By the second stipulation, clause 13.2.2, she covenanted 'not to seek to interfere with supplies to the company' [Tillman (2019): para 7]. By the fourth stipulation, clause 13.2.4, she covenanted 'not to use any name likely to be confused with any name recently used by the company' [Tillman (2019): para 7]. The third stipulation, set out in clause 13.2.3, was central to her joining a competitor and covenanted that Ms Tillman would not: [Tillman (2019): para 8].

> directly or indirectly engage or be concerned or interested in any business carried on in competition with any of the businesses of the Company or any Group Company which were carried on at the Termination Date or during the period of 12 months prior to that date and with which you were materially concerned during such period.

By clause 13.3, Ms Tillman acknowledged that the provisions of clause 13 were fair, reasonable and necessary to protect the goodwill and interests of the company. Clause 13.4 provided for severance of a void clause to keep the covenant standing: [Tillman (2019): para 9].

> If any of the restrictions or obligations contained in this clause 13 is held not to be valid as going beyond what is reasonable for the protection of the goodwill and interest of the Company ... but would be valid if part of the wording were deleted, then such restriction or obligation shall apply with such modifications as may be necessary to make it enforceable.

Ms Tillman communicated to Egon that she would fully comply with all the covenants in the agreement she had signed in 2004 other than clause 13.2.3. She conceded that the clause prevented her joining the proposed employment but claimed that it was 'unreasonable restraint of trade and therefore void' [Tillman (2019): para 11].

Egon went to the court seeking an interim injunction to restrain her from taking up the proposed employment. The judge took an undertaking from the company that they would compensate Ms Tillman if the decision went against them, and granted an interim injunction. The judge did an expedited hearing and finally concluded in favour of the company granted an injunction. Ms Tillman went in appeal to the Court of Appeal, which too did an expedited hearing and reversed the decision of the judge. The dispute came before the Supreme Court.

To understand Tillman's key argument before the Supreme Court, we need to refer to clause 4.5 of the employment contract. It was a restriction during the course of the employment. It provided: [Tillman (2019): para 10].

> 4.5. You shall not, during the course of your employment, directly or indirectly, hold or have any interest in, any shares or other securities in any company whose business is carried on in competition with any business of the Company ..., except that you may hold or have an interest in, for investment only, shares or other securities in a publicly quoted company of up to a maximum of 5% of the total equity in issue of that company.

The contention of Ms Tillman, with reference to clause 13.2.3, was: [Tillman (2019): para 15].

> … the non-competition covenant not to be "interested" in any of the competing businesses there specified was unreasonably to prohibit her from holding even a minority shareholding in such a business.

She did not claim that she aspired to hold any shares in any company which was in a competing business. But this was not relevant. The relevant consideration was if she was restrained from holding any share, it would be unreasonable and void the entire covenant. Her argument was that if clause 4.5 prohibited her from holding any shares in any competing company, during the course of her employment, it would surely apply after she left the employment. Thus, the scope of 'interested' in clause 13.2.3 would include buy shares in a competing company.

Egon raised different alternate points in its protection. It first contended that the doctrine of restraint of trade does not apply to holding shares. The court noted the contention of Egon: [Tillman (2019): para 18].

> Not every post-employment restriction agreed in a contract of employment will, says the company, restrain trade. It seeks to make its point by reference to an extreme example: what if (it asks) Ms Tillman had there agreed not to play mah-jong for six months following the end of her employment?

Thus, the first question the Supreme Court explored was on the boundaries of the scope of restraint of trade and if it included buying of shares in a competing company.

Tillman v Egon Zehnder Ltd: Scope of Restraint of Trade

The Supreme Court reasoned the court should adopt 'broad, practical, rule of reason approach' [Tillman (2019): para 30] to determine the scope of restraint of trade. The court noted that the present contract was 'of the classic type between employer and employee and, as is agreed, it does provide for a restraint of trade which falls within the doctrine' [Tillman (2019): para 30]. The only question was 'whether an assumed prohibition against holding shares forms part of the restraint' [Tillman (2019): para 30].

The company contended that the word 'interested' in the covenant fell outside the doctrine but the rest of the clause fell within. The court found this to be 'a curious proposition' [Tillman (2019): para 31]. By clause 13.3 Ms Tillman acknowledged 'that the provisions of this clause 13 are fair and reasonable' [Tillman (2019): para 32]. Another clause provided for severance of void clauses to keep the covenant standing. The Supreme Court concluded these clauses represented 'a clear acknowledgement that all the restraints in subclauses (1) and (2) fall within the doctrine' [Tillman (2019): para 32].

The Supreme Court next noted that it would not be 'in any way surprising' [Tillman (2019): para 33] that the company would aspire to prohibit her from holding shares in a company in a competitive business. A controlling shareholding would enable her to direct the operations of the competitor company. The court reasoned:[Tillman (2019): para 33].

> But even a minority shareholding, say a 25% shareholding in a company started up with three others, would enable her to influence its operations. And, even more obviously, the employment of a top executive such as Ms Tillman is frequently subject to conditions that she should hold shares in her employer or be remunerated partly in its shares or in options to purchase them.

In fact, this was the reason she was required to acquire shares in the parent company after being promoted to the position of a partner in 2009. The court concluded that in 'substance as well as in form the restraint on shareholding is part of the restraint on Ms Tillman's ability to work in the immediate aftermath of her employment' [Tillman (2019): para 33]. The focus of the court shifted on the meaning of the term 'interested'.

Tillman v Egon Zehnder Ltd: Meaning of 'Interested'

The company conceded that the meaning of the term 'interested' in some context can mean holding shares in a company. However, it contended that the meaning of the term has to be construed in its context. It argued that in the context of the contract, it did not cover Ms Tillman holding shares. The Supreme Court recognised that the term 'engaged or concerned or interested' has been 'included in standard precedents for the drafting of non-competition covenants throughout the last century' [Tillman (2019): para 51]. The courts had interpreted it to include holding of shares. The Supreme Court concluded that 'the natural construction of the word "interested", consistent with long-standing authority, is that it covers a shareholding' [Tillman (2019): para 53]. Thus, any shareholding, whether large or small, was prohibited by the covenant. This is clearly 'unreasonable restraint of trade; and that, unless it can be severed and removed from the rest of the clause' [Tillman (2019): para 53], Ms Tillman would succeed. With this, the court moved to the question if the term 'interested' could be severed from the clause and save the rest of the covenant.

Tillman v Egon Zehnder Ltd: Severance

A severance refers to removing out the invalid terms of a contract and attempting to give effect to the rest of the terms. The Supreme Court noted that where 'part of a contract is unenforceable, the enforceability of the remainder represents an issue which arises far more widely than in contracts of employment' [Tillman (2019): para 54]. It noted that even in contracts tainted with illegality, there was no public policy objection to 'enforce the contract without the illegal provision' [Tillman (2019): para 54]. The court, however, noted: [Tillman (2019): para 55].

> It is clear that considerations of public policy drove the evolution of the doctrine under common law that post-employment restraints of trade were, unless reasonable, void. It is less clear that, until the early years of the last century, considerations of public policy also

drove a more restrictive approach to severance in post-employment restraints of trade than was adopted in other areas.

The Supreme Court noted that the courts in the early twentieth century, started giving a restrictive meaning to severance in contracts in restraint of employment: [Tillman (2019): para 56].

> Early in the last century, however, a much more restrictive view was suddenly taken of the availability of severance in post-employment covenants. The reasons of public policy which drove a conclusion that, unless reasonable, they were void were adopted and expanded to suggest a further conclusion that, where parts of them were unreasonable, not even the reasonable parts should usually be enforced.

The Supreme Court, after a comprehensive review of all the cases, reformulated the principles for severance. The court noted on the present-day context of employment of senior executives: [Tillman (2019): para 82].

> High-ranking employees can do particular damage to the legitimate interests of their employers following termination of their employment; and it may be that, when they enter into their post-employment covenants, they are able to negotiate with their employers on nearly an equal footing.

However, the standard reference was not to senior executives but ordinary employees. The court noted: [Tillman (2019): para 82].

> It is clearly common practice for an employer to present a prospective employee with a substantial written contract, many terms of which, including those imposing post-employment restraints, are derived from books of precedent. … most prospective employees will not be able, even if minded, to decline to accept such terms, still less, following the end of their employment, to defend a claim that they are in breach of them. The courts must continue to adopt a cautious approach to the severance of post-employment restraints.

The court, however, noted that the principles formulated by precedence had proved 'both instantly controversial and ultimately unsatisfactory' [Tillman (2019): para 83]. It consolidated and revised the principles to advance two major tests. The first criterion is that 'the unenforceable provision is capable of being removed without the necessity of adding to or modifying the wording of what remains.' [Tillman (2019): para 85] The court noted on it that were it 'ever to be thought appropriate to confer on the court a power to rewrite a restraint so as to make it reasonable, it would surely have to be achieved by legislation along' [Tillman (2019): para 85]. Thus, the courts must not add anything to make the remaining clauses stand. The second test the court formulated was 'removal of the provision would not generate any major change in the overall effect of all the post-employment restraints in the contract' [Tillman (2019): para 87]. This was for the employer to establish.

The court found the application of the tests to 'Ms Tillman's restraint covenants now becomes straightforward' [Tillman (2019): para 88]. The court severed: [Tillman (2019): para 88].

> First, the words "or interested" are capable of being removed from the non-competition covenant without the need to add to or modify the wording of the remainder. And, second, removal of the prohibition against her being "interested" would not generate any major change in the overall effect of the restraints.

The court, thus, concluded that 'those words should be severed and removed' [Tillman (2019): para 88]. By the time the Supreme Court decided the case, the six-month period of restraint had got over. The Supreme Court directed the lower court to 'formally restore the injunction … subject only to the removal of the words "or interested" [Tillman (2019): para 91].

A non-disclosure agreement (NDA) protects against an information shared with a party getting disclosed to a third person. A non-disclosure agreement, like any other contract, is binding on the parties unless a law has prohibited it, or it is opposed to public policy or suffers from a similar vice. A non-disclosure agreement has come to be tied with a restraint of trade agreement. In this agreement, an employee undertakes restraints on his activities are leaving the employment. It also applies to a vendor selling his business and goodwill; and exclusive trade relationships. An unreasonable restraint on trade is void. The reasonableness of a restraint on trade is judged by three tests. The person to whom the promise of restraint has been made must establish that the restraint protects his legitimate interests; the undertaking goes no further than is reasonably necessary to protect those interests; and the restraint is commensurate with the interest derived by the promisor. If this is established, the promisor gets a chance to establish that the restraint is opposed to public policy. If a restraint is found to be void, it can be severed from the other clauses and tested if the contract survives to be given effect to.

References

Dorchester Project Management Limited v BNP Paribas Real Estate Advisory & Property Management UK Limited, (2013) EWCA Civ 176
Harcus Sinclair LLP v Your Lawyers Ltd, (2021) UKSC 32
Nordenfelt v The Maxim Nordenfelt Guns and Ammunition Co Ltd (1894) AC 535
Tillman v Egon Zehnder Ltd, (2019) UKSC 32

Chapter 22
Applicable Law, Jurisdiction and Arbitration

If a dispute were to arise in relation to a contract, a party would need to take it to a court for resolution. The contracts provide on the court which would have jurisdiction over a dispute arising from the contract. If the clause were not there, there would be much uncertainties, particularly in an international contract, as to which court would have jurisdiction. A clause in the contract providing on the jurisdiction of a court is called the jurisdiction clause. The jurisdiction clause may provide for an exclusive jurisdiction of a court or alternate jurisdictions. The contracting parties may be in different jurisdictions and a dispute may arise as to the law of the state which would apply to the contract. To take away this uncertainty, the contract specifies the law that will apply to the contract. This clause is called the applicable law clause. In addition, a contract may provide for resolution of disputes by arbitration. We will come to it later in the chapter. Let us first explore the working of jurisdiction and applicable law clauses with the following review of cases.

Hin-Pro International Logistics Limited v Compania Sud Americana De Vapores S.A.

Hin-Pro International Logistics Ltd (Hin-Pro) is a freight forwarder registered in Hong Kong. [Hin-Pro International Logistics Limited v Compania Sud Americana De Vapores S.A., (2015) EWCA Civ 401. Hereafter Hin-Pro (2015).] Compania Sud Americana de Vapores S.A (CSAV) is an international shipping corporation with a worldwide business. Hin-Pro began proceedings against CSAV in the Wuhan Maritime Court in China claiming that the cargo had been released without production of the original bills. CSAV initiated proceedings in the commercial court in England. The bill of lading was issued to the following applicable law and jurisdiction clause: [Hin-Pro (2015): para 4].

23 Law and Jurisdiction

A. Pathak, *Contract Terms in International Business*,
https://doi.org/10.1007/978-981-96-8146-4_22

> This Bill of Lading and any claim or dispute arising hereunder shall be subject to English law and the jurisdiction of the English High Court of Justice in London. If, notwithstanding the foregoing, any proceedings are commenced in another jurisdiction, such proceeding shall be referred to ordinary courts of law.

The Court of Appeal had to decide whether the English courts had exclusive jurisdiction over the disputes. The court emphasised on the words 'shall be subject to' and highlighted: [Hin-Pro (2015): para 61].

> the words ... are imperative and directory. They are not words which are apt simply to provide an option. That is certainly the case in relation to the applicable law and, *prima facie*, the same should be so in relation to jurisdiction.

The court then noted the phrase "This Bill of Lading and any claim or dispute arising hereunder shall be subject to English law and jurisdiction" to be 'strong' and noted: [Hin-Pro (2015): para 61].

> This is not wording which does no more than indicate consent or agreement to English jurisdiction. It is transitive in the sense that the parties agree to submit all disputes to the English court, rather than submitting themselves to its jurisdiction if that jurisdiction is invoked.

The court reasoned that more than one court can have jurisdiction but there will be only one applicable law. The 'natural commercial purpose' [Hin-Pro (2015): para 63] of a clause like the present is to stipulate the law that will govern the contract and the court that will have jurisdiction over any dispute. In this context, the court noted: [Hin-Pro (2015): para 63].

> If *"shall be subject to"* makes English law mandatory (as it does) the parties must, as it seems to me be taken to have intended (absent any convincing reason to the contrary) that the same should apply to English jurisdiction. I do not think that the reasonable commercial man would understand the purpose of the clause to be confined to a submission to English jurisdiction, if invoked, or to an underscoring of the convenience of litigation here.

In a bill of lading, a large range of countries will have jurisdiction, including the countries where the goods got loaded, transhipped or discharged; and where the bill of lading contract was formed. Some of the countries are not likely to apply the English law and some 'might apply it in an idiosyncratic way' [Hin-Pro (2015): para 64]. In this context, there is 'only limited benefit in specifying England as an optional jurisdiction' [Hin-Pro (2015): para 64]. It makes 'little commercial sense to add England as an optional additional court' [Hin-Pro (2015): para 64]. The court noted: [Hin-Pro (2015): para 64].

... there was every reason to think ... that when the parties were agreed that claims and disputes should be determined by the English High Court, by necessary inference they were agreeing that they should not be determined elsewhere. That would make good commercial sense.

The court reiterated the connection between applicable law and jurisdiction of the court. It noted: [Hin-Pro (2015): para 66].

… there is obvious sense in making both English law and English jurisdiction mandatory. Whilst foreign courts may (but will not necessarily) apply English law if that is what the parties have agreed, England is the best forum for the application of its own law.

The court recognised that the clause gave exclusive jurisdiction to the English court. The judgment was drawn from and applied in the following case.

Al Mana Lifestyle Trading L.L.C. v United Fidelity Insurance Company Psc

The Al Mana Group are in the business of food and beverages and retailing in the Middle East and Gulf region. [Al Mana Lifestyle Trading L.L.C. & Others v United Fidelity Insurance Company Psc, Societe D'Assurances Libano-Suisse Sal (Commercial Registration No. 7533) and Its Qatari Branch Lebanese-Switzerland Co. for Insurance (Commercial Registration No. 23825), Trading As "Libano-Suisse S.A.L.", Libano-Suisse Insurance Co. S.A.L.—Kuwait, (2023) EWCA Civ 61. Hereafter Al Mana (2023).] The group companies had taken insurance to cover their business losses. The insurance companies operated within Gulf Cooperation Council countries. The insurance companies had their headquarters in the United Arab Emirates, Qatar and Kuwait. The Al Mana group companies claimed indemnity totalling about US$40 m under different policies related to business disruption during the Covid-19 pandemic before Commercial Court in England. The insurance companies contended before the English court that it did not have the jurisdiction to take up the claim. The policy terms had the following clause on jurisdiction: [Al Mana (2023): para 3].

APPLICABLE LAW AND JURISDICTION:

In accordance with the jurisdiction, local laws and practices of the country in which the policy is issued. Otherwise England and Wales UK Jurisdiction shall be applied,

Under liability jurisdiction will be extended to worldwide excluding USA and Canada.

The insurance companies reasoned that within the clause, the disputes would need to be taken up in the respective countries where the policies were issued, that is, the United Arab Emirates, Qatar and Kuwait. The question before the Court of Appeal was if the jurisdiction clause gave a choice of jurisdiction to the Al Mana group of companies. The Court of Appeal stated that a policy document has to be read as to 'how the words of the contract would be understood by a reasonable policyholder' [Al Mana (2023): para 21]. The court read the 'tersely expressed' clause: [Al Mana (2023): para 21].

The fact that the first sentence deals not only with jurisdiction, but also with the governing law (i.e. the local law) and the need to apply local practices, while the second sentence is confined to jurisdiction, strongly suggests that the first sentence is intended to contain the primary rule, with the second sentence operating as a fallback.

As a result, even if the jurisdiction of an English court is invoked, the English court will be required to apply the local laws and practices. On the prospect of an English court applying a foreign law, the Court of Appeal noted: [Al Mana (2023): para 23].

> While it is possible, and not uncommon, for the English court to receive evidence of foreign law, and it would be equally possible for the English court to receive evidence about local practices, that is inevitably second best when compared with the application of local law by the local court, which can also be expected to be familiar with local practices.

The court reiterated the going together of the applicable law and jurisdiction: [Al Mana (2023): para 23].

> Just as the English courts have consistently held that "England is the best forum for the application of its own law" and that a choice of English law is itself a powerful factor showing that a choice of English jurisdiction is intended to be exclusive ... so it must be accepted that a foreign court is the best forum for the application of its law and that a choice of foreign law is a powerful factor showing that a choice of foreign jurisdiction is intended to be mandatory.

The court, on a linguistic analysis of the clause, saw the English jurisdiction as only a fallback option. The question then was when was the fallback option available? The answer is if the local court does not accept jurisdiction. But this will happen in very limited or even non-existent circumstances where a court would not accept jurisdiction. But this cannot be an objection. The court noted: [Al Mana (2023): para 31].

> I see no reason why parties should not agree to confer jurisdiction on one court, with another as a fallback in case the primary court chosen is not available, without troubling to investigate whether or in what circumstances the primary court would decline jurisdiction.

It gives comfort to the parties that a fallback option is available, if their primary choice is not available. The court also explored that England gave a common jurisdiction to the policies issued in different countries. The court noted: [Al Mana (2023): para 34].

> I can see that there may in some cases, where a common issue arises concerning policies issued in more than one country, be an advantage to both parties to have that issue decided in a single forum. However, where that is so, there is no reason why the parties should not agree on the jurisdiction to decide that issue.

The court further noted that in any case 'most of the risks giving rise to litigation would be likely to be of a local nature and the benefit' [Al Mana (2023): para 34]. And if there were any advantage, the other party could always 'sue in the local court and thereby to negate the supposed advantage' [Al Mana (2023): para 34]. The Court of Appeal concluded that the dispute should be taken to the local courts.

Arbitration

Arbitration is an alternate means of settlement of a dispute, besides approaching a court. An international contract may have an arbitration clause. Arbitration emerged with the development of trade, commerce and contract law. A contracting party could seek remedy for a breach of contract by going to a court. Going to a court, however, was not always the most effective solution for the parties. This was because, one, courts could take a long time to settle a dispute and award remedy. Two, court proceedings are always adversarial. Three, court proceedings are open to public. This makes the trade relations and terms of contracts between the parties public. This is not in the business interests of either of the parties. There was a way out for the parties. As contracts were consensual, like other terms of the contract, the parties could provide that in the case of a dispute, they would refer the dispute to persons other than a court. This came to be called arbitration.

While arbitration solved some kinds of problems, it gave rise to newer issues. The court should subject the contracting parties to arbitration, and not adjudicate, as this is what the parties have agreed to. Left to themselves, however, a strong party to a contract could subject the other to grave injustices. From the point of view of the law, it is the duty and the right of the State and courts to give justice and protection to individuals. No private party can take away this privilege from the State or the courts. For this reason, a contract restraining a person from going to a court in void. And yet, arbitration was desirable as it facilitated businesses. As access to the courts was central in seeking justice, a fine balancing had to be done between arbitration and ousting the jurisdiction of the courts; and allowing access to the courts despite an arbitration agreement. Thus, arbitration became a subject matter on its own, through the Arbitration Act, 1889 in England. Each country has an arbitration Act. It is a very detailed law providing for every aspect of arbitration. The arbitration law of the United Kingdom is the Arbitration Act, 1996.

An international arbitration is one where the parties are from different states and the award would need to be enforced in a foreign country. It can be effective only if there is certainty and uniformity across the states. To secure this, at the initiative of the United Nations, the United Nations Conference on International Commercial Arbitration on 10 June 1958 adopted a convention providing on all aspects of international arbitration. The convention is the foundation of international commercial arbitration. Almost all countries had ratified the convention and given effect to it by national law. We explore arbitration further with the following two judgments of the United Kingdom Supreme Court.

The Enka Case

A power plan in Russia was severely damaged in February 2016. [Enka Insaat VE Sanayi AS v OOO Insurance Company Chubb, (2020) UKSC 38. Hereafter Enka (2020)] The power plant was insured against the damage by a Russian company, OOO Insurance Company Chubb (Chubb Russia). The insurance company paid up the insurance claim to the owner of the power plant. A few years back, the owner of the power plant had entered into a contract with a head contractor to do the design and construction of the plant. The head contractor had engaged a company called Enka Insaat Ve Sanayi AS (Enka), a Turkish engineering company, as a subcontractor for the construction of the plant. On the completion of the construction of the plant, in May 2014, the head contractor had transferred all its rights to the owner. This included the rights of the head contractor against Enka. As Chubb Russia paid the insurance amount to the owners, the rights of the owner against Enka got subrogated to it. Chubb Russia was placing the liability for the fire in the plant on Enka and seeking to recover damages from Enka. By the subrogation, Chubb Russia had got into the shoes of the head contractor against Enka.

The construction contract between the head contractor and Enka did not contain a choice of governing law clause. The Supreme Court noted: [Enka (2020): para 148].

> In a detailed and professionally drafted commercial contract made between substantial organisations based in different countries, such a clause is an entirely standard clause, almost invariably included along with a clause specifying the forum in which any dispute is to be resolved.

The court recognised that this was not accidental or an oversight. An ‘obvious explanation’ [Enka (2020): para 148] of this was ‘the parties were not able to agree on a choice of the governing law’ [Enka (2020): para 148]. As the contract was to be performed in Russia, in the absence of a governing law clause, the parties were agreed that ‘the main body of the construction contract is governed by Russian law’ [Enka (2020): para 147]. Article 50.1 of the construction contract provided for resolution of dispute by arbitration with the Rules of Arbitration of the International Chamber of Commerce and ‘the place of arbitration shall be London, England’ [Enka (2020): para 10].

Chubb Russia proceeded with its claims against Enka in the courts of Russia in May 2019. In response, Enka brought an arbitration claim in the High Court in London claiming that Chubb Russia was in breach of the arbitration agreement in initiating proceedings in Russia. Enka sought an injunction to restrain Chubb Russia from pursuing the Russian claim. The High Court dismissed Enka’s claim on the grounds that the appropriate forum to determine to scope of the arbitration agreement was the Russian court. The Court of Appeal overturned the decision reasoning that as the arbitration was to happen in London, the courts of England had the jurisdiction and could restrain Chubb Russia from pursuing the claim in the Russian courts. The decision of the Court of Appeal was challenged by Chubb Russia before the Supreme Court.

The Supreme Court introduced the network of courts and laws in international contracts providing for arbitration: [Enka (2020): para 1].

> Where an international commercial contract contains an agreement to resolve disputes by arbitration, at least three systems of national law are engaged when a dispute occurs. They are: the law governing the substance of the dispute; the law governing the agreement to arbitrate; and the law governing the arbitration process.

The court brought out that the substantive aspects of a contract are generally governed by the law applicable to the contract. It then noted on the law for arbitration: [Enka (2020): para 1].

> The law governing the arbitration process ... is generally the law of the "seat" of the arbitration, which is usually the place chosen for the arbitration in the arbitration agreement. These two systems of law may differ from each other. Each may also differ from the law which governs the validity and scope of the arbitration agreement.

The Supreme Court introduced the question in the dispute to be 'which system of national law governs the validity and scope of the arbitration agreement when the law applicable to the contract containing it differs from the law of the seat of the arbitration' [Enka (2020): para 2]. The Supreme Court observed that this issue 'has long divided courts and commentators, both in this country and internationally' [Enka (2020): para 3]. It noted the contradictory answers to the question given by the courts: [Enka (2020): para 3].

On one side there are those who say that the law that governs a contract should generally also govern an arbitration agreement which, though separable, forms part of that contract. On the other side there are those who say that the law of the chosen seat of the arbitration should also generally govern the arbitration agreement.

In this case, Enka contends that 'unless there has been an express choice of the law that is to govern the arbitration agreement, the general rule should be that the arbitration agreement is governed by the law of the seat' [Enka (2020): para 4]. Chubb Russia puts up that 'in the absence of strong indications to the contrary, a choice of law for the contract is a choice of that law to govern the arbitration agreement' [Enka (2020): para 5]. Chubb Russia contends that as the Russian law governs the construction contract, the implication is that they 'intended the arbitration agreement included in that contract to be governed by Russian law is not displaced by their choice of London as the seat of arbitration' [Enka (2020): para 5].

The Supreme Court noted that the European Union's Regulation (Rome I Regulation), which governs jurisdiction of courts in contracts, exempts 'arbitration agreements and agreements on the choice of court' [Enka (2020): para 25] from its ambit. Thus, the Supreme Court would need to resolve the question by applying the common law principles. The court stated the common law principles to be: [Enka (2020): para 27].

> Those rules are that a contract (or relevant part of it) is governed by: (i) the law expressly or impliedly chosen by the parties; or (ii) in the absence of such choice, the law with which it is most closely connected.

The choice of law to govern the contract, like any contractual term, may be expressly stated or implied, that is, 'be a matter of necessary implication or inference from other terms of the contract and the surrounding circumstances' [Enka (2020): para 35]. A determination of the choice of law governing the contract is a question of interpretation. The Supreme Court stated that in the cases where a contract has an arbitration clause and the contract has chosen a law to govern the contract, the choice should generally apply to the arbitration agreement. This general rule encourages legal certainty, consistency and coherence.

If the contract, however, has not chosen an applicable law, the inference is not justified that the applicable law to arbitration will be the law of the seat of arbitration. In this case, the court must leave aside the intention of the parties and decide it on the basis of the law which has a close connection with arbitration. The court noted: [Enka (2020): para 118].

> This exercise is different in nature from the attempt to identify a choice (whether express or implied), as it involves the application of a rule of law and not a process of contractual interpretation.

The court started out that it is a reasonable assumption that the contracting parties do not want to spread out to different systems of law. The court noted: [Enka (2020): para 119].

> Even where the parties have not agreed what law is to govern their contract, it is reasonable to start from an assumption ... that all the terms of the contract, including an arbitration clause, are governed by the same system of law. Where, however, the parties have selected a place for the arbitration of disputes, there is authority for, as a general rule, regarding the law with which the arbitration agreement is most closely connected as the law of the seat of arbitration.

There are several reasons of 'principle and policy' which justifies that where there is no choice of law, a general rule should be 'the law of the place chosen as the seat of arbitration as the law most closely connected with the arbitration agreement' [Enka (2020): para 120]. The place of performance of a contract is taken to be the most connected for identifying the system of law governing the contract. This is justified as the states have interests in regulating transactions in their territories. As a consequence, it is a 'natural assumption that the law of the territory in which a transaction is taking place will govern it in the absence of a contrary indication' [Enka (2020): para 121]. By the same reasoning, the 'starting point is that the seat of arbitration is the place where (legally, even if not physically) the arbitration agreement is to be performed' [Enka (2020): para 121]. The court noted: [Enka (2020): para 121].

By agreeing to a seat of arbitration the parties submit themselves to the jurisdiction of the courts of that place and to its law and coercive powers for the purposes of deciding any issue relating to the validity or enforceability of their arbitration agreement.

The concerns in arbitration agreements include existence and scope of arbitration, restrain proceedings brought in breach of the arbitration agreement, arbitrator's jurisdiction and challenge to arbitral award. The court noted, the 'seat of arbitration is in these circumstances the place to whose system of law the arbitration agreement is most closely attached' [Enka (2020): para 121].

In contrast, the law of the place where the contract is to be performed, does not have significant connection with arbitration agreement. The court noted: [Enka (2020): para 122].

> the subject matter and purpose of an arbitration agreement are different from those of the contract in which it is incorporated. ... seats of arbitration are frequently chosen which have no connection with where the parties' substantive obligations are to be performed (or otherwise with the contract) and sometimes precisely because they have no such connection. Other factors connecting the main contract to a country or its laws are equally irrelevant in regard to the arbitration agreement

Another supporting factor for a close connection with the law of seat of arbitration is that the contracting parties from different nationalities, who have not chosen an applicable law of the contract but have decided on the seat of arbitration, have certain expectations. The court noted: [Enka (2020): para 142].

> ... a popular seat of international arbitration has been chosen as a neutral forum with which neither party is connected. In such circumstances, if the parties had been required to make a common choice of law to govern their arbitration agreement at the time of contracting, it is inherently unlikely that they would have agreed on either of their national systems of law and much more likely that they would have settled on the law of the place which they had chosen as the seat of arbitration.

Another reason in favour of the seat of arbitration be the applicable law for arbitration is to bring legal certainty. This, the court noted: [Enka (2020): para 144].

> ... enables the parties to predict easily and with little room for argument which law the court will apply by default. ... It is desirable that parties should be able to know with certainty what law a court will apply in this situation. If they do not like the default option, they can always choose a system of law that they prefer.

The Supreme Court determined that the contract had no choice of law to govern the contract and the arbitration agreement within it. In these circumstances, the court concluded: [Enka (2020): para 171].

> ... the validity and scope of the arbitration agreement ... is governed by the law of the chosen seat of arbitration, as the law with which the dispute resolution clause is most closely connected.

As London was the seat of arbitration, the Supreme Court affirmed that the law applicable to the arbitration agreement was English law. The next case is also a judgment of the UK Supreme Court, on the applicable law after arbitration proceedings have been completed.

Kabab-Ji S.A.L. (Lebanon) v Kout Food Group (Kuwait)

Kabaj-Ji is a Lebanese company. It entered into a Franchise Development Agreement (FDA) with a Kuwaiti company Al Homaizi Foodstuff Company (AHFC). [Kabab-Ji SAL (Lebanon) v Kout Food Group (Kuwait), (2021) UKSC 48. Hereafter Kabab-Ji (2021).] The contract was formed in July 2001 and granted Al Homaizi a licence to operate its restaurant franchise in Kuwait for ten years. The agreement was governed by the laws of England. The contract had an arbitration clause providing for arbitration at the International Chamber of Commerce, Paris. In 2005, AHFC became a subsidiary of another Kuwaiti Company, Kout Food Group (KFG) following a corporate reorganisation. The parties continued business as earlier and later, got into a dispute. Within the contract, Kabab-Ji referred the dispute in arbitration before the ICC. The arbitration was only commenced against KFG, not against AHFC.

KFG argued that it was not a party to the FDA and an arbitration proceeding against it could not be started. It took part in the arbitration under protest. The majority of arbitrators found that, applying French law, KFG was a party to the arbitration agreements. The arbitrators, applying the English law, decided that the agreement between Kabab-Ji and AHFC had got novated and KFG had become a party to the agreement. The arbitrators made an award against KFG for unpaid licence fees and damages in the principal sum of US$6.7 million. KFG applied to the Paris Court of Appeal to set aside the award. Soon afterwards, Kabab-Ji issued proceedings in the Commercial Court in London to enforce the award. KFG made a cross application for an order that recognition and enforcement of the award be refused. We can now note the terms of the contract on dispute resolution: [Kabab-Ji (2021): para 37].

Article 14: Settlement of Disputes.

...

> 14.2. Except for those matters which specifically involve the Mark, any dispute, controversy or claim between LICENSOR and LICENSEE with respect to any issue arising out of or relating to this Agreement or the breach thereof, ...shall, failing amicable settlement, on request of LICENSOR or LICENSEE, be finally settled under the Rules of Conciliation and Arbitration of the International Chamber of Commerce by one or more arbitrators appointed in accordance with the said Rules.
>
> 14.3. The arbitrator(s) shall apply the provisions contained in the Agreement. The arbitrator(s) shall also apply principles of law generally recognised in international transactions. The arbitrator(s) may have to take into consideration some mandatory provisions of some countries *i.e.* provisions that appear later on to have an influence on the Agreement. Under no circumstances shall the arbitrator(s) apply any rule(s) that contradict(s) the strict wording of the Agreement.
>
> 14.4 Nothing contained herein shall in any way deprive LICENSOR of its rights to seek and obtain a temporary restraining order, preliminary/permanent injunction or other equitable relief from a court of competent jurisdiction under any applicable law. All remedies provided in this Agreement are cumulative and not exclusive of any remedies provided by law.
>
> 14.5. The arbitration shall be conducted in the English language, in Paris, France.
>
> ...

Article 15: Governing Law.

> This Agreement shall be governed by and construed in accordance with the laws of England.

The commercial court noted that the contract was governed by English law. Applying the English law, the commercial court concluded that KFG had not become a party to the FDA or arbitration. The court, thus, did not recognising the award. The Court of Appeal upheld the decision of the judge. Kabab-Ji appealed to the Supreme Court for recognition and enforcement of the award given by the arbitrators against KFG. The Supreme Court introduced the case that in international arbitration agreement, the first question which has to be answered is as to which system of law applies to the arbitration agreement. Referring to its decision in the Enka Case, the Supreme Court noted: [Kabab-Ji (2021): para 2].

> In Enka the question of which law governed the validity and scope of an arbitration agreement arose before any arbitration had taken place. In the present case the question of which law governs the validity of an arbitration agreement arises in the different context where an arbitration has already taken place and proceedings have been brought in England to enforce an award made by the arbitral tribunal.

KFG maintain that they are not a party to the agreement and therefore are not bound by the decision of the arbitrators. The Supreme Court started that as in Enka, 'the first question is to identify which system of law the English court must apply to decide whether there is an enforceable arbitration agreement' [Kabab-Ji (2021): para 2].

As recounted earlier, the United Nations Conference on International Commercial Arbitration adopted a convention to bring certainty and uniformity to the enforcement of international arbitration. The operative parts of the convention have been transposed into the Arbitration Act, 1996. Section 100 of the Act defines a "New York Convention award" as an award made in the territory of a state, other than the United Kingdom, which is a signatory to the convention. Section 101 provides for a New York Convention award to be brought to the English court for its enforcement. Section 103 gives limited grounds for the English courts not to give effect to the award. The Supreme Court noted that the major object of the convention was 'the achievement of uniform international standards', as a result, the 'residual discretion to recognise or enforce an award is correspondingly narrow' [Kabab-Ji (2021): para 15].

The Supreme Court noted 'the Convention establishes two uniform international conflict of laws rules' [Kabab-Ji (2021): para 26]. The two rules are: [Kabab-Ji (2021): para 26].

> The first, and primary, rule is that the validity of the arbitration agreement is governed by "the law to which the parties subjected it"—in other words the law chosen by the parties. The second, default rule, which applies where no choice has been indicated, is that the applicable law is that of "the country where the award was made". Where the parties have chosen the seat of arbitration, the place where the award was made will be (or be deemed to be) the place of the seat.

The Supreme Court explored the suggestion that if the person resists that he never entered into an arbitration agreement, there can be no law to which the party could be subjected to. In these cases, the court stated: [Kabab-Ji (2021): para 27].

> The general approach in private international law, however, where there is a dispute about whether an agreement exists or is valid is to decide that question by applying the law that would govern the agreement if it exists or is valid.

The court next stated the principle: [Kabab-Ji (2021): para 35].

> 35 Once it is accepted that an express agreement as to the law which is to govern the arbitration agreement is not required and that any form of agreement will suffice, it seems difficult to resist the conclusion that a general choice of law clause in a written contract containing an arbitration clause will normally be a sufficient "indication" of the law to which the parties subjected the arbitration agreement.

The court applied to the clauses of the FDA contract and noted: [Kabab-Ji (2021): para 39].

> Clause 15 of the FDA is a typical governing law clause, which provides that "this Agreement" shall be governed by the laws of England. Even without any express definition, that phrase is ordinarily and reasonably understood … to denote all the clauses incorporated in the contractual document, including therefore clause 14.

The 'effect of these clauses is absolutely clear' [Kabab-Ji (2021): para 39]. The court concluded that the law governing the arbitration agreement is English law. As a matter of English law, KFG had not become a party to the arbitration agreement. Thus, it could not get an arbitration award enforced.

Contracts have a jurisdiction clause and an applicable law clause. The applicable law settles the question as to the law that would govern the contract. It can only be one law of a country. The jurisdiction clause settles the court to which a dispute arising from the contract would be taken. The jurisdiction clause can give exclusive jurisdiction to a court or give alternative jurisdictions for the parties to choose from. It is possible for a court to have jurisdiction over the contract with a foreign applicable law. If there is a doubt, however, it is taken that a country is the best forum for its own laws. In addition to the two clauses, a contract may provide for arbitration.

An arbitration agreement may be made separately from the main contract or it may be a part of the main substantive contract. It should settle the question as to the place where the arbitration will take place, the seat of arbitration, and the system of law that will apply to the arbitration. It is possible for arbitration to take place in a country with the substantive law of the country being another country and the applicable law to arbitration, yet another country. In the Enka case, the UK Supreme Court has settled the question if the law applicable to arbitration is not settled. In this case, the law which is most closely connected with arbitration is to be taken as the law and this is, the law of the seat of arbitration.

References

Al Mana Lifestyle Trading L.L.C. & Others v United Fidelity Insurance Company Psc, Societe D'Assurances Libano Suisse Sal (Commercial Registration No. 7533) and Its Qatari Branch Lebanese-Switzerland Co. for Insurance (Commercial Registration No. 23825), Trading As "Libano-Suisse S.A.L.", Libano-Suisse Insurance Co. S.A.L.—Kuwait, (2023) EWCA Civ 61

Enka Insaat VE Sanayi AS v OOO Insurance Company Chubb, (2020) UKSC 38
Hin-Pro International Logistics Limited v Compania Sud Americana De Vapores S.A., (2015) EWCA Civ 401
Kabab-Ji SAL (Lebanon) v Kout Food Group (Kuwait), (2021) UKSC 48

Chapter 23
Other Contract Terms

In the preceding chapters, we have explored the important terms in the General Conditions of Contract (GCC). There are several other supporting terms to contract. These clauses are on notice, language, taxes and permits, publicity, spare parts, repeat contracts, letter of credit, sampling and inspection. In this chapter, we take a few terms which are conceptually engaging or have engaged current interest of the courts. The terms covered in this chapter are warranties and representations, order of precedence, notice, good faith and agency.

Warranties and Representations

It is a principle of contracts that a party to a contract can set aside a contract if he was induced to enter into the contract by misrepresentation made by the other party. Once a contract is made, if a party breaches a contractual promise, the other party can seek remedies within the terms of the contract for the breach. This can include terminating the contract and claiming damages for the breach. Some kinds of contracts, for example service contracts and share purchase agreements, separately list what the contract is undertaking or warranting. These are listed as warranties. In addition, the contract may list all the representations which have been made under a heading of representations. The contract terms would limit representations to only those listed under the heading and also limit remedies against them. We review the following judgment on the theme of representations and warranties.

A. Pathak, *Contract Terms in International Business*,
https://doi.org/10.1007/978-981-96-8146-4_23

Idemitsu Kosan Co Ltd v Sumitomo Corp.

Idemitsu Kosan Co Ltd and Sumitomo Corp are both Japanese companies with business interests in the energy sector. [Idemitsu Kosan Co Ltd v Sumitomo Corp., (2016) EWHC 1909 (Comm). Hereafter Idemitsu (2016).] Sumitomo Corporation Europe Limited is a wholly owned subsidiary of Sumitomo Corporation. The companies entered into a share purchase agreement (SPA) where Idemitsu acquired the entire allotted and issued share capital of a company, Petro Summit Investment UK Limited. In the contract, Sumitomo gave various warranties about the past and present facts about the company. These were stated in Schedule 4 of the contract as warranties. The agreement required Idemitsu to raise a claim for breach of a warranty within 18 months of the formation of the contract.

Years later, Idemitsu discovered that Petro Summit was subject to substantial liabilities arising from a dispute between the owners of two oil and gas fields. Thus, some of the matters warranted by Sumitomo in the SPA were incorrect. As 18 months were past by the time Idemitsu discovered it, the notice period to make a claim within the SPA was over. Idemitsu claimed to terminate the contract on the grounds that a false representation was made to it, and it was entitled to terminate the contract on the grounds of misrepresentation. The commercial court noted: [Idemitsu (2016): para 14].

> When a seller, by the terms of the contract under which he sells, 'warrants' something about the subject matter sold, he is making a contractual promise. Nothing less. But also I think (and all things being equal) nothing more.

When a party makes a warranty, the party is making a promise that for a breach of the term he will be liable to pay damages within the terms of the contract. However, 'the seller is not purporting to impart information; he is not making a statement to his buyer' [Idemitsu (2016): para 14]. When something is warranted, the court took the view that it is 'quite novel, and wrong, to suggest that this would amount to a statement of fact' [Idemitsu (2016): para 14]. Thus, the question of misrepresentation and setting aside the contract on the grounds of misrepresentation does not arise. The judge noted: [Idemitsu (2016): para 19].

> I think a sound premise, is that the act of concluding a contract on terms that include contractual warranties does not amount to or involve the making by the warrantor to the counterparty of any relevant statement.

Thus, the court did not allow the claim of Idemitsu to use warranties as representations.

Contract documents have come to be voluminous. The contracting parties are alive to the prospect of a conflict arising within the contract documents. An order of precedence clause sets out the order in which the documents would be read and privileged, if a conflict or ambiguity were to arise. An example of the clause is:

> These General Conditions of Contract with apply to the extent these are not superseded by provisions of other parts of the contract.

We review the following two cases on the theme of order of precedence.

Order of Precedence: The Triple Point Case

The Triple Point Case has been reviewed earlier. To recall, Triple Point was contracted to develop a trading software platform for a Thai trading company, PTT. [Triple Point Technology, Inc. v PTT Public Company Ltd, (2019) EWCA Civ 230. Hereafter Triple Point (2019)]. Under the contract, Triple Point licenced its proprietary software to PTT towards developing the trading platform and raised three invoices for payment. The invoices specified the dates by which these were to be paid. Triple Point demanded payment of the invoices. PTT did not pay and asserted that within the contract terms, payments were to be done on achievement of milestones. As the performance by Triple Point was delayed and milestones not achieved, no payment was due. Triple Point contended that the invoices were raised within the contract and were integral part of the contract and thus, the court should 'construe the contract in such a way as to give effect to every provision, if that was possible' [Triple Point (2019): para 54]. The order forms (invoices) set out the dates on which PTT must pay for the software and the licences. Article 18 sets out the dates on which PTT must pay for implementation, including customisation of the software. Triple Point contended: [Triple Point (2019): para 54].

> In the present case, it is possible to give effect to both Article 18 (which provides for payment by milestones) and the order forms (which provide for payment on calendar dates).

The Court of Appeal found this to be 'an ingenious argument' [Triple Point (2019): para 55] but it was incorrect. The software packages on their own were of no value to PTT. The court noted: [Triple Point (2019): para 55].

> What PTT was purchasing was customised software for use in its business. The provisions in the contractual documents ... made it plain that the CTRM contract governed both the provision and the customisation of the software.

The court noted the 'natural reading of Article 18' [Triple Point (2019): para 55] was that it governed all payments and these should be by achievement of milestones. Article 29 of the contract was titled 'Order of Precedence'. It reads: 'In the event of a conflict in the provisions of this Contract, the following shall prevail in the order ... This Contract ... Exhibit 1 and 2 ... Exhibit 3'[Triple Point (2019): para 16]. The court explained the reason contracts have a precedence clause:[Triple Point (2019): para 57].

> Precedence clauses are of particular importance in substantial construction or IT contracts. Many people draft different sections of the contract and specification. The final contract is an amalgam of all these efforts. Sometimes, although not in this case, the contracts are so vast that no human being could possibly be expected to read them from beginning to end.

A contract document has to be read as a whole to give effect to its provisions. The court integrated the rule with the order of precedence clause: [Triple Point (2019): para 57].

> The traditional rule that you construe a contract as a whole must now be understood in this context. Conflicts between different parts of the contract documents are almost inevitable in such cases. Precedence clauses tell the reader how such conflicts should be resolved.

The order of precedence put the software platform development contract at the top. As noted earlier, Article 18 of the contract had provided for payment by achievement of the milestones. The order of precedence clause puts the invoices at the very bottom. The court applied the precedence clause: [Triple Point (2019): para 59].

> The dates in the order forms may well be the dates on which some individuals expected or hoped that milestones would be achieved. But the provision in Article 18 for payment by reference to milestones takes precedence over the calendar dates stated in the three order forms.

The court constructed that the payment needed to be done on achievement of milestone basis.

Order of Precedence: RWE Npower Renewables Ltd v J N Bentley Ltd

JN Bentley Limited was engaged by RWE Npower Renewables Limited to carry out civil engineering works at a hydroelectric project in Scotland. [RWE Npower Renewables Ltd v J N Bentley Ltd, (2014) EWCA Civ 150. Hereafter RWE (2014).] Clause 2 of the Contract listed the lengthy and complex contract documents. This included the NEC 3 Engineering and Construction Contract Conditions 2005 (revised 2006), Contract Data sheets Parts 1 and 2, Post Tender Clarifications, Works Information and Site Information. The documents were listed by the order of precedence. A dispute arose between the parties whether the contractor had completed a work or not. Clause 6.2 of the contract and Option X5 both provided on completion of the civil works. The Court of Appeal stated: [RWE (2014): para 15].

> … the contract documents should as far as possible be read as complementing each other and therefore as expressing the parties' intentions in a consistent and coherent manner.

The court noted that Option X5 was worded in more general terms while clause 6.2 provided in greater detail on completion of work. The court noted: [RWE (2014): para 15].

> Despite differences in detail, however, one would expect the two provisions to complement each other and that only in the case of a clear and irreconcilable discrepancy would it be necessary to resort to the contractual order of precedence to resolve it.

To resolve the differences and uncertainties posed by the two clauses, the court noted: [RWE (2014): para 16].

> … right way to resolve it … is by obtaining such assistance as one can from other parts of the contract. For that purpose clause 6.2 with its more detailed provisions is the obvious place at which to start … that the two clauses can and should be read in harmony with each other.

If it came to applying the order of precedence clause, the Court of Appeal stated the principle that it was 'intended to resolve discrepancies relating to individual obligations rather than forcing on the reader a choice between one entire clause and another' [RWE (2014): para 17]. The court noted: [RWE (2014): para 17].

> A contract is a bundle of related obligations, each of which can be separately identified. I see no reason … to adopt the rather undiscriminating approach … which involves abandoning the whole of any complex provision if it can be shown to be inconsistent in any respect with another. Only to the extent that different provisions on their true construction impose different obligations in relation to the same subject matter is it necessary to decide which takes precedence.

The court concluded that the contractor had completed the work.

Notices

A contract requires the parties to communicate with each other towards performance of the contract. GCCs have a clause on notice and communications as to how the parties will communicate with one another. It will provide that the parties would communicate in writing. It may read:

> Notice and Communications
>
> All notices, requests, demands and other communications between the parties will be in writing. Written communication can take the form of letter, fax or email.
>
> A notice will be effective only when delivered or on the notice's effective date, whichever is later.

There may notice clauses for specific purposes, for example, making claims, notifying breaches or terminating the contract. Decision Inc Holdings Proprietary Limited, Decision Inc Shareco (RF) Proprietary Limited v Stephen Garbett, Anis El-Mariesh, [Decision Inc Holdings Proprietary Limited, Decision Inc Shareco (RF) Proprietary Limited v Stephen Garbett, Anis El-Mariesh, (2023) EWCA Civ 1284. Hereafter Decision (2023).] was on a share purchase agreement. The contract gave several warranties. The notice clause stated: [Decision (2023): para 18].

> Clause 11.4
>
> The Sellers shall not be liable for a Claim unless notice in writing summarising the nature of the Claim (in so far as it is known to the Buyer) and, as far as is reasonably practicable, the amount claimed, has been given by or on behalf of the Buyer to the Sellers.

The buyer served a notice for a claim but it did not specify the amount. The Court of Appeal, on appraising the facts concluded that 'common sense suggests that it was not impossible to work out how much was claimed'[Decision (2023): para 70]. The Court of Appeal noted:[Decision (2023): para 74].

> the correct view is that clause 11.4 of the SPA required the claimants to state the "amount claimed" in respect of *each* breach of warranty alleged, not just an omnibus figure, as far as reasonably practicable.

The clause is clear that the seller is not liable if the requirement of the notice is not met. The court concluded that 'this means that a notice must summarise in respect of each claim for breach of warranty' [Decision (2023): para 74] and the amount claimed to be valid. The Court of Appeal concluded the notice 'had to include the "amount claimed" in respect of that breach and that the fact that it did not do so meant that the [seller] could not be held liable for any such breach' [Decision (2023): para 75].

Contract terms may have a clause on the parties acting in good faith in performance of their contractual duties. The meaning of good faith is to act honestly to each other, be faithful to the parties' bargain, have fair dealings and not indulge in commercially unacceptable conduct. There can be two sources of good faith. One, the contract has express terms requiring the parties to act in good faith. Two, the courts have implied good faith in relational contracts. The following case review explores both the sources of good faith.

Good Faith: The Phones4U Case

We have reviewed the case in an earlier chapter. To recapitulate, the case is between EE, a mobile network operator in the UK and a distributor of its services, P4U. P4U had three business partners. [Phones 4U Limited (In Administration) v EE Limited, Deutsche Telekom AG, Orange SA, Vodafone Limited, Vodafone Group Public Limited Company, Telefonica UK Limited, Telefonica, S.A., Telefonica O2 Holdings Limited, (2023) EWHC 2826 (Ch). Hereafter Phones 4U (2023).] Two of them left it in quick succession. EE, the only remaining business partner declared a year in advance that it would not renew its distributorship contract. Following this, P4U appointed administrators for liquidation. EE had the right to immediately terminate the contract if P4U appointed an administrator. On this basis, EE terminated the contract.

P4U initiated a separate proceeding that the mobile phone operators had acted in collusion to drive it to its insolvency [Phones 4U (2023)]. In this context, the question came up if EE had not acted in good faith towards P4U. The contract had the following express terms requiring EE to act in good faith in performance of specific duties: [Phones 4U (2023): para 648].

> 13.2 EE hereby undertakes and agrees that it will in good faith observe and perform the terms and conditions of this Agreement and in particular EE shall, and shall procure that its employees, agents and subcontractors will:
>
> 13.2.1 comply with all legislation and regulations, …
>
> 13.2.2 supply to P4U from time to time such amount of the then current technical brochures, …
>
> 13.2.3 arrange and make available to P4U, should P4U so request, sales and technical training courses ….

The court noted with reference to EE announcing it a year in advance that it would not renew the contract:[Phones 4U (2023): para 652].

> I consider that clause 13.2 is clear. The good faith obligation which it imposes is specifically in terms of the performance of the terms and conditions set out in the EE Agreement. Those conditions included the obligation on EE to make "Revenue Share Payments" (a term defined by the EE Agreement) to P4u. But it is not here alleged that EE failed to make any payments that were due.

The contract had the following clause, of a more general nature, requiring EE to act in good faith:[Phones 4U (2023): para 648].

> 13.11 EE hereby undertakes and agrees with P4U that it will act in good faith and not carry out any activity designed to reduce or avoid the making of any Revenue Share Payment(s) to P4U as contemplated by this Agreement.

In relation to clause 13.11, P4U contended that it comprised of two obligations, first, a general obligation to act in good faith and second, 'a more particular obligation to avoid any activity designed to reduce or avoid the making of revenue share payments' [Phones 4U (2023): para 653]. The judge noted that if one 'literally read' the clause, it could be taken to be 'imposing a general and then a more particular obligation.' [Phones 4U (2023): para 653]. But the contracting was 'a professionally drafted and very full contract between sophisticated parties' [Phones 4U (2023): para 653]. In this context, the court noted: [Phones 4U (2023): para 653].

If they had intended to impose a general obligation of good faith, I consider that they would have done so. And if there were to be such an express, general good faith obligation on EE, I regard it as inconceivable that the contract would not also have imposed the same obligation on P4u.

The court, thus, ruled that clause 13.11 is to be read as requiring good faith to 'activity designed to reduce or avoid' the liability under the agreement to make Revenue Share Payments and 'not more generally' [Phones 4U (2023): para 653].

Relational Contracts and Good Faith

There was another source for good faith to come in. Good faith is implied in relational contracts. Was the EE agreement a relational contract? If yes, then, should clause 13.11 be read differently and more widely. Or, should the requirement of good faith be implied independently. The judgment first reviewed the recent development of the concept of a relational contract.

The concept of relational contract was developed in the Yam Seng case [Yam Seng Pte Limited (A company registered in Singapore) v International Trade Corporation Limited, (2013) EWHC 111 (QB). Hereafter Yam Seng (2013)] by Leggatt J. The concept was there was 'no general duty of good faith in English contract law', however, it may be 'implied into a commercial contract based on the presumed intention of the parties'. This could be the case where the contract involves 'a longer-term relationship between the parties to which they make a substantial commitment'

[Yam Seng (2013): Para 142]. The court in the Yam Seng Case noted: [Yam Seng (2013): Para 142].

> Such "relational" contracts, as they are sometimes called, may require a high degree of communication, cooperation and predictable performance based on mutual trust and confidence and involve expectations of loyalty which are not legislated for in the express terms of the contract but are implicit in the parties' understanding and necessary to give business efficacy to the arrangements.

The judge illustrated such contracts to include some joint venture agreements, franchise agreements and long-term distributorship agreements. Leggatt LJ developed the concept of relational contract further in Sheikh Tahnoon Bin Saeed Bin ShakbootAl Nehayan v Kent [Sheikh Tahnoon Bin Saeed Bin Shakboot Al Nehayan v Kent (2018) EWHC 333 (Comm).] to state that these require trust and confidence between the parties. The judge elaborated on the nature of the trust required: [Sheikh Tahnoon Bin Saeed Bin Shakboot Al Nehayan v Kent (2018) EWHC 333 (Comm): para 167].

> The trust is not in the loyal subordination by one party of its own interests to those of another. It is trust that the other party will act with integrity and in a spirit of cooperation. The legitimate expectations which the law should protect in relationships of this kind are embodied in the normative standard of good faith.

In Bates v Post Office Ltd, [Bates v Post Office Ltd (No 3) (2019) EWHC 606 (QB).] the concept of relational contract was further developed. It was stated that a contract has to be seen in the circumstances of the relationship between the parties defined by the terms of the contract, set in its commercial context, to be judged to be a relational contract. The judgment set out the following factors to explore in making a determination: [Bates v Post Office Ltd (No 3) (2019) EWHC 606 (QB): para 725].

1. There must be no specific express terms in the contract that prevents a duty of good faith being implied into the contract.
2. The contract will be a long-term one, with the mutual intention of the parties being that there will be a long-term relationship.
3. The parties must intend that their respective roles be performed with integrity, and with fidelity to their bargain.
4. The parties will be committed to collaborating with one another in the performance of the contract.
5. The spirits and objectives of their venture may not be capable of being expressed exhaustively in a written contract.
6. They will each repose trust and confidence in one another, but of a different kind to that involved in fiduciary relationships.
7. The contract in question will involve a high degree of communication, co-operation and predictable performance based on mutual trust and confidence, and expectations of loyalty.
8. There may be a degree of significant investment by one party (or both) in the venture. This significant investment may be, in some cases, more accurately described as substantial financial commitment.

9. Exclusivity of the relationship may also be present.

In the current EE case, applying the concepts of a relational contract and the above factors, the court noted: [Phones 4U (2023): para 660].

> I accept that the EE Agreement has some features of a relational contract, in that it is a moderately long-term arrangement (it had a term of three years) with the potential for renewal, and in turn had replaced a previous agreement; and further that EE and P4u had to collaborate with one another extensively in the performance of the contract.

But the balance was against the contract being a relational contract. EE was collaborating with P4U but also in competition with P4U. It was EE's desire to expand its direct retailing and reduce its reliance on indirect retailers. The desire is legitimate and its decision not to renew was towards pursuit of this goal. In this context, the court noted: [Phones 4U (2023): para 662].

> … exclusivity is a supporting indication, not a necessary condition, for a relational contract, and I consider that being in direct competition is a strong factor pointing the other way. At the very least, it would substantially affect what is required by any duty of good faith.

The judge, thus, concluded that the contract was not a relational one. The judge further noted that even if the contract is taken to be a relational contract, it does not matter as there is no breach of good faith by EE. The judge observed: [Phones 4U (2023): para 722].

> It is obviously not suggested that any obligation of good faith required EE to renew or extend the EE Agreement. Nor is it suggested that any such obligation obliged EE to respond positively to P4u's requests for assistance when it was in difficulty following the decision of Vodafone UK.

It was alleged by P4U that EE declaring a year in advance that it would not renew the contract was in bad faith. The implication is, EE having made the decision not to renew the contract, it should have kept it secret from P4U for months. In the earlier cases on relational contracts, however, being secretive with the other party was stated to be in bad faith. The judge found this would be 'paradoxical to say that it was bad faith for EE to have disclosed relevant information' [Phones 4U (2023): para 723]. Thus, EE was not in breach of good faith by its letter commutating a year in advance that it would not renew the contract. The judge concluded: [Phones 4U (2023): para 724].

> EE could have offered greater support or cooperation to P4u if it had so wished, but it was entitled to give priority to its own interests and concerns. In all the circumstances, I do not consider that its decision to send the letter would be regarded as commercially unacceptable by reasonable and honest people.

The court thus concluded that EE had not breached the express terms requiring it to act in good faith. The contract was not a relational contract, requiring implying good faith in it. In any case, EE had not acted in bad faith in its conduct with P4U.

Agency: Angove's Pty Ltd v Bailey

An agency is a contract, where a principal authorises another person to act for him. An agency can be created by express terms or impliedly. The agent may be authorised to contract for the principal. In this case, the agent makes the contract between the principal and the third party and drops out, for the contract is of the principal, not the agent. We explored agency in an earlier chapter and noted that a principal can be disclosed or undisclosed. Agency is prevalent in commercial transactions. A contract itself may be an agency contract. Other times, the contract may have provided for the parties to be represented by agents or the parties could deal with third parties through agents. A specific feature of an agency is, even if the agency is irrevocable, the principal can terminate the agency. We explore the theme with the following review.

Angove's Pty Ltd is an Australian winemaker. [Angove's Pty Ltd v Bailey, United Kingdom Supreme Court, 27 July 2016, (2016) UKSC 47. Hereafter Angove's (2016).] For many years, it had employed an English company, D & D Wines International Ltd, as its agent and distributor in the United Kingdom. Angove's gave written notice terminating the agency. On this date, two invoices of two retailers, totalling A$874,929 were not paid. The termination notice also took away the authority of D & D to collect the price from the two customers. The notice declared that Angove's would collect the price directly from the customers and give commission to D & D. D & D challenged the termination of the agency and its powers to collect the pending invoices and its commission. The Supreme Court stated the principles on revocability of an agency: [Angove's (2016): para 6].

> The general rule is that the authority of an agent may be revoked by the principal, even if it is agreed by their contract to be irrevocable. The revocation is effective to terminate the agent's authority, but gives rise to a claim for damages. … the rule was said to be "so plain a doctrine of common sense and common justice that it requires no illustration or reasoning to support it.

An agent stands for the principal, as if the agent is the principal. The court noted: [Angove's (2016): para 6].

> An agent is empowered to commit his principal within the limits of his authority as if the principal had agreed personally. This is a confidential relationship importing a duty of loyalty, and normally of undivided loyalty, on the part of the agent.

The relationship between a principal and an agent is personal. No one can deprive the principal of speaking for himself and being himself. This is the reason and agency contract, even if the principal has no right to terminate it, the principal can terminate it. Of course, the principal would need to compensate for the losses caused to the agent by the termination. The principle, however, has exceptions. The main exception is where the agent 'has a relevant interest of his own in the exercise of his authority' [Angove's (2016): para 7]. The court noted on this exception: [Angove's (2016): para 7].

The exception applies if two conditions are satisfied. First, there must be an agreement that the agent's authority shall be irrevocable. Secondly, the authority must be given to secure an interest of the agent, ... In these cases, the agent's authority is irrevocable while the interest subsists.

The court explored the range of interests the agent could have in the agency. It noted one extreme of it to be where agency was granted: [Angove's (2016): para 9].

> ... solely to enable the grantee to satisfy a pre-existing debt owed to the agent, or where an owner of land gave a power of attorney to a creditor to sell the land to satisfy the debt.

No one could doubt that the agency should be irrevocable in these cases. At the opposite extreme are the cases where the only interest of the agent is to earn his commission. In these cases, the principal can terminate the agency, even if it is irrevocable. The reason for it is 'the authority is not properly speaking a security at all' [Angove's (2016): para 9]. But there may be situations between the two extremes where the interest of the agent is broader than mere collection of his commission. In these cases, the court noted: [Angove's (2016): para 9].

> There is no principled reason why a true agent employed on his principal's affairs should not also be regarded as having a personal interest in the exercise of his authority sufficient to make it irrevocable.

The court concluded the principle that an agent's authority is revocable, even if it is agreed to be irrevocable. Merely because the contract terms do not give the right to terminate the agency, the right of the principal to terminate is not excluded. What has to be agreed between the parties for it to be irrevocable is that 'it is intended to secure the financial interest of the agent' [Angove's (2016): para 15]. This is a question for construction of the agreement. Constructing the contract, the court concluded that the agent did not have financial interest and the principal could terminate the contract.

In this chapter, we have reviewed other terms in GCCs including, warranties and representation, order of precedence, good faith and agency. A warranty is a contractual promise, for whose breach, the party can claim damages within the terms of the contract. Representations are statements made towards formation of the contract. A contract can be set aside on the grounds of misrepresentation. Unless contract terms bring it out, a warranty cannot be made into representation and the reverse, a representation cannot be claimed to be a warranty. As contract documents have become numerous and voluminous, the GCCs have included an order of precedence clause. The clause lists the order of priority of documents for resolving conflicts and ambiguities. A contract may have express terms requiring the other to act in good faith. In addition, the courts have come to imply the duty of good faith in relational contracts. An agency, even if the contract terms state it to be irrevocable, can be terminated by the principal. In this case, the principal will need to pay damages to the agent. The exception to the right of the principal to terminate an irrevocable contract is if the agency itself has created more than usual interest for the agent in the agency.

References

Angove's Pty Ltd v Bailey, United Kingdom Supreme Court, 27 July 2016, (2016) UKSC 47
Bates v Post Office Ltd (No 3) (2019) EWHC 606 (QB)
Decision Inc Holdings Proprietary Limited, Decision Inc Shareco (RF) Proprietary Limited v Stephen Garbett, Anis El-Mariesh, (2023) EWCA Civ 1284
Idemitsu Kosan Co Ltd v Sumitomo Corp., (2016) EWHC 1909 (Comm)
Phones 4U Limited (In Administration) v EE Limited, Deutsche Telekom AG, Orange SA, Vodafone Limited, Vodafone Group Public Limited Company, Telefonica UK Limited, Telefonica, S.A., Telefonica O2 Holdings Limited, (2023) EWHC 2826 (Ch)
RWE Npower Renewables Ltd v J N Bentley Ltd, (2014) EWCA Civ 150
Sheikh Tahnoon Bin Saeed Bin ShakbootAl Nehayan v Kent (2018) EWHC 333 (Comm)
Triple Point Technology, Inc. v PTT Public Company Ltd, (2019) EWCA Civ 230
Yam Seng Pte Limited (A company registered in Singapore) v International Trade Corporation Limited, (2013) EWHC 111 (QB)

List of Cases

- 2 Entertain Video Limited v Sony DADC Europe Limited, [2020] EWHC 972 (TCC).
- Air Transworld Ltd v Bombardier Inc. [2012] 1 C.L.C. 145.
- Aircraft Purchase Fleet Limited v Compagnia Aerea Italiana SPA, [2018] EWHC 3315 (Comm).
- Alfred C Beatty v Guggenheim Exploration Co (1919) 225 NY 380, p 387-8.
- Aluminium Industrie Vaassen BV v Romalpa Aluminium Ltd., (1976) 1 WLR 676.
- Anglia Television Ltd. v Reed, [1972] 1 Q.B. 60.
- Ashington Piggeries v Christopher Hill Ltd [1972] AC 441.
- AXA Sun Life Services plc v Campbell Martin Ltd, [2011] EWCA Civ 133.
- Baldry v. Marshall, (1925) 1 KB 260.
- Barclays Bank plc v Quincecare Ltd [1992] 4 All ER 363.
- Barton v Morris, [2023] UKSC 3.
- BHP Petroleum Limited v British Steel PLC, 2000 WL 362480.
- BSyB Ltd v HP Enterprise Services UK Ltd [2010] EWHC 86 (TCC).
- Bunge SA v Nidera BV (2015) UKSC 43.
- Bunge SA v Nidera BV, [2015] UKSC 43.
- Burley v Joseph W Burley Partners Ltd [2002] EWCA Civ 1163.
- C&S Associates UK Limited v Enterprise Insurance Company Plc, [2015] EWHC 3757 (Comm).
- Cammell Laird and Company, Limited v. The Manganese Bronze and Brass Company, Limited, (1934) AC 402.
- Cavendish Square Holding BV v. Makdessi, 2(2015) UKSC 67.
- Channel Island Ferries Limited v Sealink UK Limited, 1988 WL 622867.
- Coys of Kensington Automobiles Limited v Tiziana Pugliese, [2011] EWHC 655 (QB).
- Dalmare SpA v Union Maritime Ltd, [2013] Bus. L.R. 810.

A. Pathak, *Contract Terms in International Business*,
https://doi.org/10.1007/978-981-96-8146-4

- Dassault Aviation Sa v Mitsui Sumitomo Insurance Co Ltd, [2024] EWCA Civ 5.
- Deepak Fertilisers Ltd v ICI Chemicals and Polymers Ltd, (1999) 1 T.C.L.R. 200.
- Diageo PLC v Vijay Mallya, [2019] EWHC 2067 (Comm).
- Donoghue v Stevenson [1932] AC 562.
- Dorchester Project Management Limited v BNP Paribas Real Estate Advisory & Property Management UK Limited, [2013] EWCA Civ 176.
- Dunlop Pneumatic Tyre Co. Ltd. v. New Garage and Motor Co. Ltd. [1915] A.C. 79.
- Electrosteel Europe SA v Edil Centro SpA, Case C-87/10.
- Energy Works (Hull) Limited v MW High Tech Projects UK Limited, [2020] EWHC 2537 (TCC).
- Fawaz Al-Hasawi v Nottingham Forest Football Club Ltd v NF Football Investments Ltd, NFFC Group Holdings Ltd, [2018] EWHC 2884 (Ch).
- Federal Republic of Nigeria v JP Morgan Chase Bank NA [2019] EWHC 347 (Comm).
- FG Wilson (Engineering) Ltd v John Holt & Co (Liverpool) Ltd,[2014] 1 W.L.R. 2365.
- Filatona Trading Limited v Vladimir Anatolevich Chernukhin, [2020] EWCA Civ 109.
- First National Trustco (UK) Limited v Bahia Blanca Holiday Club, [2020] EWCA Civ 107.
- Gilbert-Ash (Northern) Limited v Modern Engineering (Bristol) Limited [1974] AC 689.
- Gillespie Bros. & Co. v Cheney, Eggar & Co., [1986] 2 QB 59.
- Golden Ocean Group Limited v Salgaocar Mining Industries Pvt Ltd, 2011 WL 197258.
- GPP Big Field LLP v Solar EPC Solutions SL, [2018] EWHC 2866 (Comm).
- Great Dunmow Estates Limited v Crest Nicholson Operations Limited, [2019] EWCA Civ 1683.
- Gwynt y Mor OFTO Plc v Gwynt y Mor Offshore Wind Farm Ltd, [2020] 4 WLUK 129.
- Hadley v Baxendale (1854) 9 Ex. 341
- Harcus Sinclair LLP v Your Lawyers Ltd, [2021] UKSC 32.
- Hedley Byrne & Co. Ltd. v Heller & Partners Ltd., [1964] A.C. 465.
- Henderson v Merrett Syndicates Ltd [1995] 2 A.C. 145.
- Henderson v Merrett Syndicates Ltd [1995] 2 A.C. 145.
- Henry Kendall & Sons v. William Lillico & Sons, (1969) 2 AC 31.
- Hines v. Overstock.Com, Inc. 668 F.Supp.2d 362 (2009).
- Hotel Services Ltd. v Hilton International Hotels (UK) Ltd., 2000 WL 191222.
- J N Hipwell & Son v Szurek [2018] EWCA Civ 674.
- James Andrew Robinson v P.E.Jones (Contractors) Limited, [2011] EWCA Civ 9.
- JP Morgan Chase Bank, N.A. v The Federal Republic of Nigeria, [2019] EWCA Civ 1641.

- Kaefer Aislamientos SA de CV v AMS Drilling Mexico SA de CV, [2019] EWCA Civ 10.
- KG Bominflot Bunkergesellschaft für Mineraloele mbH & Co v. Petroplus Marketing AG (The Mercini Lady), (2010) EWCA Civ 1145.
- Kwei Tek Chao and Others (Trading As Zung Fu Co.) v. British Traders and Shippers LD.,[1954] 2 Q.B. 459.
- Lebeaupin v Richard Crispin and Company, [1920] 2 K.B. 714.
- L'Estrange v F Graucob, Ltd, [1934] 2 KB 394
- Linden Gardens Trust Ltd v Lenesta Sludge Disposals Ltd., [1994] 1 A.C. 85.
- Manbre Saccharine Co, Ltd v. Corn Products Co, Ltd, [1919] 1 K.B. 198.
- Marks and Spencer plc v BNP Paribas Services Trust Company (Jersey) Limited [2015] UKSC 72).
- Meyer v. Uber Techs., Inc., 868 F.3d 66 (2d Cir. 2017).
- Modern Engineering (Bristol)Ltd v Gilbert-Ash (Northern) Ltd [1974] AC 689.
- MWB Business Exchange Centres Ltd v Rock Advertising Ltd, [2018] UKSC 24.
- MWB Business Exchange Centres Ltd v Rock Advertising Ltd., [2016] EWCA Civ 553.
- National Carriers Ltd. v. Panalpina (Northern) Ltd, [1981] A.C. 675.
- Nobahar-Cookson v Hut Group Ltd., [2016] EWCA Civ 128.
- Nordenfelt v The Maxim Nordenfelt Guns and Ammunition Co Ltd [1894] AC 535.
- Omak Maritime Ltd. v Mamola Challenger Shipping Co. [2010] EWHC 2026 (Comm).
- Peekay Intermark Ltd v Australia and New Zealand Banking Group Ltd, [2006] EWCA Civ 386
- Persimmon Homes Ltd v Ove Arup & Partners Ltd, [2017] EWCA Civ 373.
- Philipp v Barclays Bank UK PLC, [2023] UKSC 25.
- Phones 4U Ltd (in administration) v EE Ltd, [2018] EWHC 49 (Comm).
- Photo Production v. Securicor Transport Ltd (1980) AC 827.
- Playboy Club London Ltd v Banca Nazionale del Lavoro SpA, [2018] UKSC 43.
- Profindo Pte Ltd v Abani Trading Pte Ltd [2013] SGHC 10.
- Proton Energy Group SA v Orlen Lietuva, [2013] EWHC 2872 (Comm).
- PST Energy 7 Shipping LLC and another v OW Bunker Malta Ltd, [2016] UKSC 23.
- PST Energy 7 Shipping LLC, Product Shipping and Trading S.A. v O.W. Bunker Malta Limited, [2015] EWHC 2022 (Comm).
- R G Grain Trade LLP (UK) v Feed Factors International Ltd, [2011] EWHC 1889 (Comm).
- Rainy Sky SA v Kookmin Bank [2011] UKSC 50.
- Robinson v. Harman (1848) 1 Exch 850.
- Ross T Smyth & Co Ltd v. T D Bailey Son & Co, (1940) 3 All ER 60.
- Ruxley Electronics and Construction Limited v. Forsyth, (1996) AC 344.
- Saint Line Ltd v Richardsons, Westgarth and Co Ltd [1940] 2 KB 99.
- Seadrill Ghana Operations Ltd v Tullow Ghana Ltd., [2018] EWHC 1640 (Comm). Hereafter Seadrill (2018).

- Seadrill Management Services Ltd and another v OAO Gazprom [2010] EWCA Civ 691.
- Sgouros v. TransUnion Corp., 817 F.3d 1029 (7th Cir. 2016).
- Shanghai Shipyard Co. Ltd. v Reignwood International Investment (Group) Company Limited, [2021] EWCA Civ 1147.
- Sheffield Teaching Hospital Foundation Trust v Hadfield Healthcare Partnerships Limited, Kajima Construction Europe (UK) Limited, Veolia Energy & Utility Services UK PLC, [2023] EWHC 644 (TCC).
- Soteria Insurance Limited (formerly Cis General Insurance Limited) v IBM United Kingdom Limited, [2022] EWCA Civ 440.
- Stevens v Publicis S.A., Judgment, Supreme Court, New York County, 2008 NY Slip Op 02880 [50 AD3d 253].
- Stocznia Gdynia SA v Gearbulk Holdings Limited, [2009] EWCA Civ 75.
- Sumitomo Mitsui Banking Corporation Europe Limited v Euler Hermes Europe SA (NV), [2019] EWHC 2250 (Comm).
- Surrey County Council and Another v Bredero Homes Ltd., [1993] 1 W.L.R. 1361.
- T/A Hamid Properties v Francis Bradshaw Partnership, [2013] EWCA Civ 470.
- Tandrin Aviation Holdings Limited v Aero Toy Store LLC., Insured Aircraft Title Service, Inc., [2010] EWHC 40 (Comm).
- Teheran-Europe v Belton [1968] 2 QB 545.
- Tennants (Lancashire) Ltd v CS Wilson & Co Ltd [1917] AC 495.
- Thames Valley Power Ltd. v. Total Gas & Power Ltd. [2006] 1 Lloyd's Rep. 441.
- The Argo Fund Ltd v Essar Steel Ltd [2005] EWHC 600.
- The Hansa Nord, Cehave NV v Bremer Handelsgesellschaft mbH, [1976] Q.B. 44.
- The Inntrepreneur Pub Company (GL) v East Crown Limited, High Court of Justice Chancery Division, 2000 WL 1151484.
- The Star Polaris [2016] EWHC 2941.
- Tillman v Egon Zehnder Ltd, [2019] UKSC 32.
- Tradax v Goldschmidt SA [1977] 2 Ll. Rep. 604.
- Triple Point Technology, Inc v PTT Public Company Ltd, [2021] UKSC 29.
- Triple Point Technology, Inc. v PTT Public Company Limited, [2017] EWHC 2178 (TCC).
- Triple Point Technology, Inc. v PTT Public Company Ltd, [2019] EWCA Civ 230.
- Vossloh Aktiengesellschaft v. Alpha Trains (UK) Limited, (2010) EWHC 2443 (Ch).
- Wallis, Son & Wells v. Pratt & Haynes, (1911) AC 394.
- Wilmington Trust SP Services (Dublin) Limited, Sabarmati Aviation Leasing Limited (formerly known as Sky Aircraft Cassia Two Limited), Falgu Aviation Leasing Limited (formerly known as Sky Aircraft Cassia One Limited) v Spicejet Limited, [2021] EWHC 1117 (Comm).
- Wood v Capita Insurance Services Limited, [2017] UKSC 24.

- Wuhan Guoyu Logistics Group Co Ltd v Emporiki Bank of Greece SA., [2012] EWCA Civ 1629.
- X v Kuoni Travel Ltd, [2021] UKSC 34.

The manufacturer's authorised representative in the EU is Springer Nature Customer Service Centre GmbH, Europaplatz 3, 69115 Heidelberg, Germany. If you have any concerns regarding our products, please contact ProductSafety@springernature.com

Printed and bound by CPI Group (UK) Ltd, Croydon, CR0 4YY
01/10/2026
02225909-0005